THE RUIN OF A PRINCESS

As told by

The Duchesse d'Angoulême, Madame Elizabeth, Sister of Louis XVI, and Cléry, the King's Valet de Chambre

Literally translated by

KATHARINE PRESCOTT WORMELEY

Illustrated with photogravures from the Original Paintings

LONDON
T. WERNER LAURIE LTD.
CLIFFORD'S INN

LIST OF

PHOTOGRAVURE ILLUSTRATIONS.

MADAME ROYALE, DUCHESSE D'ANGOULÊME . . . . *Frontispiece*
    By Danloux; Vienna.

                                                                           PAGE

MADAME ÉLISABETH AT MONTREUIL 20
    By Richard; Versailles.

LOUIS XVI 80
    By Duplessis; Versailles.

THE PRINCESS DE LAMBALLE 122
    By Mme. Vigée Le Brun; Maîtres du XIX Siècle.

THE TOWER OF THE TEMPLE 125

THE DAUPHIN AND MADAME ROYALE 182
    By Mme. Vigée Le Brun; Versailles.

MADAME ÉLISABETH DE FRANCE 210
    By Mme. Vigée Le Brun; Portraits Nationaux.

QUEEN MARIE-ANTOINETTE LEAVING THE TRIBUNAL AFTER HER CON-
    DEMNATION TO DEATH 278
    Paul Delarouche

CONTENTS.

Part First.

LIFE AND LETTERS OF MADAME ÉLISABETH DE FRANCE.

CHAPTER I.

Introductory. — Sketch of the Life of Madame Élisabeth from her Childhood until August 10, 1792 1

CHAPTER II.

Letters of Madame Élisabeth to the Marquise de Bombelles, the Marquise de Raigecourt, the Abbé de Lubersac, and others 33

CHAPTER III.

Madame Élisabeth's Life in the Tower of the Temple recorded only by her Niece, Marie-Thérèse de France, and by Cléry, Louis XVI.'s Valet. — Her Removal to the Conciergerie. — Her Examination, Condemnation, and Death 90

Part Second.

JOURNAL OF THE TOWER OF THE TEMPLE, BY CLÉRY.

CHAPTER I.

The 10th of August, 1792. Cléry permitted to serve the King and his Family. — Life and Treatment of the Royal Family in the Tower of the Temple 111

CHAPTER II.

Continuation of their Life and Treatment.— The King separated from his Family, and summoned for Trial before the Convention . . . 138

CHAPTER III.

The King's Trial.— His Will.— The Decree of the Convention condemning the King to Death.— Last Meeting with his Family.— Leaves the Temple for his Execution 175

Part Third.

NARRATIVE OF MARIE-THÉRÈSE DE FRANCE, DUCHESSE D'ANGOULÊME.

First Uprising of the Populace on the 5th and 6th of October, 1789.— Removal of my Family to the Capital 210

Flight of my Father; his Stoppage at Varennes; his Return to Paris 216

Assault on the Tuileries by the Populace, June 20, 1792 230

Massacre at the Tuileries; Dethronement of my Father.— The Days from the 10th to the 13th of August, 1792 236

Imprisonment of my Family in the Tower of the Temple, August 13, 1792, followed by the Trial and Martyrdom of my Father, January 21, 1793 243

Life in the Tower of the Temple from the Death of Louis XVI. to that of the Queen, October 16, 1793 259

Life in the Temple till the Martyrdom of Madame Élisabeth and the Death of the Dauphin, Louis XVII, June 9, 1795 278

Brief sketch of the Life of Marie-Thérèse until her death, October 18, 1851 289

THE DUCHESSE D'ANGOULÊME.

Homage to the Duchesse d'Angoulême, by C.-A. Sainte-Beuve . . . 295

APPENDIXES.

		PAGE
I.	Montreuil	311
II.	First Examination of Madame Élisabeth by Fouquier-Tinville, May 9, 1794	313
III.	Extract from the Deliberations of the Commissioners of the Commune on the Service of the Temple	317
IV.	Signs agreed upon to make known to the Princesses the Progress of the various Armies, etc.; and sundry Communications from Madame Élisabeth to M. Turgy	318
V.	Louis XVI.'s Seal and Ring	323

INDEX 325

LIFE AND LETTERS

OF

MADAME ÉLISABETH DE FRANCE.

PART FIRST.

CHAPTER I.

Introductory. — Sketch of the Life of Madame Élisabeth from her Childhood until August 10, 1792.

MANY records of Madame Élisabeth exist, but only two of real authority: the "Éloge historique de Mme. Élisabeth de France," by Antoine Ferrand, minister of State and peer of France, first published in 1814 and again in 1861; and the "Vie de Madame Élisabeth," by M. A. de Beauchesne, Paris, 1869. Both works contain a number of her letters. From these volumes the following record has been made, chiefly in their own (translated) words. The parts selected are the simple historical facts of Mme. Élisabeth's story. The other parts may not be false, — far be it from us to say they are, — but they are so romantically tender as to convey a sense of extravagance, and thus do injury to the noble figure which the truth presents. For instance, it is recorded by her biographers that as her head fell into the basket a perfume of roses was wafted over the Place Louis XV. The impression that we of the present day receive from such a statement is of folly and fulsome flattery; yet the essential truth is in the simple facts, where the undying

> actions of the just
> Smell sweet, and blossom in the dust.

This record of Madame Élisabeth is here followed by the "Journal of the Temple," written by Cléry, the valet who attended on Louis XVI. to the last hour of his life, and by the far more valuable and even precious Narrative of that embodiment of sorrow, Marie-Thérèse de France, daughter of Louis XVI. and Marie-Antoinette, and later Duchesse d'Angoulême. There we see the end of the great French monarchy (for the restored kings were not the monarchy). No one can read this series of Memoirs — Saint-Simon, d'Argenson, Bernis — without realizing the causes of that mighty fall; not to be found so much in the career of the Great Monarch as in the lowered standards he left behind him, the corruption of the regency, and the long reign of his great-grandson's vice and ineptitude which consolidated the wrongs of France.

One fact shines clear above this mass of evil; and it is allowable to call the attention of the reader to it forcibly. Beside the enervating depravity of the Regent, the personal cowardice and sloth of Louis XV., the lack of firmness and regal assertion of Louis XVI. and his brothers, stands the splendid courage, physical and moral, of the three women whose ends are here recorded.

Élisabeth-Philippine-Marie-Hélène de France, daughter of the Dauphin Louis, son of Louis XV., and Marie-Josèphe de Saxe, was born at Versailles, May 3, 1764. Her three brothers, the Duc de Berry, the Comte de Provence, and the Comte d'Artois, were taken to the chapel on the same day, immediately after the king's mass, to witness her baptism, at which were present also the king and queen, the king's sisters Mesdames Adélaïde, Victoire, Sophie, and Louise, the Duc d'Orléans, the Duc de Chartres, the Prince de Condé, the Prince and Princesse de Conti, the Duc de Penthievre, the Prince de Lamballe, and others.

At her birth Madame Élisabeth was so delicate that for months her existence was a source of continual anxiety. Her father died the following year, and her mother, the wise and excellent Dauphine Marie-Josèphe, in 1767. The little orphan was then given wholly to the care of the Comtesse de Marsan (daughter of the Prince de Soubise), governess of the Children of France, who was already bringing up Élisabeth's sister, Madame Clotilde de France, afterwards Queen of Sardinia, who was four years and eight months older than Élisabeth. The difference in character and temper was greater still. Clotilde was born with the happiest disposition, which needed only to be encouraged and aided. Élisabeth was very different; it was often necessary to oppose her nature, and always to direct it. Proud, inflexible, passionate, she had defects to be mastered which would have been regrettable in a lower rank; in a princess of royal blood they were intolerable. The task of Mme. de Marsan was a difficult one. Madame Élisabeth's self-will was powerful, proud of her birth, she exacted around her supple instruments of it; she said she had no need to learn and tire herself uselessly, inasmuch as princes had about them persons whose duty it was to think for them. She stamped with anger if one of her women did not immediately bring her the thing she asked for. The difference in the characters of the sisters made a difference in the feelings of their governess towards each. Jealousy came to increase the asperity of the younger sister's nature. "If Clotilde had asked you," she said, one day, when Mme. de Marsan had refused a request, "*she* would have had it."

But Élisabeth was taken ill, and Clotilde insisted on taking care of her. This illness developed between them feelings of the tenderest affection; Clotilde taught her little sister the alphabet and how to spell and form words, she gave her little counsels which tended to soften her character, and she inculcated in her the first notions of religion with which she was already nourishing her own soul.

Still, Mme. de Marsan felt the want of aid in seconding the reform in the child's nature which she had so much at heart to bring about, and she cast her eyes on Mme. de Mackau, whose husband had been minister of the king at Ratisbon. This lady was educated at Saint-Cyr, an establishment which kept notes of not only the character and merits of its pupils, but followed their careers in the world for which it had formed them. It was from information thus derived that Mme. de Marsan asked the king to appoint Mme. de Mackau, who was living in retirement in Alsace, as sub-governess. This choice proved to have all the elements required to work a happy change in the nature of a self-willed and haughty child. Mme. de Mackau possessed a firmness to which resistance yielded, and an affectionate kindness which enticed attachment. Armed with almost maternal power, she brought up the Children of France as she would have trained her own children; overlooking no fault; knowing, if need were, how to make herself feared; all the while leading them to like virtue. To a superior mind she added a dignity of tone and manners which inspired respect. When her pupil gave way to the fits of haughty temper to which she was subject, Mme. de Mackau showed on her countenance a displeased gravity, as if to remind her that princes, like other persons, could not be liked except for their virtues and their good qualities. Distressed and disconcerted by this sudden and unexpected change,

Élisabeth, whose nature it was to be unable to feign or to hide whatever was passing in her soul, gave in this way a great advantage to her governess, quick to profit by the knowledge she thus gained of the child's inner feelings.

Little by little, Élisabeth yielded to wise and friendly management, and the defects which retarded her progress and prevented her from getting the advantages of her education gradually effaced themselves. Her wise governesses neglected nothing that could form her mind; they accustomed her to discuss questions with ease and without pedantry; to pose an argument properly, to examine it with discernment, and to bring logic to bear upon it and solve it. As all progress is accomplished only by degrees, the young princess continued for some time to commit her early faults. On such occasions, becoming more and more rare, she met a stern look, a stiff manner; and that simple show of displeasure was an efficacious correction. The proud and violent qualities changed, little by little, into firmness of principles, into a nobility and energy of feeling which made her in after years superior to the trials that filled her life.

Deprived of her parents and of the tenderest emotions of nature, her heart turned to fraternal love, which became from childhood her dominant passion. She cherished her three brothers, but a sort of predilection drew her to the Duc de Berry, the Dauphin. Was it that she already felt he would be unhappy because he was fated to be king? This tenderness of heart, which had so far served to correct Élisabeth's defects, was destined to be the the source of her consolation, her courage, her sorrows, and her devotion.

About this time, on certain days, when serious study was over, a few young ladies of merit, of religious principles and good education, were admitted to the privacy of the young princesses. It was a circle created to utilize their leisure as well as to amuse it, to form them to the customs of the world, to teach them to express their ideas with grace and concision, to judge of things with accuracy, and state their judgments clearly. These meetings had the precious advantage of being recreations which, under youthful gayety and perfect modesty, initiated them unconsciously in that divining tact, that knowledge of the world, so difficult to acquire, which consists in discerning at first sight the value of individuals, in estimating the nature and dominant spirit of each society under whatever form it presents itself: in short, the tact of sagacity, which became in the end so trained in Élisabeth that she was rarely mistaken in the opinion she formed of persons or of the spirit of the society in which she found herself. Madame Élisabeth seldom amused herself with frivolous talk, she was never really interested in a conversation unless there was something to gain from it. Time was precious to her.

The Abbé de Montégut, canon of Chartres, who was appointed, in 1774, tutor to the Children of France, contributed to develop in Madame Élisabeth the religious sentiments which never left her in after life. He explained to her the Gospels as being both the school of duty and the source of consolations. She applied herself to their study with a penetration above her age. One might almost say that a secret inspiration warned her that she was destined to find there the best and first of knowledge. As her intelligence developed, those two precepts became deeply rooted in her. Religion seemed to her a chain of duties and consolations, the first link of which, attached in heaven, was ever drawing humanity towards its origin and its completion.

Mme. de Marsan, on her side, took her often to Saint-Cyr. That royal establishment, which bore the imprint of a saintly and majestic thought, awakened all the sympathies of the young girl, who never left it without regret and promises to return.

Louis XV. died on the 10th of May, 1774, when Élisabeth was ten years old, and the Duc de Berry, the Dauphin and his wife, Marie-Antoinette, became King and Queen of France; the first nineteen years of age, the second a year younger. That year and the next were passed by the young princesses in their secluded school life, but always accompanying the Court, whether at Versailles, Fontainebleau, Marly, Compiègne, or La Muette. The following year Madame Élisabeth was confirmed and made her first communion, and the sisters were parted by the marriage of Clotilde to the Prince of Piedmont, afterwards King of Sardinia. No sensation of sorrow had as yet affected Élisabeth's heart; her sister's departure was her first experience of it, and when the moment of separation came, she clung to her with such force that they were obliged to tear them apart. Queen Marie-Antoinette, writing a few days later to her mother, the empress, says: —

"My sister Élisabeth is a charming child, who has intelligence, character, and much grace; she showed the greatest feeling, and much above her age, at the departure of her sister. The poor little girl was in despair, and as her health is very delicate, she was taken ill and had a very severe nervous attack. I own to my dear mamma that I fear I am getting too attached to her, feeling, from the example of my aunts, how essential it is for her happiness not to remain an old maid in this country."

It was on the 12th of May, 1776, that Turgot and Malesherbes, the two ministers whom the philosophical party, the "party of progress," had brought into power to effect reforms at the beginning of the new reign, quitted their ministry. "Ah!" cried Louis XVI., as Malesherbes asked him to accept his resignation: "how fortunate you are! would that I could get away also!" It would take too long here to enter into public details which have not as yet a close connection with the life of Madame Élisabeth; suffice it to say briefly, that all efforts at reform on the part of these ministers and the young monarch miscarried. The king's edicts which suppressed the *corvée* (forced labour) and abolished corporations and their privilege, were bitterly opposed in parliament; and it required a *lit de justice* to enforce their registration. All attempts to reform the army made by the Comte de Saint-Germain, minister of war, and his auxiliary, M. de Guibert,[1] also failed. With singular unwisdom they contrived to displease the officers and discontent the troops at the very moment when it was so necessary to be able to count upon the inviolable fidelity of the army.

Nothing, therefore, of all that was attempted succeeded well, and Louis XVI. began the second portion of his reign with vanished illusions and fears for the future.

On the 17th of May, 1778, the Court went to Marly. The king having determined to give his sister an establishment, she was on that day resigned into his hands by her then governess, the Princesse de Guéménée, and His Majesty gave her the Comtesse Diane de Polignac as lady of honour, with the Marquise de Sérent as lady-in-waiting. From that moment there was question of her marriage. Her hand seemed, in the first instance, destined to the Infant of Portugal, Prince of Brazil, who was the same age as herself and would eventually have brought her the title of queen. While she saw the conveniences of this alliance, Madame Élisabeth was far from wishing it, and though she personally put no obstacle in the way, she was comforted on learning that the negotiations were broken off.

[1] The lover of Mlle. de Lespinasse. — Tr.

Shortly after, two other princes sought the honour of obtaining her hand. One was the Duke of Aosta, who was five years older than herself and could give her, in a neighbouring and friendly Court, a place on the steps of a throne beside her sister Clotilde; but the political pride of the government asserted that a secondary place at the Court of Sardinia was not becoming to a Daughter of France. Her third suitor was the Emperor Joseph II., brother of Marie-Antoinette, who on the occasion of his journey to France the preceding year had been struck by the vivacity of her mind and the sweetness of her nature. But the anti-Austrian party, which by that time (1783) prevailed at Court, where it had already sown around the queen distrust and hatreds, dreaded an alliance which might be contrary to its ascendancy, and set to work to prevent it. The intrigue succeeded. It was said, without grounds, that Madame Élisabeth felt some regret at this conclusion. The emperor had not yet shown in politics the eccentricities of his mind, and he had just lost a wife whose youth, virtues, and piety had won the love and benedictions of a whole people.[1] But Madame Élisabeth, although she assuredly possessed all the qualities that fitted her for such an inheritance, seemed to attach no greater value to this union than to the other marriages with which policy had interfered.

As time went on, Madame Élisabeth strengthened herself perceptibly against the dangers of her nature, her age, and the Court; she felt more and more what was lacking in her. Her efforts increased from her self-distrust, and the more she acquired higher qualities the less she knew herself capable of the perfection she sought to attain. It was this feeling

[1] She was the daughter of Madame Infanta Duchess of Parma, oldest twin daughter of Louis XV., consequently the first cousin of Madame Élisabeth. — Tr.

of humility which gave to her speech an exquisite restraint, to her actions a prudent reserve, and to her charity a wise discretion.

All the young girls who had been brought in contact with Madame Élisabeth or had grown up with her, sharing her studies and her pleasures, gave her a warm and sincere devotion; to them she was not the princess but the friend. "How lovable you are, my heart," she says in one place, "to wish to forget that I am princess; nothing could give me greater pleasure than to forget it myself; I say it as I think it. Friendship, you see, my Bombelles, is a second life, which sustains us in this low world."

Among these young girls were two or three whom her heart distinguished specially, and with them she corresponded steadily to the last of her living life. One was Mlle. de Mackau, the daughter of the lady to whom she owed so much, who was early married to the Marquis de Bombelles, then ambassador to Portugal, and at the time of the Revolution ambassador to Venice. Another was Mlle. Marie de Causans, third daughter of the Marquise de Causans, who was appointed by the king, at the time Madame Élisabeth's establishment was formed, as lady of honour and superintendent of his sister's household. Her second daughter, Virginie, was chanoinesse at Metz, who spent the months of her vacation in Madame Élisabeth's establishment. The love between them became so strong that the princess dreading the moment of the young girl's return to her Chapter endeavoured to make her one of her own ladies-in-waiting; but the Marquise de Causans, although a widow of small means and a large family, made it a principle that none of her four daughters should hold office at Court unless she was married, and she turned a deaf ear to Madame Élisabeth's entreaties. Then a thought came to the princess;

she went one morning to the queen and said in her coaxing, gentle way: "Promise to grant me what I am going to ask of you." The queen, before promising, wished to know the request, and a playful battle ensued. Finally Madame Élisabeth yielded and said: "I want to give Causans a *dot;* ask the king to advance me for five years the thirty thousand francs he always gives me as a New Year's gift." The queen very willingly took charge of the commission, and the king as willingly granted the request. The Marquis de Raigecourt presented himself as a husband, and Louis XVI. appointed the young wife as lady-in-waiting to his sister. Her joy knew no bounds. For five years she received no presents, and when the matter was mentioned she would say, "I have no presents yet, but I have my Raigecourt." The fifth year expired in 1789, but by that time public difficulties intervened, and the custom of years was given up.

A brother of Mme. de Raigecourt, the Marquis de Causans, a member of the States General, was also a friend of Madame Élisabeth, who kept up a close correspondence with him on the events of the time. Her letters were said by him to contain very just and lofty conceptions on passing events, and especially on what was taking place in the Assembly. That collection of letters, in which the energy of her spirit and the penetration of her views were visible, it is said, on every page, was confided by the Marquis de Causans, at the time he was compelled to emigrate, to hands which he had every reason to consider peculiarly safe; but it disappeared in one of those cataclysms of which the revolutionary tornado produced so many examples.

Madame Élisabeth's letters to Mme. de Bombelles and Mme. de Raigecourt, while somewhat cautious as to public affairs, nevertheless express, as we shall see later, a sound and independent judgment on principles and passing events, and are the only personal revelation of her heart and mind which we possess before the black pall drops forever, on the 10th of August, 1792, between the family in the Temple and the world.

The domestic happiness which Madame Élisabeth now began to enjoy in her own little circle seems to have reigned in the palace of Versailles as well. Never before did the Court of France present such a sight: a young queen living in perfect harmony with two sisters-in-law of her own age, and a young king liking to lean on the friendship of his two brothers. "The greatest intimacy," says Mme. Campan, "existed between the three households [that of the king, that of *Monsieur*, the Comte de Provence, and that of the Comte d'Artois]. " They met together at meals, and ate apart only when their dinners were in public. This manner of family living lasted until the time when the queen allowed herself to dine occasionally with the Duchesse de Polignac, but the evening meeting for supper was never interrupted, and it took place always in the apartments of the Comtesse de Provence. Madame Élisabeth took her place there as soon as she had finished her education, and sometimes Mesdames, the king's aunts, were invited. This family intimacy, which had no precedent at Court, was the work of Queen Marie-Antoinette, and she maintained it with great perseverance."

The interests and pleasures of a young Court nevertheless gave rise to intrigues which at times divided the members of the royal family. The king and his brothers were each of different natures. Louis XVI., who possessed the virtues of an honest man, was far from having all those which are required in a king. His self-distrust was extreme. While he was still dauphin, if a question arose that was difficult to decide, "Ask my brother of Provence about that," he would say. Trustful in others, he surrendered his own will readily; but if he discovered that any one deceived him he flew into fits of passion. He had neither firmness of character nor grace of manner. Like certain excellent fruits with a knotty rind, his exterior was rough, but the heart perfect. Stern to himself alone, he kept the laws of the Church rigorously, abstained and fasted during the forty Lenten days, but thought it right that the queen should not imitate him. Sincerely pious, but trained to tolerance by the influence of the century in which he lived, he was also disposed, too disposed perhaps, to yield the prerogatives of the throne whenever the interests of his people were alleged to him; forgetting that one of the first interests of a nation is the maintenance of a strong and incontestable power. A weak royalty is impotent both to do good and to prevent evil.

There was in Louis XVI. something honest which did not accept complete liability (*solidarité*) for the preceding reign; but, heir of a régime of which he bore the weight, he was ill at ease between a past which roused repugnance and a future, not threatening as yet, but full of doubts and mystery. Simple, economical, liking to read and study, seeking to forget his throne in the exercise of hunting or of manual labour, detesting women without virtue and men without conscience, he seems a stranger in his own Court, where morals were light and consciences easy. A young king, given to moderation and faithful to duty, regarding himself as the father of all Frenchmen, but especially drawn to those who were weakest, could not be appreciated by courtiers, men for the most part frivolous and in debt, corrupters or corrupted, who regarded innovations as a danger and reforms as a crime.

The Comte de Provence, whose intellect and education

were on a par, concealed beneath a prudent dignity his regret at not being put by fate in the first rank. Versed in the culture of letters, aided by a wonderful memory, he felt himself, in a literary aspect, to be far superior to the king his brother. This sentiment was born in him from childhood. One day the Duc de Berry, playing with his brothers, used the expression *il pleuva*. "What a barbarism!" cried the Comte de Provence, "a prince ought to know his own tongue." "And you ought to hold yours," retorted the elder.

Monsieur took pleasure in the society of men of letters; he endeavoured to explain to himself the source and inspiration of the new ideas that rose on the horizon, he prepared himself for events that he might not be surprised by them; he temporized with parties and united with none; he lived with his brothers without dissensions and without confidence; he toyed with opinion coldly; and when the day came that unfortunate arrangements made the king's departure a failure at Varennes, he cleverly kept out of danger and reserved himself for the future.

The Comte d'Artois was a type of the Frenchman of the olden time; careless in temperament, gay in mind, and with all the chivalrous graces. Well made, choice in his toilet, adroit at all exercises of the body, he never appreciated grandeur except for the advantages it gave him, nor fortune except for the pleasures it procures. The manner in which he regarded women followed him even into the sanctuary. "Monseigneur," said the Bishop of Limoges on one occasion, "I have a favour to ask of your Royal Highness,— it is that you will not come to mass." Born in a frivolous and voluptuous Court, he took the habits of it; but his heart was generous, and that quality survived exile, a throne, and disaster.

It is easy to see how around three such princes men of

different morals and ideas grouped themselves; honest men were near Louis XVI., politicians near the Comte de Provence, the frivolous and volatile near the Comte d'Artois. Thus the friends of the king were few, those of *Monsieur* numerous, those of the Comte d'Artois innumerable. The last had the pretension to think themselves directly under the patronage of the queen, who, lively and brilliant, wanted the pleasures of her age and took delight in the Comte d'Artois, who amused her and whose tastes were somewhat like her own. The jealous and malignant spirit of a swarm of courtiers endeavoured to make a crime of the queen's liking for the gay young brother-in-law, but they have not succeeded, to the eyes of history, in poisoning amusements witnessed by the whole Court, not to speak of the Comtesse d'Artois, whose affection for the queen remained unchanged.

Such was the interior of the palace of Versailles during the years which preceded the Revolution. The princes and princesses of the blood seldom appeared there; their tastes and habits were different. "Of the three branches of the House of Bourbon," said the old Maréchal de Richelieu, one day, "each has a ruling and pronounced taste: the eldest loves hunting; the Orléans love pictures; the Condés love war." "And Louis XVI.," some one asked, "what does he love?" "Oh, he is different, he loves the people."

Except on occasions of formal etiquette, the absence from Court of the princes of the blood was noticeable. Exception must be made, however, of the Princesse de Lamballe, whose functions, as superintendent of the queen's household and her affection for the queen herself, kept her always at Court. The princes of the blood, whom the quarrels with parliament had thrown into the Opposition, considered it advisable to add to the privileges of their birth the advantages of popularity obtained by the so-called independence of their opinions. The time was coming when the great House of Bourbon was to weaken and condemn itself to impotence by the falling apart of its sheaves.

Madame Élisabeth was now, at the age of fifteen, to find herself mistress of her actions, surrounded by the splendours of fortune, invited to share all pleasures, and observed by every eye. What is liberty at that age if not release from study, amusement, toilet, jewels, and fêtes? Such was not the programme of the king's young sister. Her conscience took upon itself the duty of exercising the same control and watchfulness over her conduct that her governesses had just laid down. "My education is not finished," she said; "I shall continue it under the same rules; I shall keep my masters, and the same hours will be given to religion, the study of languages, belles-lettres, instructive conversations, and to my walks and rides on horseback." And she kept to all that she thus planned.

Her appearance at this time has been described and painted, although she herself had a great repugnance to sitting for her picture. Her figure was not tall, neither had her bearing that majesty which was so much admired in the queen; her nose had the shape which is characteristic of the Bourbon face; but her forehead with its pure lines giving to her countenance its marked character of nobleness and candour, her dark blue eyes with their penetrating sweetness, her mouth with its smile that showed her pretty teeth, and the expression of intelligence and goodness that pervaded her whole person formed a charming and sympathetic presence.

It was at this time that she began to reflect on public affairs, and her first strong interest was in America. In spite of many difficulties, Louis XVI. had succeeded in making certain useful reforms in the interior of the kingdom. He abolished the *corvée*, substituting for it taxes in money;

he created in Paris the Mont-de-Piété (pawn or loan shops) and the Caisse d'Escompte; he also calmed the public fear of bankruptcy by securing the payment of the Funds (*rentes*) on the Hôtel-de-Ville. The first political event of his reign was the war of independence in America. By an act recently put forth, the English Parliament declared it "had the right to force the colonies to obey all its laws and in all cases." It was this act, the execution of which destroyed the very shadow of freedom, which produced the American Revolution.

The representatives of the future United States assembled and by a solemn act declared the inhabitants of the colonies free and independent and released from all relations with England. This Congress called religion to the support of the dawning liberty, and placed America beneath the immediate protection of Providence. That august dedication was made with great ceremony: a crown, consecrated to God, was placed upon the Bible; and that crown was then divided into thirteen parts for the deputies of the thirteen provinces, and medals were struck to commemorate this event. All the women of the country, at their head the wife of Washington, made themselves remarkable for their patriotic zeal; acts of an ancient chivalry and heroism signalized this memorable war, the reading of which wrung tears of admiration and enthusiasm from Madame Élisabeth.

We cannot enter into the details of the great events that follow. Our troops were fortunate in this war as auxiliaries; America threw off the British yoke and secured her independence, but our navy and that of Spain, our ally, suffered cruelly. This war, although it was, like all war, contrary to the feelings of humanity in Madame Élisabeth, nevertheless flattered her national pride, and made the sacrifices which ended in her brother's glory and that of the nation less painful to bear. But what she especially noted with warm satisfaction throughout the struggle was the generous spirit that ruled it and sometimes lessened its evils. Thus she read with pleasure in a report, addressed November 26, 1781, to the minister of the navy, by the Marquis de Bouillé, then governor of Martinique, that the French troops under his orders had, on seizing the island of Saint-Eustache, shown a spirit of justice and loyalty equal to their patience and courage.

"I found in the government house," writes M. de Bouillé, "the sum of a million sterling which was in sequestration, awaiting a decision of the court of London. It belonged to the Dutch; and I made it over to them after obtaining authentic proofs of their ownership."

And again, in another report to the minister of the navy, Captain de la Pérouse, commanding a squadron of the king, writing on board the "Sceptre" in the Hudson straits, September 6, 1782, says:—

"I took care, when burning the fort at York, to leave a rather considerable storehouse at a distance from the fire, in which I deposited provisions, powder, shot, guns, and a certain quantity of European merchandise, such as was suitable to exchange with savages, in order that the English, who I know have taken refuge in the woods, may find, on their return to their old quarters, enough for their subsistence until the English authorities have been informed of their situation. I feel certain that the king will approve my conduct in this respect, and that in thus providing for those unfortunates I have only forestalled the benevolent intentions of His Majesty." Such facts as these were collected and told by Madame Élisabeth with delight.

In the year 1781 the king bought the property of the Princesse de Guéménée, at Montreuil, which the wreck of her husband's fortunes did not allow her to retain. He asked the queen, to whom he had confided his project, to invite Élisabeth to go to Montreuil when they next drove out together, and take her (with a purpose) into the house of her former governess, of which he knew his sister was very fond. Delighted with the surprise she was to give to the young girl, Marie-Antoinette gave the invitation: "If you like," she said, "we will stop on our way at Montreuil, where you were so fond of going when a child." Élisabeth replied that it would be a great pleasure. On arriving, they found everything arranged to receive them, and as soon as they had entered the salon the queen said: "Sister, you are in your own house. This is to be your Trianon. The king, who gives himself the pleasure of giving it to you, gives me the pleasure of telling you."

The brotherly inspiration of Louis XVI. was not at fault. This gift became to Madame Élisabeth a source of infinite enjoyment; for from this moment she was able to associate her dearest friends familiarly with her daily existence, and escape from the pomps of Court whenever her duty did not require her presence there. Madame Élisabeth was born for private intimacy; lively, confiding, and expansive in her familiar circle of a few friends, she was timid, reserved, and even embarrassed, not only in the queen's salons, but in her own, surrounded by all her ladies. It was therefore to her a source of the keenest enjoyment, or rather of happiness, to have this private home of her own with its rural delights.

The park and mansion, of which she now took possession, was near the barrier at the entrance to Versailles on the road to Paris. The park itself was of twelve acres, charmingly diversified with greensward and trees, and with shrubbery paths among the copses in all directions. A large section of the property Madame Élisabeth presently devoted to a cowpasture, dairy, vegetable and fruit gardens, and a poultry-yard. In the middle of a lawn, shaded with trees and shrubs and brightened with beds of flowers, stood the house, the peristyle of which was supported by four marble columns. The first act of the young proprietor was to give a small house on the estate to Mme. de Mackau, whose permanent home it became.

The king decided that until Madame Élisabeth had reached her twenty-fifth year (she was now eighteen) she should not sleep at Montreuil; but as soon as she was put in possession of her dear domain she passed the entire day there, and was only at Versailles in the evening and at night, or for occasions of ceremony. She heard mass in the morning in the Chapel of the Château, and immediately after it went with certain of her friends in a carriage, or on horseback, an exercise of which she was very fond, or sometimes on foot to Montreuil. The life she led there was uniform, like that of a family in some country château a hundred leagues from Paris. Hours for study, work, and rambles, either alone or with friends, occupied her time; the dinner-hour brought them all together around the same table.

Little by little her occupations increased. She laid out her farm, her dairy, her kitchen-gardens and poultry-yard, and became herself the farmer of the place; she loved all rural interests. She had an overseer, to whom she gave full authority under herself; and this man and those under him fulfilled her orders with such care and assiduity that no disputes and no complaints ever troubled that happy solitude.

But Madame Élisabeth was not satisfied with her own enjoyment of the place. Soon she became the friend and providence of the neighbouring village and its environs. She knew all the inhabitants personally; their interests became hers; young girls were dowered and married, the old

and the worthy were cared for, the sick were nursed and doctored. The milk of her dairy went to the children, the vegetables and fruits to the sick; often she could be seen attending to the distribution herself. All this was not done without personal sacrifice. Her means were comparatively small; she had only the pension which she received as sister of the king, but she eked it out by economy,— economy on herself, be it said. "Yes, that is very pretty," she replied, when urged to buy a jewel which she fancied, "but with that money I could set up two little homes." Various other anecdotes of this kind have come down to us, but Madame Élisabeth herself frowned on any notice being taken of such deeds. On one occasion, when the Bishop of Alais made her a fulsome speech of admiration, she said, blushing, that he judged her far too favourably. "Madame," he replied, "I am not even on the level of my subject." "You are right," she said, with a certain little sarcasm that was all her own; "you are very much above it."

One pleasure which she derived from her new way of living was that of seeing her brothers with greater freedom. *Monsieur* would often drive out to Montreuil and spend hours with her. "My brother, the Comte de Provence," she said one day, "is the most enlightened of advisers. His judgment on men and things is seldom mistaken, and his vast memory supplies him with an inexhaustible source of interesting anecdotes." The society of the Comte d'Artois gave her interests of another kind. More sensible than he, she often permitted herself to lecture him. Gay and heedless, he laughed at her advice, but as he advanced in life he began to love her with a tenderness mingled with veneration, a feeling which increased as misfortunes closed down upon them. After he had left France, those about him could guess when he received a letter from her; emotion showed on his features and his hands trembled as he opened it. Reciprocal affection between a brother and sister was never keener, truer, or more expansive.

Madame Élisabeth's relation to Louis XVI. was of still another character. They both seemed aware that she was, and would be, necessary to him. She liked to visit her aunt Louise, the Carmelite nun at Saint-Denis. The king became uneasy at the frequency of these visits. "I am very willing," he said to her one day, "that you should go and see your aunt, but only on condition that you will not imitate her. Élisabeth, I *need you.*" Her heart had told her that already, and the time was swiftly approaching when she obeyed the inward call and gave up her life to him.

Thus flowed the days of the happy young princess until the terrible winter of 1788–89, when the sufferings of the poor exhausted her means and made her run in debt to advance to the starved and frozen people what she called "their revenue." Her letters show that already she foresaw, and rightly, the public troubles that were soon to appear. She knew the character of the king; she believed that his impolitic action on the 8th of May, 1788, could end only in the recall of the parliament, of M. Necker, and the convocation of the States-General. In a letter of hers dated June 9, 1788, she says: "The king returns upon his steps, as did our grandfather. He is always afraid of being mistaken; his first impulse passed, he is tormented by a fear of doing injustice. . . . It seems to me," she continues, "that it is in government as it is in education: one should not say *I will,* unless one is sure of being right; then, once said, nothing should be given up of what has been ordained." Madame Élisabeth would fain have had the king take that principle as his rule of conduct, and she foresaw the evils that his kindness and his weakness would produce. "I see a thousand things," she says, "which he does not even suspect, because his soul is so good that intrigue is foreign to it." The note of foreboding, not, perhaps, fully comprehended by her own mind, is in much that she says and writes at this period. Instinctively she turns to the support of her life — to the spirit of faith — and we find her inmost thoughts in a prayer to the Sacred Heart of Jesus, written at this time and given to Mme. de Raigecourt, the manuscript of which, in her own handwriting, is preserved in the Bibliothèque Nationale: —

"Adorable heart of Jesus, sanctuary of the love that led God to make himself man, to sacrifice his life for our salvation, and to make of his body the food of our souls: in gratitude for that infinite charity I give you my heart, and with it all that I possess in this world, all that I am, all that I shall do, all that I shall suffer. But, my God, may this heart, I implore you, be no longer unworthy of you; make it like unto yourself; surround it with your thorns and close its entrance to all ill-regulated affections; set there your cross, make it feel its worth, make it willing to love it. Kindle it with your divine flame. May it burn for your glory; may it be all yours, when you have done what you will with it. You are its consolation in its troubles, the remedy of its ills, its strength and refuge in temptation, its hope during life, its haven in death. I ask you, O heart so loving, the same favour for my companions. So be it."

"*Aspiration.*

"O divine heart of Jesus! I love you, I adore you, I invoke you, with my companions, for all the days of my life, but especially for the hour of my death.

O vere adorator et unice amator Dei, miserere nobis. Amen."

It was on the 5th of October, 1789, the day when the Parisian mob of men and women marched to Versailles and compelled the king to take the fatal step of going to Paris, that Madame Élisabeth was suddenly, without warning, hurried from her dear Montreuil, never to enter it again. From the terrace of her garden she saw the first coming of the populace, and, mounting her horse, she rode to the palace. The king was out hunting, but messengers had gone for him, and when he returned she urged him to stand firm against this vanguard of anarchy, saying that a vigorous and immediate repression would avert great future evils, and advising with true instinct that if the royal family left Versailles at all, it should be for a town at a distance from Paris, where loyal men could rally to the king and enable him to break through the tyranny that the factions were beginning to exercise.

For a moment he seemed to listen to her and to the counsels of M. de Saint-Priest, minister of the interior, whose opinions agreed entirely with hers. But his firmness gave way before the views of M. Necker, and he consented to negotiate, as power to power, with the rioters. Prompted by its leaders, the mob demanded that the king should instantly fix his residence in Paris, and M. de la Fayette sent message after message urging him to comply. Madame Élisabeth expressed her contrary opinion: "It is not to Paris, Sire, that you should go. You have still devoted battalions and faithful guards to protect you. I implore you, my brother, not to go to Paris."

The king, pulled this way and that by conflicting opinions, hesitated too long; the moment for resistance went by; the troops, indignant at a thoughtless neglect of them, lost ardour, and the king, without initiative, without will, deferred to the clamour of the multitude and gave his promise to depart. As the miserable procession passed Montreuil, Madame Élisabeth bent forward in the carriage to look at the trees of her dear domain. "Are you bowing to Montreuil, sister?" asked the king. "Sire, I am bidding it farewell," she answered gently.

From this time she shared the captivity — for such it was — of her brother and his family. At first a semblance of social life was kept up at the Tuileries. The Princesse de Lamballe tried to gather a society about her, and the queen for a while appeared at her assemblies; but confidence and safety were gone; this last effort of gayety, begun by the princess to brighten the queen's life, ceased, and the royal family took up a system of living which they followed ever after, even in the Temple. During the mornings the queen and Madame Élisabeth superintended the lessons of Madame Royale and the dauphin, and worked at large pieces of tapestry. Their minds were too preoccupied by the events of the day, the perils of the present and the threats of the future, to allow them to read books, as they did later in the awful silence and monotony of the Tower; needlework became their sole distraction. Mlle. Dubuquois, who kept a shop for wools and tapestries, long preserved and exhibited a carpet made by the two princesses for the large room of the queen's apartment on the ground floor of the Tuileries.

During this time Madame Élisabeth continued whenever the opportunity came to her to urge the king to assert himself and firmly maintain his power and the monarchy. When M. de Favras was executed (February 19, 1790) and the king did not, or could not, interfere to save him, she exclaimed in the bitterness of her heart: "They have killed Favras because he tried to save the king, and the days of October 5th and 6th remain unpunished! Oh, if the king would only *be* king, how all would change!" She saw with dread the coming crisis which, breaking the lines of government, would render the king's will impotent and repression impossible. This conviction appears in many details of her life. Noticing that one of her ladies looked attentively into the garden of the Tuileries (May, 1791), she asked what attracted her attention. "Madame, I am looking at our good master, who is walking there." "Our master!" she exclaimed. "Ah! to our sorrow, he is that no longer."

The queen shared the anxiety that the king's weakness inspired in Madame Élisabeth, but she had a hope which Madame Élisabeth did not share. She was convinced that the safety of the royal family and the French monarchy would be undertaken by Austria, and that some efficacious succour would come from that direction, without her making any appeal for it. This was attributing to her brother and the cabinet of Vienna a generosity they were far from having, and admitting a hope which her enemies were not slow in turning into a crime.

It should here be remarked that Madame Élisabeth judged the politics of the European cabinets with severity. She was very far from approving the official advice and crafty insinuations which made their way to Queen Marie-Antoinette. Having a profound aversion for all that did not seem to her upright, just, and straightforward, she was convinced that the secret proceedings of the Comte de Mercy — "that fox," as she called him — would prove fatal; but being without power to combat that influence, she could only pity Marie-Antoinette for enduring it, and for lending an ear to counsels which, without serving the family welfare, compromised, in her opinion, the stability of her brother's throne. To be just, we must here remark that Madame Élisabeth had been brought up, like all the princesses of the House of France, to distrust Austria. The same feelings could not be expected of the daughter of Maria Theresa. Equitable history will recognize that Marie-Antoinette never dreamed of sacrificing France to her native country; but she did hope and believe that the alliance with the House of Austria, of which her marriage had been a pledge, would serve the interests of the two nations, and be a support to the French monarchy now shaken to its foundations.

The day came at last when Louis XVI., goaded by his virtual captivity and exposed to the virulent actions of the clubs as well as to the monstrous insults of the street populace, attempted to recover power. He resolved to leave Paris and raise his standard elsewhere in France, thus following, on the 20th of June, 1791, the advice his sister had given him October 5, 1789.

The story of the escape from Paris and the stoppage at Varennes is too fully told elsewhere to repeat it here. Madame Élisabeth makes only brief allusion to it in her letters of that date. After their return to Paris M. de la Fayette, appointed by the National Assembly governor of the Tuileries and keeper of the king and royal family, offered to allow Madame Élisabeth to leave the kingdom. This she refused to accept, and that decision sealed her fate. Nevertheless, she shuddered as she contemplated with clear eyes the position of the king and queen, deprived of all military support, reduced to beg their friends to go away from them, isolated henceforth on a throne without power, captives in a palace which was really a prison, and forbidden the last right of misfortune, that of complaint. She saw that in vain the king had sacrificed his prerogatives, given up his rights, abandoned his honours; the factions by this time disputed even his right to think, and measured out to him and his family the very air they breathed. Madame Élisabeth made herself no illusions as to the projects of the anarchists; on the 20th of June, 1792, the anniversary of the capture at Varennes, they justified her fears.

She relates the events of that day in a letter, omitting, however, certain acts of her own which redound to her glory. As the king left his family to face the mob, she followed him, and darting through the door, which was instantly locked behind her, she placed herself beside him as he stood on a table which the pressure of the mob had forced him to mount with the *bonnet rouge* upon his head. The populace took her for the queen and threatened her. "Do not undeceive them," she said. There she remained for several hours, exposed to the vilest insults. Once when a bayonet almost touched her breast, she turned it aside with her hand, saying: "Take care, monsieur, you might wound me, and I am sure you would be sorry for that."

A woman of the people, speaking the next day of the failure of the attack, said: "We could do nothing; they had their Sainte Geneviève with them," giving her the name the fish-wives applied to her as the carriage entered Paris on the fatal 5th of October, the last day of the French monarchy.

It was on the day following this 20th of June, that Louis XVI. wrote to his confessor: "Come and see me this evening, I have done with men; I can now concern myself only with heaven."

In spite of the vast emigration of nobles and gentlemen who abandoned their country and their king from the time of the first revolutionary alarms in 1789,— which has been, perhaps, too much condoned by history in view of their great misfortunes,— a few faithful men remained in Paris after June 20th, resolved to save the king and his family if it were still possible. They knew that the attack of June 20th was an organized blow, missed for the moment, but certain to be repeated. As early as the morning of the

7th of August they had precise information as to what was to happen on the 10th, and they formed a definite plan for the rescue of the royal family. Malouet, in his "Memoirs of the Constituent Assembly," of which he was a member, gives a clear account of this.

Even the Constitutional party, alarmed at the rapidity with which the Revolution was rushing towards anarchy, was ready to rally to the king, and would have supported any action that removed him from Paris and placed him with the army; it was even proposed among them to bring a division under General de la Fayette to Compiègne to favour the escape of the royal family. This plan, conceived as early as May, 1792, failed, owing to the king's incurable distrust of the constitutionals and his remembrance that to them he owed the failure at Varennes. Malouet says:—

"M. de la Fayette, who now judged the state of things more soundly than he did at the beginning of the Revolution, was sincere in his desire to devote himself to the king and the Constitution, after having contributed to put them in great peril. He was sure of his army and that of his colleague Luckner, if the king decided to put himself at their head. He came to Paris in May to make the proposal, and as he knew the king had confidence in me he asked me to meet him."

Louis XVI. rejected this proposal, and Malouet adds: "Whatever were the desires, the hopes of the royal family, nothing justifies the imprudence of the king in isolating himself without defence in the midst of his enemies, and in not being willing, or not knowing how, to rally to himself a national party. . . . Can it be believed that the king, whose judgment was accurate, that the queen, who did not lack enlightenment or courage, that Madame Élisabeth, who had much of both, should have willingly reduced themselves

in the midst of the greatest dangers to complete inaction?
... I do not doubt that the security and hopes of the queen and Madame Élisabeth fastened themselves on help from the foreign Powers, which the king never invited except with much circumspection and always in hopes of averting a national war. These tentatives were as inconsequent as all else that he did. There was nothing precise, nothing complete in his plan; the secret powers given to the Baron de Breteuil were only contingent; more vague than unlimited, they appealed neither to the foreign armies, nor to the great body of *émigrés* assembled on the frontier; they simply tended to the mediation of the allies of France."

Meantime the crisis was approaching. The 5th of October and the 20th of June foretold it; on the 10th of August it came. There is comfort in feeling that a few generous hearts remained in Paris watching for a chance to save the royal family even at the last moment. Malouet was one of them, and he thus tells of their final effort, their forlorn hope: —

"M. de Lally [Tollendal]," he says, "came frequently to our meetings at the house of M. de Montmorin with MM. de Malesherbes, Clermont-Tonnerre, Bertrand, la Tour-du-Pin, Sainte-Croix, and Gouverneur Morris, envoy of the United States, for whom the king had a liking, and who gave His Majesty (but as uselessly as the rest of us) the most vigorous advice. It was on the 7th of August that we dined together for the last time. Our conference had for its object to attempt a fresh effort to carry off, by means of the Swiss Guard, the royal family and take them to Pontoise. Being fully warned in detail of all the preparations for the 10th of August, we had been assembled in consultation ever since the morning at M. de Montmorin's. He had written to the king informing him of everything, and saying that now there could be no holding back; that we should be the next morning before daylight, to the number of seventy, at the royal stables, where the order must be given to have saddle-horses ready for us; that the National Guard of the Tuileries, commanded by Acloque, would aid our expedition; that four companies of the Swiss Guard would start at the same hour from Courbevoie and come to meet the king; that we ourselves should escort him to the Champs-Élysées and put him in a carriage with his family. The bearer of the letter came back without reply. M. de Montmorin went at once to the king. Madame Élisabeth informed him that the insurrection would not take place; that Santerre and Pétion had pledged themselves to that; that they had received seven hundred and fifty thousand francs to prevent it and to bring the Marseillais over to the king's side. The king was none the less anxious and agitated, though fully decided not to leave Paris. . . . He said he preferred to expose himself to all dangers than begin civil war."

This is not the place to relate the public events of those days, so well known, with their causes and actors, to history; suffice it to say that the plan which miscarried June 20th was carried out on the 10th of August, when the king was persuaded, against the will of his wife and sister, to seek refuge in the National Assembly, while the Swiss Guard, believing he was still in the palace, fought to defend him and were butchered to a man. " Nail me to that wall," said Marie-Antoinette, "if I consent to go."

But before this day Madame Élisabeth had abandoned hope; she no longer sought to arm the king with courage; the lines of her face, and the look from her eyes now said, " Resignation," and such was her history from that moment. Her last letter bore date August 8, 1792, — two days before the fatal 10th; in it she spoke of the "death of the executive power," adding, "I can enter into no details." The last glimpse we have of her as a comparatively free woman on her way through the Tuileries to the National Assembly, is given by M. de La Rochefoucauld, in his unpublished Memoirs:—

"They issued," he says, "by the centre door [of the Tuileries]. M. de Bachmann, major of the Swiss Guard, came first through two ranks of his soldiers. M. de Poix followed him at a little distance, walking immediately before the king. The queen followed the king, leading the dauphin by the hand. Madame Élisabeth gave her arm to Madame the king's daughter; the Princesse de Lamballe and Mme. de Tourzel followed. I was in the garden, near enough to offer my arm to Madame de Lamballe, who was the most dejected and frightened of the party; she took it. The king walked erect; his countenance was composed, but sorrow was painted on his face. The queen was in tears; from time to time she wiped them and strove to take a confident air, which she kept for a while; nevertheless, having had her for a moment on my arm, I felt her tremble. The dauphin did not seem much frightened. Madame Élisabeth was calm, resigned to all; it was religion that inspired her. She said to me, looking at the ferocious populace: 'All those people are misguided; I wish their conversion, but not their punishment.' The little Madame wept softly. Madame de Lamballe said to me, 'We shall never return to the Château.'"

The Tower of the Temple, that historical purgatory of the royalty of France, is now to be the last scene and witness of the virtues of Madame Élisabeth; and it is also to witness a transformation in the character of its chief captive. Louis XVI., no longer feeble and irresolute, blundering and inert, becomes a patient, tranquil man, brave unto death, with charity to all, a true Christian, the innocent expiator of the crimes and faults of other reigns.

CHAPTER II.

Letters of Madame Élisabeth to the Marquise de Bombelles, the Marquise de Raigecourt, the Abbé de Lubersac, and others, from 1786 to August 8th, 1792.

To the Marquise de Bombelles.

September, 1786.

I possess in the world two friends, and they are both far away from me. That is too painful; one of you must positively return. If you do not return, I shall go to Saint-Cyr without you, and I shall still further avenge myself by marrying our *protégée* without you. My heart is full of the happiness of that poor girl who weeps with joy — and you not here! I have visited two other poor families without you. I pray to God without you. But I pray for you, for you need his grace, and I have need that he should touch you — you who abandon me! I do not know how it is, but I love you, nevertheless, tenderly. ÉLISABETH-MARIE.

November 27, 1786.

You see that I obey you, my child, for here I am again. You spoil me; you write to me punctually; that gives me pleasure, but I am afraid it may give you a headache. I preach against my interests, for I am very happy when I see your handwriting; I love you, but I love your health better than all. You say that Fontainebleau has not spoilt me; I like to believe it. Perhaps you will think that rather vainglorious, but I assure you, my heart [*mon cœur*], that I am very far from thinking I can remain good; I feel I have very much to do to be good according to God. The world judges lightly; on a mere nothing it gives us a good or a bad reputation. Not so with God; he judges us internally; and the more the outward imposes, the sterner he will be to the inward. . . . I have been at Montreuil since nine o'clock, the weather is charming. I have walked about with Raigecourt for an hour and three-quarters. Mme. Albert de Rioms is coming to dine with me, so that my letter cannot be long.

March 15, 1787.

You ask me, my friend, how I pass my time; I shall answer: Rather sadly, because I see many things that grieve me. The famous Assembly of Notables has met. What will it do? Nothing, except make known to the people the critical situation in which we are. The king is sincere in asking their advice. Will they be the same in giving it? I think not. I have little experience, and the tender interest I take in my brother alone induces me to concern myself with these subjects, much too serious for my nature. I do not know, but it seems to me they are taking a course directly the opposite of that they ought to take. . . . I have a presentiment that all will turn out ill. As for me, if it were not for my attachment to the king I would retire to Saint-Cyr. Intrigues fatigue me; they are not in accordance with my nature. I like peace and repose; but it is not at the moment when my brother is unfortunate that I will separate from him.

The queen is very pensive. Sometimes we are hours together alone without her saying a word. She seems to fear me. Ah! who can take a keener interest than I in my brother's happiness?

April 9, 1787.

M. de Calonne was dismissed yesterday; his malversation was so proved that the king decided upon it; I do not fear to tell you the extreme joy I feel, which is shared by every one. He is ordered to remain at Versailles until his successor is appointed, so as to render him an account of affairs and of his projects. One of my friends said to me some time ago that I did not like him, but that I should change my opinion before long. I don't know if his dismissal will contribute to that; he would have to do a good many things before I could change in regard to him. He must feel a little anxious about his fate. They say his friends put a good face upon it; but I believe the devil loses nothing and that they are far from being satisfied. It was M. de Montmorin who gave him his dismissal. I hoped the Baron de Breteuil would not take that upon himself; it does him honour not to have done so.[1]

The Assembly continues as before and with the same plans. The Notables talk with more freedom (though they have never cramped themselves in that), and I hope good may come of it. My brother has such good intentions, he desires the right so much and to make his people happy, he has kept himself so pure, that it is impossible God should not bless his good qualities with great successes. He did his Easter duties to-day. God will encourage him, God will show him the right way: I hope much. The preacher in his address encouraged him immensely to take counsel of his own heart. He was right, for my brother is very good and very superior to the whole Court united.

[1] The Baron de Breteuil, then minister of the king's household and of the department of Paris, had been the representative of the king towards the Elector of Cologne, Catherine II., Empress of Russia, Gustavus III., King of Sweden, and the Emperors Joseph II. and Leopold. In the various phases of his career he had won the esteem of all honourable men. —FR. ED.

He was later sent by Louis XVI. to negotiate measures with all the European Powers for the rescue of the king and his family and the restoration of the monarchy. See Diary and Corr. of Count Fersen, of the present Hist. Series. — TR.

I am at Montreuil since midday. I have been to vespers in the parish church. They were quite as long as they were last year, and your dear vicar sang the *O filii* in a manner quite as agreeable. Des Escars expected to burst out laughing, and I the same.

I am in despair at the sacrifice you make me of your monkey, and all the more because I cannot keep it; my Aunt Victoire has a dread of those animals and would be angry if I had one. So, my heart, in spite of all its graces and of the hand that gives it to me, I must relinquish it. If you like, I will send it back to you; if not, I will give it to M. de Guéménée. I am in despair, I feel it is very churlish, that it will vex you very much, and so I am all the more sorry. What consoles me is that you would have had to get rid of it soon on account of your children, because it might become dangerous.

Your philosophy enchants me, my heart; you will be happier, and you know how I desired you to be that. I do not understand why you say that M. de C—— [Maréchal de Castries] is a bad politician; they seem to me well satisfied with him; he has done rather fine things, and M. de Ségur has just committed the most egregious blunder in accompanying the Empress Catherine on her journey to the Crimea. She is terribly restless, that good lady, which displeases me much. I am a partisan of repose.[1]

June 25, 1787.

The queen is very kind to me just now; we are going together to Saint-Cyr, which she calls my cradle. She calls Montreuil my little Trianon. I have been to hers the last few days with her, without any consequences, and there was no attention she did not show me. She prepared for me one

---

[1] See the account of this journey in the Memoirs of the Prince de Ligne vol. v. of this Hist. Series.— Tr.

of those surprises in which she excels; but what we did most was to weep over the death of my poor little niece [Madame Sophie de France, daughter of Louis XVI., who died an infant]. . . .

I am in a state of enchantment at the enormous gratuity they have given you. I am afraid the king will ruin himself with such liberalities. If I were your husband I would leave it with M. d'Harvelay to prove to M. de Vergennes that you demand more because you have an actual need of it; let him see it is to pay your debts for the embassy, and that as he gives you so little on account, when you get more you will have to employ it in the same way. I began by reading M. de Vergennes' letter first, thinking I was to see superb things, and I was rather shocked. However, after reflecting upon it well, I believe it is not ill-will on his part, but being obliged to give gratuities for the fêtes, he is hampered and is forced to diminish this one.

Adieu, my heart. I hope your medicine will do you good. Try to calm yourself.

June 6, 1788.

The king returns upon his steps, just as our grandfather did. . . . It seems to me that government is like education. We should not say *I will* until we are sure of being right. But once said, there should be no yielding of what has been ordained.

I think that my sister-in-law would act thus; but she does not yet know the soul of my brother, who fears always to make a mistake, and who, his first impulse over, is tormented by the dread of doing injustice. You will see that the parliament will be recalled within six months, and with it Necker and the States-General; that is an evil we shall not escape, and I wish they had been convoked a year ago that we might have them over and done with. Instead of that everybody wrangles and all are getting embittered. What the king does from clemency they will say he does from fear, for they will not do him the justice he deserves. As for me, who read his heart, I know well that all his thoughts are for the welfare of his people. But he would make that more sure by isolating himself less from his nobles. He is advised to the contrary. God grant he may never repent it! I dare not speak to him openly about many things that I see and that he does not suspect because his soul is so fine that intrigue is foreign to it. Ah! why cannot I get away and live as I like!

To Mlle. Marie de Causans.[1]

March, 1789.

Yes, certainly, my heart, I will write to you before you enter the novitiate; but I hope that you will not be forbidden to receive letters afterwards. It is true that we shall be hampered by the inspection of a mistress, but that will not prevent me from saying to you what I think. You will perhaps be astonished, my heart, when I tell you that in spite of all the reflections, consultations, and tests that you have made, I am not yet sufficiently convinced of the solidity and reality of your vocation to escape a fear that you have not reflected duly. In the first place, my heart, we cannot know whether a vocation is really the work of God until, with a desire to follow his will, we have nevertheless combated, in good faith, the inclination which leads us to consecrate ourselves to him; otherwise, we run the risk of deceiving ourselves, and of following a transient fervour that is often only a need of the heart which, having no objects of attachment, thinks to save itself from the danger of forming

[1] The third daughter of Mme. de Causans, and next younger sister of Mme. de Raigecourt. The Revolution, which broke up the convents, prevented her from becoming a nun. — Tr.

any that Heaven may disapprove by consecrating itself to God. That motive is praiseworthy, but it is not sufficient; it comes from passion, it comes from the desire and need of the heart to form a tie which shall fill it, for the moment, wholly. But, I ask you, my heart, will God approve of that offering? can he be touched by the sacrifice of a soul that gives itself to him only to rid itself of responsibility? You know that in order to make any vow of any kind we must have a free, reflecting will, devoid of all species of passion; it is the same in making the religious vows, and even more essential. The world is odious to you; but is that disgust or regret? Do not think that if it is the latter your vocation is true or natural. No, my heart, Heaven sent you a temptation; you ought to bear it, and not take a resolution to consecrate yourself to God until it has passed.

Secondly, my heart, we must have our minds humbled before taking the engagements you wish to take. This is the essential thing, the true vocation. All that concerns the body costs little, one can get used to that; but not so with all that belongs to the mind and heart. . . .

If d'Ampurie [her younger sister] is not married within three years, and is obliged to go to her Chapter, can you trust to her eighteen years and believe that she will always lead a virtuous and decorous life, that she will never need the counsel of a friend, of a sister who stands in place of her mother, and for whom she has all the feelings of a daughter? Do you think that in abandoning her to herself you fulfil the most sacred duty you have ever had to fulfil, — that to a dying mother who relied upon you, who chose you as the one most fitted to replace her, a mother who would certainly not have abandoned her children to the seductions of the world that she might yield to a taste for retreat and devotion which she would never have thought incumbent upon her?

No, my heart, it will be impossible for me to think that you fulfil your duty, that you accomplish the will of God by consecrating yourself to him at this time. In the name of that God you seek to serve in the most perfect manner, consult with others once more; but, my heart, let it be with more enlightened persons, persons who have no interests either for or against the course you wish to take; explain to them your position; let yourself be examined in good faith; you would be as wrong to exaggerate your desire as to conceal it. . . .

Reassure me, my heart, by telling me the tests to which you have put yourself. I do not speak of those of the body; those are absolutely null to me because they belong to mere habits; but have you struggled against your vocation? have you felt perfectly calm and free from all pains of mind? are you sure it is not from excitement that you give yourself to God? . . . Do not suppose, my heart, that a convent is exempt from evils in the eyes of a nun; the more perfect she may be, the more she will want to find the same sentiments in others, and you will not be safe from that temptation, for, I admit, it is one. There are very few convents in which charity reigns sufficiently for that fault to be unknown there.

Nevertheless, my heart, in whatever position you find yourself, rely upon my friendship and the keen interest that I feel in you, and speak to me with confidence of all that touches you. I dare to say that I deserve it, because of the true feelings that I have for you, and the tender interest inspired in me by all the children of your honoured and loving mother. I kiss you and love you with all my heart. I ask of you the favour not to be satisfied by reading my letter once.

To the Marquise de Bombelles.

May 29, 1789.

My heart is so full of the king's troubles that I cannot write to you of other things. All goes worse than ever. The king alone seems satisfied with the turn that things are taking. Few sovereigns in his place would be; but he has about it all a manner of seeing which is too lucky for him. The deputies, victims of their passions, of their weakness, or of seduction, are rushing to their ruin, and that of the throne and the whole kingdom. If at this moment the king has not the necessary sternness to cut off at least three heads, all is lost.

I do not ask you to return; you might find the roads all bloody. As for me, I have sworn not to leave my brother, and I shall keep my oath.

VERSAILLES, July 15, 1789.

How kind you are, my heart! All the dreadful news of yesterday [storming and destruction of the Bastille by the populace] did not make me weep, but your letter, bringing consolation into my heart through the friendship you show me, made me shed many tears. It will be sad for me to go without you. I do not know if the king will leave Versailles. I will do what you wish if there is a question of it. I do not know what I desire as to that. God knows the best course to take. We have a pious man at the head of the Council [Baron de Breteuil] and perhaps he will enlighten it. Pray much, my heart; spare yourself, take care of yourself, do not trouble your milk. You would do wrong I think, to go out; therefore, my dear, I make the sacrifice of seeing you. Be convinced of how much it costs my heart. I love you, dear, more than I can tell. At all times, in all moments I shall think the same.

I hope the evil is not as great as they think it. What makes me believe this is the calmness at Versailles. It was not very certain yesterday that M. de Launay was hanged; they had mistaken another man for him in the course of the day. I will attach myself, as you advise, to the chariot of *Monsieur*, but I think its wheels are worthless. I don't know why it is, but I am always ready to hope. Do not imitate me; it is better to fear without reason than to hope without it; the moment when the eyes open is less painful.

Paris, October 8, 1789.

My date alone will tell you to what a point our misfortunes have come. We have left the cradle of our childhood — what am I saying? left! we were torn from it. What a journey! what sights! Never, never will they be effaced from my memory. . . . What is certain is that we are prisoners here; my brother does not believe it, but time will prove it to him. Our friends are here; they think as I do that we are lost.

To the Abbé de Lubersac.
October 16, 1789.

I cannot resist, monsieur, the desire to give you news of me. I know the interest that you are kind enough to feel, and I doubt not it will bring me help. Believe that in the midst of the trouble and horror that pursued us I thought of you, of the pain you would feel, and the sight of your handwriting has brought me consolation. Ah! monsieur, what days were those of Monday and Tuesday [5th and 6th of October]! But they ended better than the cruelties that took place during the night could have made us expect. As soon as we entered Paris we began to feel hope in spite of the dreadful cries that we heard. But those of the people who surrounded our carriage were better. The queen, who has incredible courage, begins to be better liked by the people. I hope that with time and steadily sustained conduct we may recover the affection of the Parisians, who have only been misled.

But the men of Versailles, monsieur! Did you ever know a more frightful ingratitude? No, I think that God in his anger has peopled that town with monsters from hell. How much time will be needed to make them conscious of their crimes! If I were king, I should need much to make me believe in their repentance. How ungrateful to an honest man! Will you believe, monsieur, that our misfortunes, far from bringing me to God, give me a positive disgust for all that is prayer. Ask of Heaven for me the grace not to abandon it wholly. I ask of you this favour; and also, preach to me a little, I beg of you; you know the confidence that I have in you. Pray also that all the reverses of France may bring back to their better selves those who have contributed to them by their irreligion. Adieu, monsieur; believe in the esteem I have for you, and the regret I feel at your being so far away from me.

To the Marquise de Bombelles.

December 8, 1789.

I am very glad, Mademoiselle Bombelinette, that you have received my letter, as it gives you pleasure, and I am angry with it for being so long on the way. You have no idea what an uproar there has been to-day at the Assembly. We heard the shouts in passing along the terrace of the Feuillants. It was horrible. They wanted to rescind a decree passed Saturday; I hope they will not do it, for the decree seems to me very reasonable. You will see it all in the newspapers.

I have not made it a point of courage to refrain from

speaking to you of Montreuil. You judge me, my heart, too favourably. Apparently I was not thinking of it when I wrote to you. I often have news of it. Jacques comes daily to bring my cream. Fleury, Coupry, Marie, and Mme. du Coudray come to see me from time to time. They all seem to love me still; and M. Huret — I forgot him — is not very bad. Now, about the house. The salon was being furnished when I left it; it promised to be very pleasant. Jacques is in his new lodging. Mme. Jacques is pregnant; so are all my cows; a calf has just been born. The hens I will not say much about, because I have rather neglected to inquire for them. I don't know if you saw my little cabinet after it was finished. It is very pretty. My library is almost finished.[1] As for the chapel, Corille is working there all alone; you can imagine how fast it goes on! It is out of charity to him that I let him continue to put on a little plaster; as he is quite alone it cannot be called an expense. I am grieved not to go there as you can easily believe; but horses are to me a still greater privation. However, I think as little as I can about it; though I feel that as my blood grows calmer, that particular privation makes itself more and more felt; but I shall have all the more pleasure when I can satisfy that taste.

And that poor Saint-Cyr, ah! how unfortunate it is! Do you remember Croisard, the son of my sister's wardrobe woman? Well, he is to-day attached to my steps in the quality of captain of the guard. I say *attached*, because the guards never quit us more than the shadow of our bodies. You need not think it annoys me. As my movements are not varied, I do not care. After all, I can walk in the garden as much as I like. To-day I walked a full hour.

[1] See Appendix.

February 20, 1790.

You will only have a line from me to-day, my poor Bombe; I was told too late of an opportunity, and besides, my head and heart are so full of what happened yesterday that I have no possibility of thinking of anything else. Poor M. de Favras was hanged yesterday. I hope that his blood may not fall back upon his judges. No one (except the populace, and that class of beings to whom we must not give the name of men — it would be to degrade humanity) understands why he was condemned. He had the imprudence to wish to serve his king; that was his crime. I hope that this unjust execution will have the effect of persecutions, and that from his ashes will arise men who still love their country, and will avenge it on the traitors who are deceiving it. I hope also that Heaven, in favour of the courage he showed during the four hours he was kept at the Hôtel-de-Ville before his execution [when he was tortured and insulted], will have pardoned him his sins. Pray to God for him, my heart; you cannot do a better work.

The Assembly is still the same; the monsters are the masters. The king — can you believe it? — is not to have the necessary executive power to keep him from being absolutely null in his kingdom. For the last four days they have discussed a law to pacify the disturbances, but they have not ceased to busy themselves about other things far less essential to the happiness of men. Well, God will reward the good in heaven, and punish those who deceive the people. The king, and others, from the integrity of their own natures, cannot bring themselves to see the evil such as it is.

Adieu, my little one; I am well; I love you much; be the same, for love of your princess, and let us hope for happier days. Ah! how we shall enjoy them. I kiss your little children with all my heart.

You know the rules just made for monks and nuns. Say nothing to any one, but I think many men, and even nuns will leave their convents. I hope that Saint-Cyr will undergo no change; but its fate is not yet decided.

March 1, 1790.

Since the king has taken that step [his appearance before the Constituent Assembly Feb. 4, 1790], a step which puts him, they say, at the head of the Revolution, and which, to my mind, takes from him the remains of the crown that he still had, the Assembly has not once thought of doing anything for him. Madness follows madness, and good will certainly never come of it. . . . If we had known how to profit by occasions, believe me, we could have done well. But it was necessary to have firmness, it was necessary to face danger; we should have come out conquerors. . . . I consider civil war as necessary. In the first place, I think it already exists; because, every time a kingdom is divided into two parties, every time the weaker party can only save its life by letting itself be despoiled, it is impossible, I think, not to call that civil war. Moreover, anarchy never can end without it; the longer it is delayed, the more blood will be shed. That is my principle; and if I were king it would be my guide; and perhaps it would avert great evils. But as, God be thanked, I do not govern, I content myself, while approving my brother's projects, with telling him incessantly that he cannot be too cautious and that he ought to risk nothing.

I am not surprised that the step he took on the 4th of February has done him great harm in the eyes of foreigners. I hope, nevertheless, that it has not discouraged our allies, and that they will at last take pity on us. Our stay here is a great injury to our prospects. I would give all the world to be out of Paris. It will be very difficult, but still, I hope it may come about. Though I thought for a moment that we did right in coming to Paris, I have long changed my mind. If we had known, my heart, how to profit by that moment, be sure that we could then have done great good. But it needed firmness, it needed not to fear that the provinces would rise against the capital; it needed that we should face dangers; had we done so, we should have issued victors.

May 18, 1790.

You will have seen by the public papers, my dear child, that there has been some question of your husband in the Assembly, but you will also have seen that they would not even listen to M. de Lameth. So, my heart, you need not be uneasy. Some one said, apropos of M. de Lameth's speech, that he apparently feared that your husband would make Venice aristocratic, and so, wanted to get him away. I thought that charming. Your mother, who assuredly is not cold as to your interests, is not at all troubled by what took place. Therefore, my heart, let the storm growl, and do not worry.

At last we are let out of our den. The king is to ride out on horseback to-day for the third time; and I have been out once. I was not very tired, and I hope to go again on Friday. I am going this morning to Bellevue. I want to see an English garden and I am going for that. During that time the Assembly will probably be busy in taking from the king the right to wear his crown, which is about all that is left to him.

June 27, 1790.

It is long since I have written to you, my little Bombelinette; so I do it to-night in advance, not to be taken short by the post, which often happens to those who have a taste for sacred idleness. I shall not talk to you about the decrees that are issued daily, not even of the one put forth on a certain Saturday [abolition of titles of nobility]. It does not grieve the persons it attacks, but it does afflict the malevolent and those who issued it, because in all societies it has been made a subject of much diversion. As for me, I expect to call myself Mademoiselle Capet, or Hugues, or Robert, for I don't think I shall be allowed to take my real name, — de France. All this amuses me much, and if those gentlemen would issue only such decrees as that, I would add love to the profound respect I already feel for them.

You will think my style a little frivolous, considering the circumstances, but as there is no counter-revolution in it, I can be forgiven. Far from thinking of counter-revolutions we are about to rejoice (two weeks hence) with all the militia of the kingdom and celebrate the famous days of July 14 and 15, of which you may perhaps have heard. They are making ready the Champs de Mars, which can contain, they say, six hundred thousand souls. I hope for their health and mine, that it will not be as hot as it is this week, otherwise, with the liking that I have for heat, I believe I should explode. Pardon this nonsense; but I was so suffocated last week, at the review and in my own little room, that I am still dazed. Besides, one must laugh a little, it does one good. Mme. d'Aumale always told me, when I was a child, to laugh, because it dilated the lungs.

I finish my letter at Saint-Cloud; here I am, established in the garden, with my desk and a book in my hand, and here I get patience and strength for the rest that I have to do. Adieu; I love and kiss you with all my heart. Have you weaned your little monster, and how are you?

July 10, 1790.

I received your letter by the gentleman who has returned to Venice, but too late to answer it by him. We touch, my dear child, as the song says, the crucial moment of the Federation. It will take place Wednesday, and I am convinced that nothing very grievous will happen. The Duc d'Orléans is not yet here; perhaps he will come to-night or to-morrow; perhaps he will not come at all. I am of opinion that it is of no consequence. He has fallen into such contempt that his presence will cause but little excitement. The Assembly seems decidedly separated into two parties: that of M. de la Fayette, and that of the Duc d'Orléans formerly called that of the Lameths. I say this because the public believes it; but, I myself am of opinion that they are not as ill together as they want it to appear. Whether that is so, or is not so, it seems that M. de la Fayette's party is much the more considerable; and that ought to be a good thing, because he is less sanguinary, and seems to wish to serve the king by consolidating the immortal work to which Target gave birth February 4, of this year 90. All the reflections you make on the stay of the king [in Paris] are very just; I have long been convinced of it. But nothing of all that will happen, unless Heaven takes part therein. Pray for that strongly, for we need it much.

To the Marquise de Raigecourt.
July 20, 1790.

Do not come here, my heart; all is calm, but you are better in the country; I do not need you for the week's service; your husband wishes you to stay with your sister-in-law; therefore as a submissive wife, do not stir.

Paris was in great disturbance yesterday, but to-night all is very quiet. The States-General are still issuing decrees that have not common-sense. I am anxious lest the little line I wrote you may bring you back; reassure me and tell me you are still at Marseille [the château de Marseille in Picardy]. Be at ease about your husband, your brother, and all who are dear to you; they run no risks, and will run none. Adieu; I kiss you with all my heart; I am very tranquil, and you can be so entirely.

To the Marquise de Montiers.[1]

August 20, 1790.

I have received your letter, my dear child; it touched me very much; I have never doubted your feelings for me, but the signs you show of it give me great pleasure. It would have been infinitely agreeable to me to have seen you again this autumn, but I feel the position of your husband and I consent strongly to the plan he has formed of spending the winter in foreign countries. I will even own that your position makes me desire it; this country is tranquil, but from one moment to another it may be so no longer. You are too excitable to allow of your confinement in a place where from day to day an uprising is to be feared; your health could not resist it; moreover, with your disposition, recovery from confinement would be much more serious. Use all these reflections to aid you, my heart, in making the sacrifice that your husband's fortune and his position oblige you to make. If telling you that I approve of it can

---

[1] The Marquise des Montiers (Mlle. de la Briffe) had grown up from childhood with the princess; she was gay, vivacious, and full of imagination. Madame Élisabeth's letters to her take an almost maternal tone in advising, warning, and directing "my dear Demon," as she often called her. These friends were all Madame Élisabeth's ladies-in-waiting, and all were anxious to return to her in her cruel isolation; but although she was so dependent herself on friendship she would not, *for their sakes*, let them come to her. — Tr.

ke you bear it better, I shall repeat it to you incessantly.
t, my heart, what I cannot repeat to you too often, what I
h could be engraved upon your heart and mind, is that this
, decisive moment for your happiness and your reputation.
u are about to be trusted to yourself in a foreign country,
ere you can receive no counsel but your own. Perhaps
ı will meet there Parisian men whose reputations are not
y good; it is difficult in a foreign country not to receive
:'s compatriots, but do so with such prudence and regulate
ır actions with so much reason that no one can make talk
ıut you.

Above all, my heart, seek to please your husband. Though
ı have never spoken to me about him, I know enough of
a to know that he has good qualities, though he may also
ve some that do not please you so well. Make to yourself
ıw not to dwell upon those, and above all, not to let any
 speak of them to you; you owe this to him, and you owe
to yourself. Try to fix his heart. If you possess it, you
l always be happy. Make his house agreeable to him;
him find in it a wife eager to give him pleasure,
erested in her duties and her children, and you will
n his confidence. If you once have that, you can do,
h the intelligence that Heaven has given you and a
le skill, all that you wish. But, dear child, above all
ıctify your good qualities by loving God; practise your
igion; you will find strength in that, a resource in all
ır troubles, and consolations that it alone can give.
.! is there a happiness greater than that of being well
h one's conscience? Preserve it, that happiness, and
ı will see that the tortures of life are little, indeed, com-
:ed to the tortures of those who give themselves up to all
 passions.

Do not let the piety of your mother-in-law disgust you.

There are persons to whom Heaven has not given the grace of knowing it in its true light; pray to Heaven to enlighten her. I am glad that your husband sees her defects, but I should be sorry if by jesting or otherwise, you made him remark upon them. Forgive, my dear heart, all this prating; but I love you too well not to say to you that which I think will be useful to your happiness. You tell me with the amiability of which you are so capable, that if you are worth anything in life you owe it to me; take care, that is encouraging me to tire you again.

Adieu, my heart; write me as often as you have the desire to do so. If you have need to open your heart, open it to me, and believe that you cannot do so to any one who loves you more tenderly than I.

I am forgetting to reply about M. d'A. Not being able, in view of the present position of my affairs to do anything for him just now, I desire you to tell the person who spoke to you to send you word if he should be in a more critical position; then, I will do what I possibly can. Say many things from me to your mother-in-law, to whom I will write before long.

To the Marquise de Raigecourt.

August 29, 1790.

Good-morning, my poor Raigecourt; here we are back at Saint-Cloud to my great satisfaction; Paris is fine, but in perspective; here I have the happiness of seeing as much of it as I wish; indeed, in my little garden I can scarcely see more than the sky. I no longer hear those villanous criers who, of late, not content with standing at the gates of the Tuileries, have roamed the gardens, that no one might fail to hear their infamies.

For the rest, if you want news of my little health I shall

l you that I still have torpor in my legs.[1] Still, if I may st the symptoms of that horrid malady, I fancy the cure at hand. But I have already been mistaken so many ies, that I dare not flatter myself much; in fact, sincerely, lo not believe in it. Perhaps, if I had courage, I might n say I do not desire it; but you know that I am weak, l that I dread to expose myself to great pain. . . .

: am very impatient to get news of you, to know you are :led; I wish I could say happy, but that, I feel, is very icult [Mme. de Raigecourt had just lost a little son]. :tunately, you can give yourself up to devotion. That l be your consolation, your strength. Do not burden ir spirit with scruples; that would insult God who has ie you so many favours, and who deserves that you should to him with the confidence of a child. Make use of the :ructions you have received and of your rector's counsels juiet the over-sensitiveness of your feelings towards God.

. Yes, your soul is too sensitive: a trifle hurts it; l is more indulgent to his creatures; he knows our weaks, but in spite of it, he wants to crown us with all his ours, and, in return for so much kindness he asks for our fidence and our complete abandonment to his will. Ah! ʒ, at this present moment do we need to repeat to ourʒes that truth! You will often need to have recourse to ɪ to fortify yourself; do not therefore put yourself in a ition to be deprived of the divine nourishment. This is ɜal temptation which you ought to fight at its birth; if . let it make progress you will be very unhappy, you

---

[1] This expression, and others of the same kind, Madame Élisabeth uses ːpress her wish that the king would leave Paris, the hopes he gave her , and the efforts made to prevent it. Her letters to Madame de Raige‑ ‑t, who was in France, where correspondence might be dangerous, seem free than those to Madame de Bombelles, which went probably in the assador's bag, or by private hand. — TR.

will offend God ceaselessly. Here am I preaching like the peasant to his priest! but when the public news worries me I fling myself into sermonizing.

October 24, 1790.

I have just received your second letter. Make ready to receive a reproach in my style. Tell me why you think yourself obliged to be always in violent states? That is bad judgment, my dear child. You will make yourself ill, and give your child an inevitable tendency towards melancholy. And why? because you are not in Paris or at Raigecourt, and because all the stories people tell you seem truths in your eyes. For pity's sake, do not do so. Put into the hands of Providence the fate of those who interest you, and rub your eyes very hard to prevent their seeing black![1]

As for news, I only know that infamous tales are still told of the queen. Among others, they say there is an intrigue with Mir [abeau], and that it is he who advises the king! My patient [the king] still has stiffness of the legs, and I am afraid it will attack the joints and there will be no cure for it. As for me, I submit myself to the orders of Providence. To each day its own evil. I shall await the last moment to fall into despair, and in that moment I hope I shall do nothing. . . . We are going to-morrow, H. and I, to Saint-Cyr, to feed a little on that celestial food, which does me much good.

November 3, 1790.

Well, my poor Rage, are you getting accustomed to the life you lead? The late master of this place is being persecuted by his creditors who will end by killing all his friends

---

[1] Madame Élisabeth had exacted that Mme. de Raigecourt, who was pregnant, should leave Paris, events becoming more and more alarming. Mme. de R. fell into a sort of despair at the separation, and wanted to be allowed to return to Madame Élisabeth at any cost. — Fr. Ed.

with grief. Nothing that happens can decide him to part from his property: offers are made on all sides; nothing comes of them. What is to be done? we must pray to Providence to be with him.

Here we are back in Paris; if we knew how to profit by it I would not complain; but, as you know, the château of the Tuileries will be our habitual promenade. Well, as God wills; if I thought of myself only I do not know what I should prefer. Here I am more conveniently placed for my little devotions: but for walks and the gaiety of the place, Saint-Cloud is preferable; and then the neighbourhood of Saint-Cyr. On the other hand, the evenings were very long; you know I have a horror of lights, or rather they make me so sleepy that I cannot read long at a time. So on the whole I conclude that God arranges all for the best, and that I ought to be very glad to be here.

December 1, 1790.

Mon Dieu, my poor Raigecourt, what extraordinary thing have they been telling you? I puzzle my head to guess, and cannot do so. Nothing has happened here. We are still in perfect tranquillity, and I cannot conceive what you mean.

I have made a mistake of twenty-four hours as to the post-day, which is the reason this letter did not go by the last courier. You now know the decree about the clergy, and I can see from here, all that you are saying, all that you are thinking, how you are wringing your arms, and shutting your eyes, and saying, "Ah! God wills it; it is well, it is well, we must submit;" and then you do not submit any more than others. Do not go and think you do because you are so resigned at the first moment; my Raigecourt's head will heat; this reflection will agitate her, that fear will torture her; such a person runs risks, what will happen to him? will they force him to act against his duty and his conscience? etc., etc. And then, behold my Raigecourt beside herself, all the while saying: "My God, I offer you submission." Have the goodness, mademoiselle, not to torture yourself in that way. M. de Condorcet has decided that the Church is not to be persecuted because it would make the clergy interesting; and that, he says, would do an infinite injury to the Constitution. Therefore, my heart, no martyrdom, thank God, for I own that I have no fancy for that sort of death.

December 30, 1790.

I see persecution coming, being in mortal anguish at the acceptance that the king has just given. God reserved us this blow; may it be the last, and may he not suffer that schism be established: that is all I ask. But if the days of persecution do return, ah! I should ask of God to take me from this world, for I do not feel within me the courage to bear them. This acceptance [of the decree against the clergy] was given on Saint Stephen's day; apparently that blessed martyr is now to be our model. Well, as you know, I am not afraid of stones; so that suits me. They say that seven of the rectors of Paris have taken the oath. I did not think the number would be so large. All this has a very bad effect on my soul; far from rendering me devout, it takes away from me all hope that God's anger will be appeased. Your rector decides to follow the law of the Gospel and not the one just made. I am told that a member of the Commune, wanting to persuade the rector of Sainte-Marguerite, said to him that the esteem felt for him, the preponderance that he had in the world, would do much to restore peace by influencing minds. To which he answered, "Monsieur, the reasons that you give me are the very ones that oblige me to refuse the oath and not act against my conscience."

May God not abandon us wholly; it is to that we must limit our hopes. I have no taste for martyrdom; but I feel that I should be very glad to have the certainty of suffering it rather than abandon one iota of my faith. I hope that if I am destined to it, God will give me strength. He is so good, so good! he is a Father, so concerned for the true welfare of his children that we ought to have all confidence in him. Were you not touched on the Epiphany with God's goodness in calling the Gentiles to him at that moment? Well, we are the Gentiles. Let us thank him well; let us be faithful to our faith; let us not lose from sight what we owe to him; and as to all the rest, let us abandon ourselves to him with true filial confidence.

February 15, 1791.

I am grieved at the unnecessary fear that M. de B. has caused you. We are still far from all those evils he has put into your head. . . . I am sorry to be so far from you and to be unable to talk as I would like to do; but, my heart, calm yourself. I know that that seems difficult, but it is necessary. You excite your blood; you make yourself more unhappy than you need be: all that, my heart, is not in the order of Providence. We must submit to God's decrees, and that submission must bring calmness. Otherwise, it is on our lips only, not in our heart. When Jesus Christ was betrayed, abandoned, it was only his heart which suffered from those outrages; his exterior was calm, and proved that God was really in him. We ought to imitate him, and God ought to be in us. Therefore, calm yourself, submit, and adore in peace the decrees of Providence, without casting your eyes upon a future which is dreadful to whose sees with human eyes alone. Happily, you are not in that case; God has crowned you with so many favours that you will apply your virtue to wait patiently for the end of his wrath.

As for me, I am not in your condition. I will not say that virtue is the cause of this; but in the midst of many troubles and anxieties, I am more within reach of consolations; I am calm, and I hope for a happy eternity. . . . As for what you say of me, believe, my heart, that I shall never fail in honour, and that I shall always know how to fulfil the obligations that my principles, my position, and my reputation impose upon me. I hope that God will give me the light necessary to guide me wisely, and to keep me from wandering from the path that he marks out for me. But to judge of all that, my heart, others must be near me. From a distance, a chivalrous act appears enchanting; seen near-by it is often found to be an act of vexation, or of some other feeling not worth more in the eyes of the wise and good.

March 2, 1791.

I have received your little letter. I do not think that the person of whom you speak ever had the intention towards others that is attributed to her. She has defects, but I never knew her to have that one. If D. [d'Artois] would break off his alliance with Calonne, by travelling in another direction, that would give pleasure, I am sure. As for me, I desire it eagerly for the good of one I love so well, and for whom, I own to you, I dread the intimacy with Calonne. Do not say this to the man you have seen, but you can send word of it under the greatest secrecy, to her whose ideas you approve, even for interested persons; I cannot myself enter into any explanation with them, and you would do me a kindness to take charge of this.

March 18, 1791.

I profit by the departure of M. de Chamisot to tell you many things. I am infinitely uneasy at the course my brother is about to take. I believe that the wise counsels that have been given him are not to be followed. The little unity, the little harmony that there is among the persons who ought to be bound together by an indissoluble tie, make me tremble. I wish I could see in all that only God's will; but I own to you that I often put *self* into it. I hope that M. de Firmont will make me attain, by his counsels, to that necessary point of safety. You will see from this that it is he whom I have chosen to take the place of the Abbé Madier in my confidence. I confessed yesterday, and I was perfectly content with him. He has intelligence, gentleness, a great knowledge of the human heart. I hope to find in him what I have long lacked to enable me to make progress in piety. Thank God for me, my heart, that he has thus, by a peculiar stroke of his providence, led me to M. de Firmont, and ask him to make me faithful in executing the orders he may give me through that organ.

I have no news to send you from here; all is much the same. The evil-minded amuse themselves at our expense. France is about to perish. God alone can save it. I hope he will.

Extract from a letter of the Abbé Edgeworth de Firmont to a friend, published in his Memoirs.[1]

Though a foreigner, and very little worthy to be distinguished by the princess, I soon became her friend. She gave me her unlimited confidence, but I was known to neither the king nor the queen. Nevertheless, they often heard me mentioned, and during the last period of their reign they several times expressed their surprise at the facility with which I was allowed to enter the palace, while around them there was nothing but surveillance and terror. It is a fact that I never saw the danger for what it really was; and while no other

---

[1] He was an Irishman, and was recommended to Madame Élisabeth, for her confessor, by the Superior of Foreign Missions. It was to him that Louis XVI. sent in his last extremity. — TR.

ecclesiastic could appear at Court unless completely disguised, I went there in open day, two or three times a week without changing my dress. In truth, when I remember those days of horror I am surprised at my courage, but I suppose that Providence blinded me to danger intentionally. Though my presence excited some murmurs among the guards, I never received the slightest insult from them. I continued thus until the fatal day of the arrest of the royal family. On the 9th of August, 1792 — I remember it well! — Madame Élisabeth desired to see me, and I spent the greater part of the morning in her room, not imagining the scene of horror that was then being prepared for the next day.

To the Marquise de Raigecourt.

April 3, 1791.

Ah! my heart, you ought not to complain, your pregnancy has brought you great good luck in keeping you away from schism and these awful divisions. . . . I ask no better than to be godmother to your little one. If you like, I will give her the name of Hélène; and if you will be pleased to give birth to her at one o'clock in the morning of the 3rd of May [her own birthday and hour] it will be very well, provided it gives her a happier future than mine, where she will never hear of States-Generals or schisms.

Mirabeau has taken the course of going to see in another world if the Revolution is approved of there. Good God! what an awakening his will be. They say he saw his rector for an hour. He died tranquilly, believing himself poisoned; though he had no symptoms of it. They showed him to the people after his death; many were grieved; the aristocrats regret him much. For the last three months he had put himself on the right side, and they hoped in his talents. For my part, though very aristocratic, I cannot help regarding his death as a mercy of Providence to this country. I do not believe that it is by men without principles and without morals that God intends to save us. I keep this opinion to myself, as it is not policy — but I prefer a thousand times religious policy, and I am sure you will be of my opinion.

I counted on having the happiness to take the communion on Holy Thursday and at Easter; but circumstances will deprive me of it; I fear to cause disturbance in the château, and have it said that my devotion was imprudent; a thing that above all others I desire to avoid, because I have always thought it should be a means to make one's self loved. The rumour is spread about Paris that the king is going to-morrow to high-mass in the parish church; I cannot bring myself to believe it until he has actually been there. All-powerful God! what just punishment are you reserving for a people so misguided?

May 1, 1791.

I think the reflections you make are perfectly just; we ought to guard ourselves from extremes in all opinions. I am far from thinking that to be attached to those I love forms an exclusive claim to put them in offices . . . I think it needs perfect equality in merit, or some great distinction to give a veritable claim to preference. In all things I want justice alone to guide my choice; I will even go further and say that I want it to carry the day over any desire I may have to prefer one person to another person, and that friendship should yield to it. A disinterested friendship is the only kind that touches me (yours is that, and therefore I can speak thus freely to you). I feel that in my position (of other days) my influence was employed to obtain favours, and I lent myself to it too zealously.

May 18, 1791.

I have received your letter; it gives me great pleasure in spite of its gloom. Believe, my heart, that I am less unhappy than you imagine; my vivacity sustains me, and in crucial moments God overwhelms me with kindness. I suffered much in Holy Week, but that over, I have calmed myself. ... The more the moment approaches,[1] the more I become, like you, incredulous. Nevertheless the news my brother receives is satisfactory. Every one says that the principalities [German States] are interested for us. I desire it eagerly, perhaps too eagerly. ... It seems to me that our Court is rather badly informed as to the policy of the cabinets of Europe. I do not know if they distrust us, or whether we have flattered ourselves too much. I own to you that if I see the end of this month arrive with no appearance of anything, I shall have need of great resignation to the will of God, to bear the thought of passing another summer like that of 1790; and all the more because things have grown much worse since then; religion is weakened, and those who were attached to us have left for other countries where it still exists. What will become of this one, if Heaven be not merciful! ...

We take so few precautions that I believe we shall be here when the first drum beats. If things are managed wisely I do not think there will be much danger; but up to this moment, I do not see clear to bid farewell to my dear country. Nevertheless, I would not answer that it may not happen some day, when no one thinks of it. Lastic, Tily, Sérent, [her ladies] they will all be gone within a month, forced away by circumstances; would that I were gone too! I am

---

[1] This is evidently an allusion to the approaching effort of the king to leave Paris. The parts omitted are omitted by the French Editor, not by the translator. — Tr.

not sustained by your fine zeal; I feel the need of addressing myself to some one who will shake (as you call it) my soul. I see that, perfect as I thought myself, I should have had to spend at least some centuries in purgatory if Providence had not interfered. Happily it has sent me a confessor gentle without being weak, educated, enlightened, knowing me already better than I do myself, and who will not let me stay in my languor. But it is now, my little one, that I need prayers; for if I do not profit by this mercy I shall have a terrible account to render. I regret I did not know him earlier, and if I have to leave him soon it will be a great disappointment.

June 29, 1791.[1]

I hope, my heart, that your health is good, and that it does not suffer from the situation of your friend. Hers is excellent; you know that her body is never conscious of the sensations of her soul. This latter is not what it should be towards its Creator, the indulgence of God is its only hope of mercy. I neither can nor will I enter into details as to all that concerns me; let it suffice you to know that I am well, that I am tranquil, that I love you with all my heart, and that I will write to you soon — *if I can.*

July 9, 1791.

I have just received from you the tiniest letter it is possible to see; but it gives me great pleasure because you send me word that Hélène and you are both well; try to have it last. For that reason do not think of coming here. No, my heart, the shocks to the soul are less dangerous where you are than in Paris. Stay there until minds are calmer than they are now. What should I

[1] This letter is written directly after the fatal return from Varennes. — Tr.

do if anything happened here and you were here, too? I should be doubly unhappy, for with your acute sensibility your milk would flow into your blood, and you would be very ill.

Paris is tranquil in appearance. They say that minds are in fermentation. But, in fact, I know nothing. There is some excitement, — to-day the women of one of the clubs came to present a petition which the Assembly would not receive. They said they would return to-morrow. The petition is to be read at the opening of the Assembly; I think it demands that there shall be no longer a king. It seems to me impossible to foresee the action of the Assembly. Duport, Lameth, Barnave, Dandré, La Fayette, are for the monarchy, but I do not know if they can carry the day.

I have been very unhappy, my heart; I am still, especially in not being able to get sure news from foreign countries. I was able to see my abbé yesterday; I talked very deeply with him and that wound me up again. At present I suffer much less than you would do in my place; therefore be tranquil about me. Try to discover if a staff-officer named Goguelat, escaped with M. de Bouillé; we are uneasy about him.

Ah! my heart, pray for me, but especially for the salvation of those who may be the victims of all this. If I were sure about that, I should not suffer so much; I could say to myself that an eternity of happiness awaits them. Collect for this prayer all the souls you know; some are more interested than others, and have certainly thought of this. What troubles each individual is enduring! More fortunate than some, I have this week resumed my usual way of life, but my soul is far from being able to take pleasure in it. Yet I am calm, and if I did not fear more for others than for myself, it seems to me that I could support with ease my position, which, though I am not a prisoner, is nevertheless annoying. Adieu, my heart; I love and kiss you tenderly.

To the Abbé de Lubersac.[1]

July 29, 1791.

I have just received your letter. I hope, monsieur, that you do not doubt the interest with which I have read it. Your health seems to me less bad: but I fear that the last news you will have received from this country will make too keen an impression on you. More than ever is one tempted to say that a feeling heart is a cruel gift. Happy he who can be indifferent to the woes of his country, and of all that he holds most dear! I have experienced how desirable that state is for this world, and I live in the hope that the contrary will be useful in the other. Nevertheless, I own to you that I am far from the resignation I desire to have. Abandonment to the will of God is so far only on the surface of my mind. Still, having been for nearly a month in a violent state, I am beginning to return to my usual condition; events seem to be calming down and that has caused it. God grant that this may last awhile and that Heaven will pity us. You cannot imagine how fervent souls are redoubling their zeal. Surely Heaven cannot be deaf to so many prayers, offered with such trustfulness. It is from the heart of Jesus that they seem to await the favours of which they are in need; the fervour of this devotion appears to redouble; the more our woes increase, the more those prayers are offered up. All the communities are making them; but indeed the whole world ought to unite to petition Heaven. Unhappily,

[1] The Abbé de Lubersac, being Madame Victoire's chaplain, had accompanied her to Rome. Madame Élisabeth's last letter to him is dated (as we shall see) July 22, 1792. His heart clung passionately to France. Unable to live away from it he returned to Paris in August and perished in the massacres of September 2 and 3. — Tr.

it is much easier to speak strongly as to this than to execute it; I feel this constantly, and it angers me instead of humiliating me.

You ask me for my advice on the project you have formed. If you wish me to speak to you frankly, I shall say that I would not, if I were you, take the subject you have chosen. We are still too corrupted for the virtues in which many persons do not believe at all to have much effect. It would be impossible for me to give you any information upon it, for I possess none. But I believe that if you have the desire to write, all subjects of Christian morality would be well treated by you; and if you are willing that I should still further give you my opinion I shall say that, if I were you, I would choose a subject strong in reason rather than in sentiment; it is more suited to the situation in which your soul now is. Remember, in reading this, that you wished me to say to you what I think; and do not doubt, I entreat you, the perfect esteem I have for you, or the pleasure your letters give me.

To the Marquise de Bombelles.

July 10, 1791.

I have received your little letter, dear Bombe; I answer it in the same way. Though we differ in opinion the signs it contains of friendship give me great pleasure. You know I am always sensitive to that, and you can imagine that in a moment like this friendship has become a thousand-fold more precious to me . . . . Paris and the king are still in the same position; the former tranquil, the second guarded and not lost sight of a moment, and so is the queen. Yesterday a species of camp was established under their windows, for fear they might jump into the garden which is hermetically closed and full of sentinels; among them two or three under my windows. Adieu, my heart, I kiss you tenderly, as well as your little one. They say that the affair of the king will be reported on soon, and that he will then be set at liberty. The law against the *émigrés* is very severe; they forfeit three-fifths of their property. (*The end of this letter is written in " white ink."*)

No, my heart, I am very far from permitting your return. It is not, assuredly, that I should not be charmed to see you, but because I am convinced that you would not be safe here. Preserve yourself for happier times, when we may perhaps enjoy in peace the friendship that unites us. I have been very unhappy; I am less so. If I saw an end to all this I could more easily endure what is taking place; but now is the time to give ourselves wholly into the hands of God — a thing that indeed the Comte d'Artois ought to do. We ought to write to him and urge it. Our masters wish it. I do not think it will influence him.

Our journey with Barnave and Pétion went on most ridiculously. You believe, no doubt, that we were in torture; not at all. They behaved well, especially the first, who has much intelligence and is not ferocious as people say. I began by showing them frankly my opinion as to their actions, and after that we talked for the rest of the journey as if we ignored the whole thing. Barnave saved the *gardes du corps* who were with us and whom the National guards wanted to massacre.

September 8, 1791.

The Constitution is in the hands of the king since Saturday, and he is reflecting on the answer he will make. Time will tell us what he decides upon in his wisdom. We must ask the Holy Spirit to give him of its gifts; he has great need of them.

I wish I had something amusing to tell you, but we do not abound in that commodity; all the more because the price of bread is rising and makes us fear many riots this winter, not counting those with which the autumn threatens us. It is very sad, and there is no way to make ourselves illusions because the Assembly itself speaks of them, the riots, as an evil it expects. It is true that the strength given by the love of liberty is very reassuring, and patriotism can easily take the place of order and the subordination of troops. . . .

Yes, my heart, I wish I could transport myself near you. How sweet it would be to me! But Providence has placed me where I am; it is not I who chose it; Providence keeps me here and to that I must submit. We are still quite tranquil. A letter has appeared from the Prince, and a declaration from the emperor and the King of Prussia [at Pillnitz]. The letter is strong, but the other is not. Yet some persons think they see the heavens opening. As for me I am not so credulous; I lift my hands to heaven and ask that God will save us from useless evils. You will do the same, I think.

To the Marquise de Raigecourt.

September 12, 1791.

At last I have an opportunity to write to you; I am charmed, for I have a hundred thousand things to say; but I do not know where to begin; besides, I do not want to have to render an account of this letter in the next world, for, just now, charity is a difficult virtue to put in practice.

I begin by telling you that the Constitution is not yet signed, but it is safe to wager that it will be by the time this letter reaches you, perhaps before I close it, even. Is it a good, is it an evil? Heaven alone knows which it is. Many persons think, from their point of view, that they are certain about it.

I am in no way called upon to give my advice, or even to speak of the matter. I am still floating as to the view to take; there are so many *fors* and *ifs* and *buts* to be considered that I remain uncertain. One must see all things very near to judge; these are too far-off to be able to bring them enough into one's thoughts to fix one's ideas.

To speak to you a little of myself, I will tell you that I am about what you have always seen me; rather gay, though there are moments when my position makes me feel keenly; nevertheless, on the whole, I am more calm than agitated or anxious, as you certainly fancy I am. The knowledge you have of my nature will make you understand what I say. The life I lead is about the same. We go to mass at midday; dine at half-past one. At six I return to my own apartments; at half-past seven the ladies come; at half-past nine we sup. They play billiards after dinner and after supper, to make the king take exercise. At eleven everybody goes to bed, to begin again on the morrow. Sometimes I regret my poor Montreuil, especially when the weather is warm and fine; there may come a time, perhaps, when we shall all be there again; what happiness I should then feel! but everything tells me that moment is very far-off; we are walking on a quicksand.

One thing alone affects me deeply. It is that they are trying to put coldness into a family whom I love sincerely.[1] Consequently, as you are in the way of seeing a person who might have some influence, I wish you would talk to him in private and fill him with the idea that all will be lost if *the son* should have other ideas for the future than those of confidence and submission to the orders of *the father*. All

---

[1] Between the king and his brothers. In the above letter the name *father* means the king; that of *mother-in-law*, the queen; that of *son* the Comte d'Artois. — Fr. Ed.

views, all ideas, all feelings ought to yield to that. You must feel, yourself, how necessary this is. To speak quite clearly: remember the position of that unfortunate father; events which prevent him from any longer managing his own estate throw him into the arms of his son. That son has always had as you know, a perfect conduct towards his father, in spite of all that has been done to make him quarrel with his mother-in-law. He always resisted it. I do not think it made him bitter, because he is incapable of bitterness; but I fear that those who are now allied with him may give him bad advice. The father is nearly well; his affairs are recovering; he may shortly take back the management of his estate, and *that* is the moment that I fear. The son, who sees the advantages of leaving them in the hands *in which they now are,* will hold to that idea; the mother-in-law will never allow it; and this struggle must be averted by making the young man feel that, even for his personal interests, he ought not to put forward that opinion, and so avoid placing himself in a painful position.

I wish therefore that you would talk this over with the person I indicated, and make him enter into my meaning (without telling him I have spoken thus) by making him believe the idea is his own, and then he will more readily communicate it. He ought to feel better than any one the rights of the father over his sons, for he has long experienced it. I wish also that he could persuade the young man to be a little more gracious to his mother-in-law, if only by the charm a man can employ when he chooses, and thus convince her that he wants to see her what she has always been. In this way he would avoid much vexation and could enjoy in peace the friendship and confidence of his father. But you know very well that it is only by talking tranquilly to that person, without closing the eyes or lengthening the face, that you can make him feel what I say. For that you must be convinced yourself. Therefore, read my letter over again, try to understand it thoroughly, and start from that to do my commission. They will tell you harm of the mother-in-law; but the sole means of preventing that from becoming a reality is the one I tell you. The young man made a blunder in not allying himself with a friend of the said lady. If no one speaks to you of this do not mention it.

P. S. I knew it! here is the Constitution settled and accepted in a letter which you will certainly hear of soon. In reading it, you will know all that I think of it, therefore I will say no more. I have much anxiety as to the results. I wish I could be in all the cabinets of Europe. The conduct of Frenchmen becomes difficult. One single thing supports me, it is the joy of knowing that those gentlemen are out of prison.[1] I go to the Assembly at midday, to follow the queen; were I mistress of myself, I certainly would not go. But, I do not know how it is, all this does not cost me as much as it does others, though assuredly I am far from being constitutional. M. de Choiseul came out of prison to-day, the others yesterday. Adieu; give me, in white ink, all the news you know, but try to have it true. That about the imperial troops does not please me. What is said in your region? The colonies are not to be subjected to the decrees. Barnave spoke with such force that he carried the day. That man has much talent; he has intellect, he might have been a great man had he willed it; he may still be one; but heaven's anger is not over. How should it be? what are we doing to make it so?

[1] All the gentlemen captured during the flight to Varennes were released on the king's accepting the Constitution. — TR.

October 4, 1791.

They say there is to be a congress at Aix-la-Chapelle; they even quote an extract of a letter from Maréchal de Broglie saying positively that the emperor has received answers from all the other Courts, adhering to the declaration of Pillnitz, and that in consequence their ministers and ambassadors are to assemble at Aix-la-Chapelle. God grant it may be so! Then, indeed, we might have a hope of seeing our evils at an end. But this slow progress demands great prudence, much union of wills; to this all our desires should tend. I own to you that this position works upon my mind more than it should. I am pursued in my prayers with counsels that I want to give; I am very discontented with myself; I wish to be calm — but that will come.

October 12, 1791.

Very happy news is being spread here. The emperor has, they say, recognized the National flag; thus, all fears are calmed. It must be owned that in the eyes of the centuries, present and future, such pacific moderation will have a superb effect. Already I see histories relating it with enthusiasm, the people blessing it for their happiness, peace reigning in my hapless country, constitutional religion fully established, philosophy enjoying its work, and we, poor Roman-apostolicals, moaning and hiding ourselves; for if this Assembly is not driven out by the Parisians, things will be terrible for non-conformists. But, my heart, God is master of all; let us work to save ourselves; let us pray for the evil-doers, and not imitate them; God will reward us how and when he will.

All is tranquil here, but who knows how long it will last? I think it may last long, because the people, meeting with no resistance, have no reason for excitement. The king is at this moment the object of public adoration; you cannot form an idea of the uproar there was on Saturday night at the Italian comedy; but we must wait and see how long such enthusiasm will last.

I do not number my letters any longer, because I burned all the papers I did not care to have read on my return here.

I think, as you do, that the young man of whom you speak [Comte d'Artois] will never be happy in his family; but I do not think that his mother-in-law is altogether the cause of it; I think he is tricked by the old fox [Comte de Mercy] who is the intimate friend of her brother. If the young man did wisely he would try to win him over, but there are so many conflicting interests to defeat it! What is greatly to be feared is that the mother-in-law should be as much the fox's victim as any one.

An extraordinary thing has happened within a day or two; a corporal took it upon himself to lock the king and queen into their rooms from nine o'clock at night till nine the next morning. This went on two days before it was discovered. The guard is furious, and there is to be a council of war. By rules, the corporal ought to be hanged; but I do not think he will be, and I should be sorry for it. The rumour in Paris is that the king is under arrest.

No doubt you read the newspapers, therefore I give you no news when I tell you that the decree on the priests passed yesterday, with all possible severity. It was taken to the king in spite of its unconstitutional faults. At the same time there came a deputation of, I believe, twenty-four members, to beg the king to take steps towards the Powers inviting them to prevent the great assemblages of *émigrés*, or else to declare war against them. In their speech they assured the king that Louis XIV. would not have suffered such assemblages. What do you think of that? — a pretty thing of them to talk in these days of Louis XIV., "that despot!"

To the Marquise de Bombelles.

November 8, 1791.

Do you know, my Bombe, that if I did not rely on your friendship, your indulgence, I should be rather ashamed of the long time since I have written to you. But it was to do better that I did wrong. I wanted to write you a long letter and I never have found time. Your mother wrote you a week ago, so that you know that all with us is still standing, and that, in spite of the blasphemies they never cease to vomit against God and his ministers, the skies have not yet fallen upon us. . . . [*The rest is in white ink.*]

At last they feel here the necessity of drawing closer to Coblentz [the headquarters of the princes and *émigrés*]. Some one is to be sent from here who will remain there, and will be in correspondence with the Baron de Breteuil.[1] But I feel one fear as to this step; I am afraid it is taken only

---

[1] Louis XVI.'s confidential agent towards the Courts of Europe. The following is a copy of his full powers:—

"Monsieur le Baron de Breteuil, knowing your zeal and your fidelity, and wishing to give you a proof of my confidence, I have chosen you to confide to you the interests of my crown. Circumstances do not allow me to give you instructions on this or that object, nor to hold with you a continuous correspondence. I send you the present to serve you as full powers [*pleins pouvoirs*] and authorization towards the different Powers with whom you may have to negotiate for me. You know my intentions; and I leave it to your prudence to make what use you judge necessary of these powers for the good of my service. I approve of all that you may do to attain the end that I propose to myself, which is the re-establishment of my legitimate authority and the welfare of my people. On which, I pray God, M. le Baron de Breteuil, etc."

The Baron de Breteuil's headquarters were at Brussels. See "Diary and Correspondence of Count Axel Fersen," the preceding volume of this Hist. Series. — TR.

to stop rash enterprises, which are much to be dreaded, and not to bring about deserved confidence. Yet, if that confidence does not exist what will happen? We shall be the dupe of all the Powers of Europe. I hope your husband will urge the Baron de Breteuil to enter sincerely into this new order of things. Here we are at the gates of winter; this is the moment for negotiations; they might have a happy issue, but only if done with harmony of action. If that does not exist, remember what I tell you: in the spring, either the most dreadful civil war will be established in France, or each province will set up its own master. Do not think that the policy of Vienna is disinterested; it is far short of that. Austria never forgets that Alsace once belonged to her. All the other Powers are very glad to have a reason to leave us in a state of humiliation. Think of the time that has passed since our return from Varennes! Did those events stir the emperor? Has he not been the first to show uncertainty as to what he would do? To believe, as many persons assert, that it is the queen who holds him back, seems to me devoid of sense, and almost a crime. But I do permit myself to think that the policy pursued towards that Power has not been conducted with sufficient skill. If that is so, I think there is some blame; but it would be unpardonable if, after the decree given yesterday against the *émigrés*, the present danger were not felt. Judge by the quantity of Frenchmen who are over there how impossible it will be to restrain them; and what will become of France and her king if they take such a course without foreign help? Reflect on all this, my Bombe; and if your husband sees there is real danger that . . . [*the paper is torn at this place*] . . . or that he urges his friend to act in good faith; I expect that at first the man sent to Coblentz will meet with some difficulties; but he must not be alarmed; speaking in the king's name and putting no inflexibility into his manner of maintaining his opinion while arguing it well, he will lead the others.

Adieu; let me know that you receive this letter; if your husband takes any steps towards the baron he must not let him know that I asked it, or that I have even written to you on the subject.

To the Comte d'Artois.

February 19, 1792.

You know, my dear brother, what my friendship is for you, and how I rejoice to hear of your well-being. I believe, I who am here on the spot, that you are unjust towards that person; you have not at bottom a better friend. I pray God that he will shed upon you his blessing and his light, and you will then judge better. This estrangement is on all sides a calamity and a suffering; for it casts shadows where friendship ought to shine. I will write to you more at length by the opportunity you know of, and I will prove to you that you will never find a truer, tenderer, more devoted friend than I am to you.

To the Marquise de Raigecourt.

February 22, 1792.

I will see, my heart, when my purse is a little less empty, what I can do for those good and saintly Fathers of the sacred Valley [La Trappe]. What a life is theirs! how we ought to blush in comparing it with ours! But perhaps a part of those saints have not as many sins to expiate as we have. What ought to console us is that God does not require from everybody what he does from them, and that, provided we are faithful in the little we do, he is content.

The queen and her children were at the theatre last night, where the audience made an infernal uproar of applause. The Jacobins tried to make a disturbance, but they were beaten. The others called for the repetition four times of the duet between the valet and the maid in "Événements imprévus," in which they tell of the love they feel for their master and mistress; and at the passage where they say, "We must make them happy," the greater part of the audience cried out, "Yes, yes!"—Can you conceive of our nation? It must be owned, it has its charming moments. On which, good-night. Your sister spent a happy day lately at the "Calvaire." *Vive la Liberté!* As for me, who enjoy as much as I can of it for the last three years, I envy the fate of those who can turn their steps where they will; if I could only spend a few calm days it would do me great good. It is a year since I *have dared* to go to Saint-Cyr.

To the Comte d'Artois.

February 22, 1792.

Your last letter was brought to me this morning, my dear brother, and I have been made very happy by finding it less bitter than the one that preceded it. Nevertheless, I promised to add a few words to one I wrote you three days ago, and I am too sincerely your friend not to do so.

I think that the son has too much severity towards his mother-in-law. She has not the faults for which he blames her. I think she may have listened to suspicious advice; but she bears the evils that overwhelm her with strong courage; and she should be pitied far more than blamed, for she has good intentions. She tries to fix the vacillations [*incertitudes*] of the father, who, to the misfortune of the family, is no longer master, and—I know not if God wills that I deceive myself, but—I greatly fear that she will be one of the first victims of what is taking place, and my heart is too wrung with that presentiment to allow me to blame her.

God is good; he will not suffer discord to continue in a family to which unity and a good understanding would be so useful. I shudder when I think of it; it deprives me of sleep, for discord will kill us all. You know the difference in habits and societies that your sister had always had with the mother-in-law; in spite of that she feels drawn to her when she sees her unjustly accused, and when she looks the future in the face. It is very unfortunate that the son has not been willing, or perhaps able, to win over the intimate friend of the mother-in-law's brother [Comte de Mercy]. That old fox is tricking her; and the son ought to have taken the duty upon himself, if possible, and made the sacrifice of being on terms with him in order to foil him and prevent an evil which has now become alarming. Of two evils, the least. All men of his sort frighten me; they have intellect, but what good is it to them? Heart is needed as well, and they have none. They have nothing but intrigue; into which it is unfortunate that they drag so many persons. Others should have been more shrewd than they. . . .

The idea of the emperor racks me: if he makes war upon us there will be an awful explosion. May God watch over us! He has heavily laid his hand on this kingdom in a visible manner. Let us pray to him, my dear brother; he alone knows hearts, in him alone is our worthy hope. I have passed this Lent in asking him to look with pity upon us, and to arrange these matters in the family I love so much. I have that so deeply at heart that I would consecrate my life to asking it on my two knees, if that would make me worthy of being heard. It is only God who can change our fate, make the vertigo of this nation (good at bottom) cease, and restore it to health and peace. Adieu — what was it you asked me? how I pass my time? what are my occupations? whether I ride on horseback? whether I still go to Saint-Cyr? I scarcely dare for a whole year past to do my duties. I kiss you with all my heart. *Miserere nobis.*

To the Marquise de Raigecourt.

April 6, 1792.

As I do not wish you to scold me, I write on Holy Thursday, but only a little line. The King of Sweden is assassinated! Every one has his turn. He had incredible courage. We do not yet know if he is dead; but it is likely that he is from the way the pistol was loaded. Adieu, my heart; when you wean the baby I will busy myself in finding you a lodging in the château, for yours has been given to others.

April 18, 1792.

You think perhaps we are still in the agitation of the fête at Châteauvieux; not at all; everything is very tranquil. The people flocked to see Dame Liberty tottering on her triumphal car, but they shrugged their shoulders. Three or four hundred *sans-culottes* followed her shouting: "The Nation! Liberty! The Sans-Culottes!" It was all very noisy, but flat. The National guards would not mingle; on the contrary, they were angry, and Pétion, they say, is ashamed of his conduct. The next day a pike with a *bonnet rouge* walked about the garden, without shouting, and did not stay long.

The King of Sweden died with much courage. What a pity that he was not Catholic; he would have been a true hero. His country seems tranquil. Adieu, my heart.

June 23, 1792.

For three days before the 20th a great commotion was felt to exist in Paris, but it was thought that all necessary precautions were taken to ward off danger. Wednesday morning the courtyards and garden were full of troops. At midday we heard that the faubourg Saint-Antoine was on the march; it bore a petition to the Assembly, and did not propose to cross the Tuileries. Fifteen hundred persons filed into the Assembly; few National guards and some Invalids, the rest were *sans-culottes* and women. Three municipal officers came to ask the king to allow the troops to enter the garden, saying that the Assembly was hampered by the crowd, and the passages so incumbered that the doors might be forced. The king told them to arrange with the commandant to defile along the terrace of the Feuillants and go out by the gate of the riding-school.

Shortly after this the other gates of the garden were opened in spite of these orders. Soon the garden was filled. The pikes began to defile in order under the terrace in front of the château where there were three lines of National guards. They went out by the gate to the Pont Royal and seemed to intend to pass through the Carrousel on their way back to the faubourg Saint-Antoine. At three o'clock they showed signs of wishing to force the gate of the grand courtyard. Two municipal officers opened it. The National Guard, which had not been able to obtain any orders since the morning, had the sorrow of seeing them cross the courtyard without being able to bar the way. The department had given orders to repulse force by force, but the municipality paid no attention to this.

We were, at this moment, at the king's window. The few persons who were with his *valet de chambre* came and joined us. The doors were closed. A moment later we heard raps. It was Acloque with a few grenadiers and volunteers whom he had collected. He asked the king to show himself, alone. The king passed into the first antechamber. There M.

Louis XVI

d'Hervilly came to join him, with three or four grenadiers whom he had induced to come with him.

At the moment when the king passed into the antechamber the persons attached to the queen forced her to go into her son's room. More fortunate than she, no one tore me from the king's side. The queen had scarcely gone when the door was burst in by the pikes. The king, at that instant, mounted one of the coffers which stand in the windows. The Maréchal de Mouchy, MM. d'Hervilly, Acloque, and a dozen grenadiers surrounded him. I stood against the wall with the ministers, M. de Marcilly, and some National guards around me. The pikes entered the chamber like a thunderbolt; they looked for the king, especially one of them, who used the most dangerous language. A grenadier turned aside his weapon, saying, "Unhappy man! this is your king." All the grenadiers then began to shout *Vive le Roi!* The rest of the pikes responded mechanically to the cry; the chamber was filled in less time than I can tell it, the pikes demanding the sanction, and the dismissal of the ministers.[1]

During four hours the same shouts were repeated. Members of the Assembly came. M. Vergniaud and Isnard spoke well to the people; told them they did wrong to demand the king's sanction thus, and urged them to withdraw; but it was as if they did not speak at all. At last Pétion and the municipality arrived. The first harangued the people, and after praising the "dignity" and "order" with which they had come, he invited them to retire with "the same calm-

---

[1] This was the moment, recorded by all other witnesses and forgotten by Madame Élisabeth, when, being mistaken for the queen and threatened with death, she stopped those who wished to correct the blunder. "No, no," she said, "let them think I am she." One witness mentions that she added, "Their crime would be less."

It was on this occasion that a woman of the people said, the next day: "We could do nothing then; they had their Sainte Geneviève with them." — TR.

ness," in order that they might not be reproached for committing excess at "a civic fête." At last the populace began to depart.

I forgot to tell you that, shortly after the crowd entered, the grenadiers made a space and kept the people from pressing on the king. As for me, I had mounted the window-seat on the side towards the king's room. A great number of persons attached to the king had come to him that morning; but he sent them orders to go away, fearing another 18th of April. I should like to express myself as to that, but not being able to do so, I will simply say that I shall recur to it. All that I say now is that he who gave the order did well, and that the conduct of the others was perfect.

But to return to the queen, whom I left dragged against her will to my nephew's room; they had carried the latter so quickly into hiding that she did not see him on entering his apartment. You can imagine her despair. But M. Huë, usher, and M. Saint-Vincent were with him and soon brought him to her. She did everything possible to return to the king, but MM. de Choiseul and d'Haussonville, also those of our ladies who were there, prevented it. A moment later they heard the doors burst in, all but one which the people did not find. Meantime the grenadiers had entered the Council Chamber, and there they placed her, with her children, behind the Council table. The grenadiers and other attached persons surrounded her, and the populace defiled before her. One woman put a *bonnet rouge* upon her head, also on that of my nephew. The king had worn one from almost the first moment. Santerre, who conducted the procession, harangued her, and told her they deceived her by saying that the people did not love her. He assured her she had nothing to fear. "We fear nothing," she replied, "when we are with brave men." So saying, she stretched out her hand to the grenadiers who were near her, and they fell upon it. It was very touching.

The deputies who came, came with good-will. A true deputation arrived which requested the king to return to his own room. I was told of this, and not being willing to stay behind in the crowd, I left about an hour before he did, and rejoined the queen. You can judge with what joy I embraced her, though I was then ignorant of the risks she had run. The king returned to his room, and nothing could be more touching than the moment when the queen and his children threw themselves into his arms. The deputies who were there burst into tears. The deputations relieved each other every half-hour until quiet was completely restored. They were shown the violences that had been committed. They behaved very well in the apartment of the king, who was perfect to them. At ten o'clock the château was empty, and every one went to bed.

The next day, the National Guard, after expressing the greatest grief at its hands being bound, and having had before its eyes, helplessly, all that had taken place, obtained an order from Pétion to fire, if necessary. At seven o'clock it was said that the faubourgs were marching, and the Guard put itself under arms with the greatest zeal. Deputies of the Assembly came with good-will and asked the king to let the Assembly come to him, if he thought there was danger. The king thanked them. You will see their dialogue in the newspapers, also the one with Pétion, who came to tell the king that the crowd was only a few persons who wanted to plant a May tree.

At this moment we are tranquil. The arrival of M. de la Fayette from the army creates a little excitement in people's minds. The Jacobins are sleeping. These are the details of the 20th of June. Adieu; I am well; I kiss you, and I am thankful you are not here in the fray.

To the Abbé de Lubersac.

June 25, 1792.

This letter will be rather long on its way; but I prefer not to let this opportunity of talking with you pass. I am convinced that you will feel almost as keenly as ourselves the blow that has just been struck us; it is all the more dreadful because it lacerates the heart, and takes away our peace of mind. The future seems an abyss, from which we can only issue by a miracle of Providence. Do we deserve it? At that question I feel my courage fail me. Which of us can expect the answer, " Yes, you deserve it "? All suffer, but alas! none are penitent, none turn their hearts to God. As for me, what reproaches I have to make to myself! Swept along by the whirlwind of misfortune I have not asked of God the grace we need; I have relied on human help; I have been more guilty than others, for who has been as much as I the child of Providence? But it is not enough to recognize our faults; we must repair them. I cannot alone. Monsieur, have the charity to help me. Ask of God, not a change which it may please him to send us when, in his wisdom, he thinks suitable, but let us limit ourselves and ask him only to enlighten and touch all hearts, and especially to speak to two most unhappy beings, who would be more unhappy still if God did not call them to him. Alas! the blood of Jesus Christ flowed for them as much as for the solitary hermit who mourns for trivial faults incessantly. Say to God often, " If thou wilt, thou canst cure them," and give to him the glory of it. God knows the remedies to be applied.

I am sorry to write to you in so gloomy a style; but my

heart is so dark that it is difficult for me to speak otherwise. Do not think from this that my health suffers; no, I am well; and God has given me grace to keep my gaiety. I earnestly hope that your health may be restored; I wish I could know that it was better; but how can one hope that with your sensibilities? Let us think that there is another life where we shall be amply compensated for the troubles of this one; and let us live in the hope of meeting there once more — but not until after we have the pleasure of seeing each other again in this world; for, in spite of my excessive gloom, I cannot believe that all is hopeless. Adieu, monsieur; pray for me, I beg of you, after having prayed for those others, and send me news of yourself at times; it is a consolation to me.

To the Marquise de Raigecourt.

July 8, 1792.

It would really require all the eloquence of Mme. de Sévigné to describe what happened yesterday; for it is, indeed, the most surprising thing, the most extraordinary, the grandest, the pettiest, etc., etc. Happily, experience aids comprehension. In short, behold the Jacobins, the Feuillants, the Republicans, the Monarchists, all abjuring their discords, and, uniting beneath the immovable arch of the Constitution and Liberty, promising one another very sincerely to walk together, laws in hand, and never to deviate from them! Happily, the month of August is approaching, when, its foliage being fully developed, the tree of liberty will offer a safer shade. The city is tranquil and will be so during the Federation. I tremble lest there be no religious ceremonies; you know my taste for them. Ask of God, my heart, that he will give me strength and counsel. Adieu; I embrace and love you with all my heart.

July 11, 1792.

Our good patriots in the Assembly have just, my heart, declared the country to be in danger, in view of the conduct of the kings of Hungary and Prussia (not to speak of others) towards poor peaceable beings like us; for why should any one blame us? However that may be, the nation is about to rise as one man.

Our ministers have taken the course of resigning, all six at once; which astonishes many persons, — all the more because their determination was sudden and confided to no one. I had attached myself to two of them, and you will agree that that was hardly worth while.

Our Federation is making ready quietly. A few Federals are already here; they do not come in troops as they did two years ago, but gradually. I have just seen some disembarking, and they have not an elegant appearance.

Adieu; I kiss you with all my heart, and I beg of you the favour of not fretting because you are not here; the reasons are good why you should stay where you are, and you must think of the matter no longer.

July 18, 1792.

Your prayers, unworthy as you pretend they are, brought us good fortune, my heart; the famous day of the 14th [fête of the Federation] passed off tranquilly. There was much shouting of *Vive Pétion!* and the *Sans Culottes!* As we returned the whole guard which accompanied the king never ceased shouting, *Vive le roi!* they were all heart and soul for us; that did good. Since then Paris is very calm. They have just sent away three regiments and two battalions of the Swiss Guards to the camp at Soissons.

I am well, my heart, except for the heat, which is scarcely endurable just now. We had a frightful storm the night before last; it lasted an immense time; the lightning fell upon the gardens at Versailles. Adieu, my heart; my letters must tire you; I think that before long you will not have patience to read them; but how can I help it? I do not know what to tell you. I kiss you with all my heart.

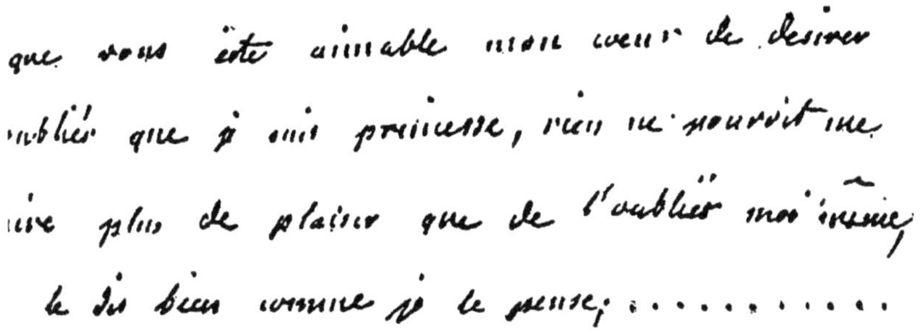
que vous êtes aimable mon cœur de désirer
oublier que je suis princesse, rien ne pourroit me
...ire plus de plaisir que de l'oublier moi même,
le dis bien comme je le pense; . . . .

To the Abbé de Lubersac.

July 22, 1792.

You will soon receive a letter from me which is a perfect jeremiad. From its style one would think I had foreseen what was to follow. I do not wish you to think, monsieur, that that is my habitual state. No, God grants me the grace to be quite otherwise; but at times my heart has need to let itself go, and I must speak of the agitations that fill it; it seems as if, by giving relaxation to the nerves, they gained more strength. You, who are more sensitive than others, must feel this need.

Since the dreadful day of the 20th we are more tranquil; but we do not the less need the prayers of saintly souls. Let those who, sheltered from the storm, feel only, so to speak, its repercussion, lift their hearts to God. Yes, God has given them the favour to live in quiet that they may make that use of their freedom. Those on whom the storm lowers meet at times with such shocks that it is difficult to practise the great resource — that of prayer. Happy the heart of whoso can feel in the great agitations of this world that God is with it! happy the saints who, pierced by stabs, can yet praise God in every moment of their day! Ask that grace, monsieur, for those who are feeble and little faithful like me; it would be a true work of charity to do.

My aunt thanks me often for making her know you [the Abbé de Lubersac was with Madame Victoire in Rome]. It seems to me very simple that she should be pleased, and I think myself fortunate to have procured for her that advantage — or, to speak more truly, to have been one of the instruments that God has used for that work of salvation. I will not say as to that all that I think; but I am very glad to be able to speak of it to you in order that you may put your shyness more to one side, if you are still a victim to it — I can use that expression, for shyness is a real affliction.

Paris is in some fermentation; but there exists a God who watches over the city and its inhabitants. Therefore be tranquil. I wish I could think that the great heats will not make you suffer; but that is difficult. Adieu, monsieur, I hope that you do not forget me before God, and that you are convinced of the esteem I have for you.

To the Marquise de Raigecourt.

July 25, 1792.

Good-day, my Raigecourt. Your Hélène must be a jewel. I do not doubt it, but I am charmed to hear it; though I should be still more charmed, I assure you, if I could see her instead of believing what you say of her. But patience! your health, I hope, will not be long in getting strong, and then you might soon come and join me. What a fine moment, my heart, will that be! we shall have bought it by a very long parting. But there is an end to all things. I do not flatter myself that I can see you before the autumn; but it is always sweet to be able to talk of it.

Our days pass tranquilly. The last few have not been quite the same; the people tried to force the gates; but the National Guard behaved admirably and stopped it all. There is talk of suspending the executive power to pass the time. To pass mine in another manner I go, in the mornings, for three or four hours into the garden, — not every day, however; but it does me a great deal of good. Adieu; I kiss you with my whole heart and end because there is nothing I am able to tell you.

Madame Élisabeth's last letter bore date August 8, 1792; two days before the fatal 10th, when silence fell forever between her and her friends. In that letter she spoke of the "death of the executive power," adding, "I can enter into no details."

CHAPTER III.

Madame Élisabeth's Removal to the Conciergerie. — Her Examination, Condemnation, and Death.[1]

[THE only authentic records of Madame Élisabeth's life from the day she entered the Tower of the Temple, August 13, 1792, to May 9, 1794, the day when she was torn from the arms of her young niece, are in the simple Narrative of that niece, Marie-Thérèse de France, and in the Journal of the Temple by Cléry, Louis XVI.'s valet. These narratives could be, and have been rewritten and elaborated in tender words by loving hearts, but their plain simplicity is more befitting the sacred figure of this brave, self-forgetting, wise, and *truly* Christ-like woman. They are given later.

We take her now as she emerges from the Temple, for a last brief moment, into the sight and hearing of men.]

On the 25th of November, 1793, the municipality of Paris addressed to the National Assembly the following petition:

"LEGISLATORS

"You have decreed Equality; source of public welfare; it is established on foundations henceforth immovable; nevertheless, it is violated, this Equality, and in the most revolting manner, by the vile remains of tyranny, by the prisoners in the Tower of the Temple. Could they still, those abominable remains, be of any account under present circumstances, it could be only from the interest the country has

---

[1] Madame Élisabeth's Life in the Temple, being recorded only by her niece and by Cléry, will be found later, in their narratives. — TR.

in preventing them from rending her bosom, and renewing the atrocities committed by the two monsters who gave them birth. If, therefore, such is the sole interest of the Republic in respect to them, it is beneath her sole surveillance that they ought to be placed. We are no longer in those horrible days when a Liberticide faction (on whom the blade of the law has already done justice) assumed, as a means of vengeance against a patriotic Commune which it abhorred, a responsibility which outraged all laws, and has weighed for more than fifteen months on every member of the Commune of Paris.

"Reason, justice, equality cry to you, legislators, to make that responsibility cease.

"And as it is more than time to return to their regular work two hundred and fifty *sans-culottes*, now unjustly employed in guarding the prisoners of the Temple, the Commune of Paris expects of your wisdom:—

"1st, That you will send the infamous Élisabeth before the Revolutionary tribunal at the earliest moment.

"2d, That in regard to the posterity of the tyrant you will take prompt measures to transfer them to a prison chosen by you, there to be locked up with suitable precautions and treated by the system of equality in the same manner as all other prisoners whom the Republic has need to secure.

"DROUY, RENARD, LE CLERC, LEGRAND, DORIGNY."

Referred to the Committee on Public Safety, this petition slumbered there for six months, but it was not forgotten in that hotbed of the Revolution.

Madame Élisabeth had, from the hour that she left Montreuil, expressed the resolution to share the trials and the perils of her brother and his family. She kept that resolution: at Versailles on the 6th of October; in Paris, through years of gloomy solitude in the Tuileries; on the road to and from Varennes; on that day of evil omen, the 20th of June; on the bloody night of the 10th of August; in the box at the Assembly, facing insults and threats; in the Tower of the Temple, witness and actor in those heart-rending farewells. Yes, she kept all the promises she made to God, and God was now about to keep all his to her: strength and faithfulness unto death were hers, and pity passes from our minds as we read of these last scenes, so all-triumphant are they.

In a pouring rain she was taken on foot across the garden and courtyard of the Temple, placed in a hackney-coach, and driven to the Conciergerie, May 9, 1794. It was then eight o'clock in the evening. At ten she was taken to the council hall of the Revolutionary tribunal, and there subjected to her first examination before Gabriel Deliége, judge, Fouquier-Tinville, prosecutor, and Ducray, clerk.[1]

After placing her signature with that of the three men at the foot of each page of her indictment, Madame Élisabeth was taken back to prison. She made herself no illusions as to the fate that awaited her. She knew it would be in vain to ask for the help of a Catholic priest; she resigned herself to that deprivation, and offered direct to God the sacrifice of her life, drawing from her living faith the strength to make that sacrifice worthily. She was alone; no human help could reach her. It is said that, unknown to her, a lawyer, M. Chauveau-Lagarde, hearing of her arraignment, went to the prison to offer himself for her defence. He was not permitted to see her. He appealed to Fouquier-Tinville, who replied: "You cannot see her to-day; there is no hurry; she will not be tried yet." Nevertheless, spurred by a vague anxiety, M. Chauveau-Lagarde went the next morning to the assize court,

[1] See Appendix II.

and there, according to his presentiment, was Madame Élisabeth seated, among twenty-four other prisoners, on the upper bench, where they had placed her that she might be conspicuously in view of every one. It was then impossible to confer with her, and she was ignorant that one man stood in that court seeking to defend her.[1]

René-François Dumas, president of the Revolutionary tribunal, opened the session; Gabriel Deliége and Antoine-Marie, judges, were seated beside him.

Gilbert Liendon, deputy public prosecutor, read the accusation; Charles-Adrien Legris, clerk, wrote down the examination.

The jurors, to the number of fifteen, were the following citizens [names given].

The Indictment.

"Antoine-Quentin Fouquier, Public Prosecutor of the Revolutionary Tribunal, established in Paris by the decree of the National Assembly, March 10, 1793, year Two of the Republic, without recourse to any Court of Appeal, in virtue of the power given him by article 2 of another decree of the said Convention given on the 5th of April following, to the effect that 'the Public Prosecutor of said Tribunal is authorized to arrest, try, and judge, on the denunciation of the constituted authorities, or of citizens,' —

"Herewith declares that the following persons have been, by various decrees of the Committee of general safety of the Convention, of the Revolutionary committees of the different sections of Paris, and of the department of the Yonne, and by virtue of warrants of arrest issued by the said Public Prosecutor, denounced to this Tribunal: —

[1] The following account of the proceedings is taken from the official report in the "Moniteur."

"1st, Marie Élisabeth Capet, sister of Louis Capet, the last tyrant of the French, aged thirty, and born at Versailles."

[*Then follow the names and description of twenty-four other prisoners.*]

"And, also, that it is to the family of the Capets that the French people owe all the evils under the weight of which they have groaned for so many centuries.

"It was at the moment when excessive oppression forced the people to break their chains, that this whole family united to plunge them into a slavery more cruel than that from which they were trying to emerge. The crimes of all kinds, the guilty deeds of Capet, of the Messalina Antoinette, of the two brothers Capet, and of Élisabeth, are too well known to make it necessary to repaint here the horrible picture. They are written in letters of blood upon the annals of the Revolution; and the unheard-of atrocities exercised by the barbarous *émigrés* and the sanguinary Satellites of despots, the murders, the incendiarisms, the ravages, the assassinations unknown to the most ferocious monsters which they have committed on French territory, are still commanded by that detestable family, in order to deliver a great nation once more to the despotism and fury of a few individuals.

"Élisabeth has shared all those crimes; she has co-operated in all the plots, the conspiracies formed by her infamous brothers, by the wicked and impure Antoinette, and by the horde of conspirators collected around them; she associated herself with their projects; she encouraged the assassins of the nation, the plots of July, one thousand seven hundred and eighty-nine, the conspiracy of the 6th of October following, of which the d'Estaings, the Villeroys, and others, who have now been struck by the blade of the law, were the agents, — in short, the whole uninterrupted chain of conspiracies, lasting four whole years, were followed and seconded by all the means which Élisabeth had in her power. It was she who in the month of June, 1791, sent diamonds, the property of the nation, to the infamous d'Artois, her brother, to put him in a condition to execute projects concerted with him, and to hire assassins of the nation. It was she who maintained with her other brother, now become an object of derision and contempt to the coalized Powers on whom he imposed his imbecile and ponderous nullity, a most active correspondence; it was she who chose by the most insulting pride and disdain to degrade and humiliate the free men who consecrated their time to guarding the tyrant; it was she who lavished attentions on the assassins, sent to the Champs Élysées by the despot to provoke the brave Marseillais; it was she who stanched the wounds they received in their precipitate flight.

"Élisabeth meditated with Capet and Antoinette the massacre of the citizens of Paris on the immortal day of the 10th of August. She watched all night hoping to witness the nocturnal carnage. She helped the barbarous Antoinette to bite the cartridges; she encouraged by her language, young girls whom fanatical priests had brought to the château for that horrible occupation. Finally, disappointed in the hope of all this horde of conspirators, namely, — that the citizens who came to overthrow tyranny would be massacred, — she fled in the morning, with the tyrant and his wife, and went to await in the temple of National sovereignty that the horde of slaves, paid and committed to the crimes of that parricide Court, should drown Liberty in the blood of citizens and cut the throats of its representatives among whom she had sought a refuge.

"Finally, we have seen her, since the well-deserved punishment of the most guilty of the tyrants who have ever dishonoured human nature, promoting the re-establishment of tyranny by lavishing, with Antoinette, on the son of Capet homage to royalty and the pretended honours of a king."

The president, in presence of the auditory composed as aforesaid, then put to the said jurors, each individually, the following oath:—

"Citizen, you swear and promise to examine with the most scrupulous attention the charges brought against the accused persons, here present before you; to communicate with no one until after you declare your verdict; to listen to neither hatred nor malignity, fear, nor affection; to decide according to the charges and the means of defence, and according to your confidence and inward conviction, with the impartiality and firmness which becomes free men."

After swearing the said oath, the said jurors took their seats in the centre of the audience chamber, facing the accused and the witnesses.

The president told the accused that they might sit down: after which he asked their names, age, profession, residence, and place of birth, beginning with Madame Élisabeth.

Q. What is your name?

A. Élisabeth-Marie.

[The report in the "Moniteur" does not say, but a large number of persons present have declared that Madame Élisabeth answered: "I am named Élisabeth-Marie de France, sister of Louis XVI., aunt of Louis XVII., your king."]

Q. Your age? A. Thirty.

Q. Where were you born? A. Versailles.
Q. Where do you live? A. Paris.

. . . .

The president then put the following questions to Madame Élisabeth:

Q. Where were you on the 12th, 13th, and 14th of July, 1789, that is, at the period of the first plots of the Court against the people?

A. I was in the bosom of my family. I knew of no plots such as you speak of. I was far from foreseeing or seconding those events.

Q. At the time of the flight of the tyrant, your brother, to Varennes did you not accompany him?

A. All things commanded me to follow my brother; I made it my duty on that occasion, as on all others.

Q. Did you not figure in the infamous and scandalous orgy of the Gardes-du-corps, and did you not make the circuit of the table with Marie-Antoinette and induce each guest to repeat the shocking oath to exterminate the patriots, to smother liberty at its birth, and re-establish the tottering throne?

A. I am absolutely ignorant if the orgy mentioned took place; and I declare that I was never in any way informed of it.

Q. You do not tell the truth, and your denial is not of any use to you, because it is contradicted on one side by public notoriety, and on the other by the likelihood, which convinces every man of sense, that a woman so closely allied as you were with Marie-Antoinette, both by ties of blood and those of intimate friendship, could not avoid sharing her machinations and helping with all your power; you did therefore, necessarily, and in accord with the wife of the tyrant, instigate the abominable oath taken by the satellites of the Court to assassinate and annihilate liberty at its birth; also you instigated the bloody outrages done to that precious sign of liberty, the tri-colour cockade, by ordering your accomplices to trample it under foot.

A. I have already declared that all those acts are unknown to me; I have no other answer.

Q. Where were you on the 10th of August?

A. I was in the château, my usual and natural residence for some time past.

Q. Did you not pass the night of the 9th and 10th in your brother's room; and did you not have secret conferences with him which explained to you the object and motive of all the movements and preparations which were being made before your eyes?

A. I spent the night you speak of in my brother's room; I did not leave him; he had much confidence in me; and yet I never remarked anything in his conduct or in his conversation which announced to me what happened later.

Q. Your answer wounds both truth and probability; a woman like you, who has manifested through the whole course of the Revolution so striking an opposition to the present order of things, cannot be believed when she tries to make us think that she was ignorant of the cause of those assemblages of all kinds in the château on the eve of the 10th of August. Will you tell us what prevented you from going to bed on the night of the 9th and 10th of August?

A. I did not go to bed because the constituted bodies had come to tell my brother of the agitation, the excitement of the inhabitants of Paris, and the dangers that might result from it.

Q. You dissimulate in vain: especially after the various

confessions of the widow Capet, who stated that you took part in the orgy of the Gardes-du-corps, that you supported her under her fears and alarms on the 10th of August as to the life of Capet. But what you deny fruitlessly is the active part you took in the conflict that ensued between the patriots and the satellites of tyranny; it is your zeal and ardour in serving the enemies of the people, in supplying them with cartridges, which you took pains to bite, because they were directed against patriots and intended to mow them down; it is the desire you have publicly expressed that victory should belong to the power and partisans of your brother, and the encouragement of all kinds which you have given to the murderers of your country. What answer have you to these last facts?

A. All those acts imputed to me are unworthy deeds with which I was very far from staining myself.

Q. At the time of the journey to Varennes did you not precede the shameful evasion of the tyrant by the subtraction of the diamonds called crown diamonds, belonging then to the nation, and did you not send them to d'Artois?

A. Those diamonds were not sent to d'Artois; I confined myself to giving them into the hands of a trustworthy person.

Q. Will you name the person with whom you deposited those diamonds?

A. M. de Choiseul was the person I selected to receive that trust.

Q. What have become of the diamonds you say you confided to Choiseul?

A. I am absolutely ignorant of what was the fate of those diamonds, not having had an opportunity to see M. de Choiseul; I have had no anxiety, nor have I concerned myself about them.

Q. You do not cease to lie on all the questions made to you, and especially on the matter of the diamonds; for a *procès-verbal* of September 12, 1792, drawn up with full knowledge of the circumstances by the representatives of the people at the time of the theft of those diamonds, proves, in a manner that cannot be denied, that those diamonds were sent to d'Artois. Have you not kept up a correspondence with your brother, the *ci-devant Monsieur?*

A. I do not remember having done so since it was prohibited.

Q. Did you not yourself stanch and dress the wounds of the assassins sent to the Champs Élysées by your brother against the brave Marseillais?

A. I never knew that my brother did send assassins against any one, no matter who. Although I gave succour to some wounded men, humanity alone induced me to dress their wounds; I did not need to know the cause of their ills to occupy myself with their relief. I make no merit of this, and I cannot imagine that a crime can be made of it.

Q. It is difficult to reconcile the sentiments of humanity in which you now adorn yourself with the cruel joy you showed on seeing the torrents of blood that flowed on the 10th of August. All things justify us in believing that you are humane to none but the murderers of the people, and that you have all the ferocity of the most sanguinary animals for the defenders of liberty. Far from succouring the latter you instigated their massacre by your applause; far from disarming the murderers of the people you gave them with your own hands the instruments of death, by which you flattered yourselves, you and your accomplices, that tyranny and despotism would be restored. That is the humanity of despots, who, from all time, have sacrificed millions of men to their caprices, to their ambition, and to their cupidity. The prisoner Élisabeth, whose plan of defence is to deny all that is laid to her charge, will she have the sincerity to admit that she nursed the little Capet in the hope of succeeding to his father's throne, thus instigating to royalty?

A. I talked familiarly with that unfortunate child, who was dear to me from more than one cause, and I gave him, in consequence, all the consolations that I thought might comfort him for the loss of those who gave him birth.

Q. That is admitting, in other terms, that you fed the little Capet with the projects of vengeance which you and yours have never ceased to form against liberty; and that you flattered yourself to raise the fragments of a shattered throne by soaking it in the blood of patriots.

The president then proceeded to the examination of the other prisoners, confining himself to a few insignificant questions.

[Here the "Moniteur," and after it historians, omit all mention of the speech of Madame Élisabeth's defender, thus leaving it to be supposed that no voice was raised in her behalf. Though the trial was rapid, and all communication was prevented between her and her defender, it is a known fact that Chauveau-Lagarde rose after the president had ended Madame Élisabeth's examination, and made a short plea, of which he has given us himself the substance:

"I called attention," he says, "to the fact that in this trial there was only a bold accusation, without documents, without examination, without witnesses, and that, consequently, as there was in it no legal element of conviction there could be no legal conviction at all.

"I added that they had nothing against the august prisoner but her answers to the questions just put to her, and that those answers, far from condemning her, ought to honour her to all eyes, because they proved absolutely nothing but the goodness of her heart and the heroism of her friendship.

"Then after developing those ideas I ended by saying that as there was no ground for a defence, I could only present for Madame Élisabeth an apology, and even so, I found it impossible to make more than one that was worthy of her, namely: that a princess who had been a perfect model of virtue at the Court of France could not be the enemy of Frenchmen.

"It is impossible to paint the fury with which Dumas apostrophized me; reproaching me for having had the 'audacity to speak' of what he called 'the pretended virtue of the accused, thus attempting to corrupt the public morals.' It was easy to see that Madame Élisabeth, who until then had remained calm, as if unconscious of her own danger, was agitated by that to which I was exposing myself.]

The report in the "Moniteur" continues:—

After the Public Prosecutor and the defenders had been heard, the president declared the debate closed. He then summed up the cases and gave to the jury the following written paper:—

"Plots and conspiracies have existed, formed by Capet, his wife, his family, his agents and his accomplices, in consequence of which external war on the part of a coalition of tyrants has been provoked, also civil war in the interior has been raised, succour in men and money have been furnished to the enemy, troops have been assembled, plans of campaign have been made, and leaders appointed to murder the people, annihilate liberty, and restore despotism.

"Is Élisabeth Capet an accomplice in these plots?"

The jury, after a few moments' deliberation, returned to

the audience chamber and gave an affirmative declaration against Madame Élisabeth and the other prisoners [here follow the names], who were then condemned to the *Penalty of Death*. . . . It was then ordered that, by the diligence of the Public Prosecutor, the present judgment shall be executed within twenty-four hours on the Place de la Révolution of this city, and be printed, read, published, and posted throughout the extent of the Republic.

As Madame Élisabeth left the Tribunal, Fouquier turned to the president and said: "It must be owned she never uttered a complaint." — "What has she to complain of, that Élisabeth de France?" replied Dumas, with ironical gaiety; "haven't we just given her a court of aristocrats who are worthy of her? There will be nothing to prevent her from fancying she is back in the salons of Versailles when she finds herself at the foot of the guillotine surrounded by all those faithful nobles."

When Madame Élisabeth returned to the prison she asked to be taken to the common room, in which were the twenty-four persons condemned to die with her on the morrow. This room, long, narrow, and dark, was separated from the office of the Conciergerie by a door and a glass partition. It had no furniture but wooden benches fastened to the walls. These, and the following details are given by two eye-witnesses who happened to be in the room that night though not among the number condemned to death.[1]

---

[1] One was Geoffroy Ferry, who was there as usual to take an inventory of the clothes and other articles on the condemned persons; he gave these details to his nephew, attached in 1825 to the École des Beaux Arts, who gave them to the author of the "Vie de Madame Élisabeth." The other was Marguerite, a maid in the service of the Marquis de Fenouil, imprisoned in the Conciergerie for refusing to testify against her master. The same author obtained these facts from her own lips in 1828. — Fr. Ed.

Joining the poor unfortunates, who were now in different stages of agony and fear, Madame Élisabeth took her place among them naturally. Such as she had been at Versailles and at Montreuil in the midst of other friends, she was here, forgetful of herself, mindful of them, and dropping into each poor heart by simple words the balm of God's own comfort. She seemed to regard them as friends about to accompany her to heaven. She spoke to them calmly and gently, and soon the serenity of her look, the tranquillity of her mind subdued their anguish. The Marquise de Sénozan, the oldest of the twenty-four victims, was the first to recover courage and offer to God the little that remained to her of life. Madame de Montmorin, nearly all of whose family had been massacred in the Revolution, could not endure the thought of the immolation of her son, twenty years of age, who was doomed to die with her. "I am willing to die," she said sobbing, "but I cannot see him die." — "You love your son," said Madame Élisabeth, "and yet you do not wish him to accompany you; you are going yourself to the joys of heaven and you want him to stay upon earth, where all is now torture and sorrow." Under the influence of those words Mme. de Montmorin's heart rose to a species of ecstasy, her fibres relaxed, her tears flowed, and clasping her son in her arms, "Yes, yes!" she cried," we will go together."

M. de Loménie, former minister of war, and lately mayor of Brienne, whom that town and its adjoining districts had vainly endeavoured to save, was indignant with a species of exaltation, not at being condemned to die, but at hearing Fouquier impute to him as a crime the testimony of affection and gratitude shown for him by his department. Madame Élisabeth went to him and said gently: "If it is fine to merit the esteem of your fellow-citizens, think how much finer it is to merit the goodness of God. You have shown your compatriots how to live rightly; show them now how men die when their conscience is at peace."

It sometimes happens that timid natures, the most susceptible of fear in the ordinary course of life, will heroically brave death when a great sentiment inspires them. Madame Élisabeth's presence conveyed that inspiration. The Marquise de Crussol-Amboise was so timid that she dared not sleep without two women in her room; a spider terrified her; the mere idea of an imaginary danger filled her with dread. Madame Élisabeth's example transformed her suddenly; she grew calm and firm, and so remained till death. The same species of emotion was conveyed to all the others. The calm presence of Madame Élisabeth seemed to them in that terrible hour as if illumined by a reflection from the Divine. "It is not exacted of us," she said, "as it was of the ancient martyrs, that we sacrifice our beliefs; all they ask of us is the abandonment of our miserable lives. Let us make that feeble sacrifice to God with resignation."

So, in these last moments of life a great joy was given to her; she revived the numbed or aching hearts, she restored the vigour of their faith to fainting souls, she blunted the sting of death, and brought to eyes despairing of earth, the light of the true deliverance.

The next morning the gates of the prison opened and the carts of the executioner, called by Barère "the biers of the living," came out. Madame Élisabeth was in the first with others, among them Mme. de Sénozan and Mme. de Crussol-Amboise, to whom she talked during the passage from the Conciergerie to the Place Louis XV. Arriving there, she was the first to descend; the executioner offered his hand, but the princess looked the other way and needed no help. At the foot of the scaffold was a long bench on which the victims were told to sit. By a refinement of cruelty Madame Élisabeth was placed nearest the steps to the scaffold, but she was the last of the twenty-five called to ascend them; she was to see and hear the killing of them all before her turn should come. During that time she never ceased to say the *De profundis;* she who was about to die prayed for the dead.

The first to be called was Mme. de Crussol. She rose immediately; as she passed Madame Élisabeth she curtsied, and then, bending forward, asked to be allowed to kiss her. "Willingly, and with all my heart," replied the princess. All the other women, ten in number, did likewise. The men, as they passed her, each bowed low the head that an instant later was to fall into the basket. When the twenty-fourth bowed thus before her, she said: "Courage, and faith in God's mercy." Then she rose herself, to be ready at the call of the executioner. She mounted firmly the steps of the scaffold. Again the man offered his hand, but withdrew it, seeing from her bearing that she needed no help. With an upward look to heaven, she gave herself into the hands of the executioner. As he fastened her to the fatal plank, her neckerchief came loose and fell to the ground. "In the name of your mother, monsieur, cover me," she said. Those were her last words.

At this execution alone, no cries of " Vive la Revolution!" were raised; the crowd dispersed silently. The eye-witness from whose lips this account was written down, added: "When I saw the cart on which they were placing the bodies and heads of the victims, I fled like the wind." The cart held two baskets; into one of which they threw the mound of bodies; into the other the heap of heads. These were taken to the cemetery at Monçeaux, and flung into a grave twelve feet square, one upon another, naked, because the clothes were a perquisite of the State. In 1816, Louis XVIII., wishing to give his sister Christian burial, ordered a search to be made for her remains. The searchers fancied they discovered her body, but her head was never found.

JOURNAL OF THE TOWER OF THE TEMPLE
DURING THE CAPTIVITY OF LOUIS XVI.
BY CLÉRY,
His Valet de Chambre.

PART SECOND.

JOURNAL OF THE TOWER OF THE TEMPLE

DURING THE CAPTIVITY OF LOUIS XVI.
BY CLÉRY.

CHAPTER I.

The 10th of August, 1792.— Cléry permitted to serve the King and his Family.— Life and Treatment of the Royal Family in the Tower of the Temple.

I SERVED the king and his august family five months in the Tower of the Temple; and in spite of the close watching of the municipal officers who were the keepers of it, I was able, either in writing or by other means, to take certain notes on the principal events which took place in the interior of that prison.

In combining these notes in the form of a journal, my intention is more to furnish materials to those who may write the history of the deplorable end of the unfortunate Louis XVI. than to compose memoirs myself; for which I have neither talent nor pretension.

Sole and continual witness of the injurious treatment the king and his family were made to endure, I alone can write it down and affirm the exact truth.

Though attached since the year 1782 to the royal family, and witness, through the nature of my service, of the most disastrous events during the course of the Revolution, it would be going outside of my subject to describe them; they are, for the most part, already collected in different works. I shall begin this journal at the period of August 10, 1792, dreadful day, when a few men overturned a throne of fourteen centuries, put their king in fetters, and precipitated France into an abyss of horrors.

I was on service with the dauphin at that period. From the morning of the 9th the agitation in the minds of all was extreme; groups were forming throughout Paris, and we heard with certainty in the Tuileries that the conspirators had a plan. The tocsin was to ring at midnight in all parts of the city, and the Marseillais, uniting with the inhabitants of the faubourg Saint-Antoine, were to march at once and besiege the château. Detained by my functions in the apartment of the young prince and beside his person, I knew only in part what was happening outside. I shall here relate none but events which I witnessed during that day when so many different scenes took place even in the palace.

On the evening of the 9th at half-past eight o'clock, having put the dauphin to bed, I left the Tuileries to try to learn what was the state of public opinion. The courtyards of the château were filled with about eight thousand National guards from the different sections, placed there to defend the king. I went to the Palais-Royal, of which I found all the exits closed; National guards were there under arms, ready to march to the Tuileries and support the battalions already there; but a populace, excited by factious persons, filled the neighbouring streets, and its clamour resounded on all sides.

I re-entered the château towards eleven o'clock through the king's apartments. The persons belonging to the Court, and those on duty were collected there in a state of anxiety. I passed on to the dauphin's apartment, where, an instant later, I heard the tocsin rung and the *générale* beaten in all quarters of Paris. I remained in the salon until five in the morning with Mme. de Saint-Brice, waiting-woman to the young prince. At six o'clock the king went down into all the courtyards of the château and reviewed the National Guard and the Swiss Guard, who swore to defend him. The queen and her children followed the king. A few seditious voices were heard in the ranks, but they were soon smothered by the shouts, repeated hundreds of times, of "Vive le roi! Vive la nation!"

The attack on the Tuileries not seeming near as yet, I went out a second time and followed the quays as far as the Pont Neuf. I met everywhere collections of armed men whose bad intentions were not doubtful; they carried pikes, pitchforks, axes, and pruning-hooks. The battalion of the Marseillais marched in fine order with cannon, matches lighted; they invited the people to follow them "to aid," they said, "in dislodging the tyrant and proclaiming his dethronement before the National Assembly." Too certain now of what was going to happen, but consulting only my duty, I went ahead of this battalion and re-entered the Tuileries. A numerous body of National guards were pouring out in disorder through the gate of the gardens opposite the Pont-Royal. Distress was painted on the faces of most of them. Several said: "We swore this morning to defend the king, and at the moment when he runs the greatest danger we abandon him!" Others, on the side of the conspirators insulted and threatened their comrades and forced them to go away. The good men let themselves be ruled by the seditious; and this culpable weakness, which, so far, had produced all the evils of the Revolution, was the beginning of the misfortunes of that fatal day.

After many fruitless attempts to re-enter the château, I was recognized by the Swiss Guard of one of the gates, and I succeeded in entering. I went at once to the king's apartment, and begged that some one on service would inform His Majesty of what I had seen and heard.

At seven o'clock, anxiety was greatly increased by the baseness of several battalions which successively abandoned the Tuileries. Those of the National Guard who remained at their post, in number about four or five hundred, showed as much fidelity as courage. They were placed, indiscriminately with the Swiss, about the interior of the palace, on the staircases, and at all the exits. These troops had passed the night without food; I hastened, with other servants of the king, to carry them bread and wine, and encourage them not to abandon the royal family. It was then that the king gave the command of the interior of his palace to the Maréchal de Mailly, the Duc du Châtelet, the Comte de Puységur, the Baron de Viomesnil, the Count d'Hervilly, the Marquis du Pajet, etc. The persons of the Court, and those on service were distributed into the different rooms, after swearing to defend till death the person of the king. We were, in all, about three or four hundred, but without other arms than swords and pistols.

At eight o'clock the danger became pressing. The Legislative Assembly held its meetings in the Riding-school, which looked upon the garden of the Tuileries. The king sent several messages informing it of the position in which he was placed, and inviting it to appoint a deputation which would aid him with advice. The Assembly, although the attack on the château was preparing before its eyes, made no reply.

A few moments later the department of Paris and several municipals entered the château, with Rœderer, then prosecutor-general, at their head. Rœderer, doubtless in collusion with the conspirators, urged His Majesty eagerly to go with his family to the Assembly; he assured the king that he could no longer rely on the National Guard, and that if he remained in the palace, neither the department nor the municipality of Paris would be answerable for his safety.

The king listened without emotion; he retired to his chamber with the queen, the ministers, and a small number of persons; and, soon after, came out of it to go with his family to the Assembly. He was surrounded by a detachment of the Swiss and the National Guard. Of all the persons on duty, the Princesse de Lamballe and Mme. de Tourzel were the only ones who had permission to follow the royal family. Mme. de Tourzel was obliged, in order that the young prince might not go unattended, to leave her daughter, seventeen years of age, in the Tuileries among the soldiers. It was then nearly nine o'clock.

Forced to remain in the apartments, I waited with terror the results of the king's action; I was near the windows that looked into the garden. It was more than an hour after the royal family had entered the Assembly, when I saw on the terrace of the Feuillants four heads on pikes which were being carried towards the Assembly. That was, I think, the signal for the attack on the château, for, at the same moment, a terrible fire of cannon and musketry was heard. The balls and the bullets riddled the palace. The king no longer being there, every one thought of his own safety; but all the exits were closed and certain death awaited us. I ran hither and thither; already the apartments and the staircases were heaped with dead; I determined to spring upon the terrace through one of the windows of the queen's apartment. I crossed the parterre rapidly to reach the Pont-Tournant. A number of the Swiss Guard who had preceded me were rallying under the trees. Placed thus, between two fires, I returned upon my steps to reach the new stairway to the terrace on the water-side. I meant to jump upon the quay, but a continual fire from the Pont-Royal prevented me. I went along the same side to the gate of the dauphin's garden; there, some Marseillais who had just massacred several Swiss were stripping the bodies. One of them came to me. "What, citizen," he said, "have you no arms? Take this sword and help us to kill." Another Marseillais snatched the weapon. I was, in fact, without arms and wearing a plain coat; had anything indicated that I was on service in the palace, I should certainly not have escaped.

Several Swiss, being pursued, took refuge in a stable not far off. I myself hid there; the Swiss were soon massacred at my side. Hearing the cries of those unhappy victims, the master of the house, M. le Dreux, rushed in. I profited by that moment to slip into his house. Without knowing me, M. le Dreux and his wife asked me to remain until the danger was over.

I had in my pocket some letters and newspapers addressed to the young prince; also my entrance-card to the Tuileries, on which was written my name and the nature of my service; these papers would have made me known. I had barely time to throw them away before an armed troop searched the house to make sure that no Swiss were hidden there. M. le Dreux told me to pretend to be working at some drawings lying on a large table. After a fruitless search, the men, their hands stained with blood, stopped to coldly relate their murders. I remained in that asylum from ten in the morning till four in the afternoon, having before my eyes the horrors committed on the Place Louis XV. Some men murdered, others cut off the heads of the bodies, women, forgetting all decency, mutilated the bodies, tore off the fragments, and carried them in triumph.

During this interval, Mme. de Rambaut, waiting-woman to the dauphin, who had with difficulty escaped from the massacre at the Tuileries, came to take refuge in the same house; a few signs that we made to each other enjoined silence. The sons of our host, coming in at that moment from the National Assembly, informed us that the king, "suspended from his functions," was closely guarded, with the royal family, in the box of the reporter of the "Logographe," and that it was impossible to approach him.

That being so, I resolved to go to my wife and children, in a country place, five leagues from Paris, where I had had a house for two years; but the barriers were closed, and, moreover, I could not abandon Mme. de Rambaut. We agreed to take the route to Versailles, where she lived; the sons of our host accompanied us. We crossed the bridge, Louis XV., which was covered with naked dead bodies, already putrefying in the great heat, and after many dangers we left Paris through a breach which was not guarded.

On the plain of Grenelle, we were met by peasants on horseback, who shouted at us from a distance, and threatened us with their guns: "Stop, or death!" One of them, taking me for a guard, aimed and was about to shoot me, when another proposed to take us to the municipality of Vaugirard. "There is already a score of them there," he said; "the killing will be all the greater." Reaching the municipality, our host's sons were recognized: the mayor questioned me: "Why, when the country is in danger, are you not where you belong? Why are you leaving Paris? That shows bad intentions." "Yes, yes," cried the populace, "to prison, those aristocrats, to prison!" "It is precisely because I am on my way to where I belong, that you find me on the road to Versailles, where I live; that is my post just as much as this is yours." They questioned Mme. de Rambaut; our host assured them we spoke the truth, and they gave us passports. I ought to render thanks to Providence for not having been taken to the prison of Vaugirard; where they had just put twenty-three of the king's guards, who were afterwards taken to the Abbaye and massacred there, on the 2d of September.

From Vaugirard to Versailles, patrols of armed men stopped us continually to examine our passports. I took Mme. Rambaut to her parents, and then started to return to my family. A fall I had in jumping from the window of the Tuileries, the fatigue of a tramp of twelve leagues, and my painful reflections on the deplorable events which had just taken place, overcame me to such a degree that I had a very high fever. I was in bed three days, but, impatient to know the fate of the king, I surmounted my illness and returned to Paris.

On arriving there I heard that the royal family, after being kept since the 10th at the Feuillants, had just been taken to the Temple; that the king had chosen to serve him M. de Chamilly, his head *valet de chambre*, and that M. Huë, usher of the king's bedchamber, was to serve the dauphin. The Princesse de Lamballe, Mme. de Tourzel, and her daughter, Mlle. Pauline de Tourzel, had accompanied the queen. Mmes. Thibaut, Bazire, Navarre, and Saint-Brice, waiting-women, had followed the three princesses and the young prince.

I then lost all hope of continuing my functions towards the dauphin, and I was about to return to the country when, on the sixth day of the king's imprisonment, I was informed that all the persons who were in the Tower with the royal family, had been removed, and, after examination before the council of the Commune of Paris, were consigned to the prison of La Force, with the sole exception of M. Huë, who was taken back to the Temple to serve the king. Pétion, then mayor of Paris, was charged with the duty of selecting two others. Learning of these arrangements, I resolved to try every possible means to resume my place in the service of the young prince. I went to see Pétion; he told me that as I had belonged to the household of the king, I could not obtain the consent of the Commune. I cited M. Huë, who had just been sent by the council itself, to serve the king. Pétion promised to support a memorial which I gave him, but I told him it was necessary above all, that he should inform the king of this step. Two days later, he wrote to His Majesty as follows: —

"SIRE, — The *valet de chambre* attached to the prince-royal from infancy asks to be allowed to continue his service with him; as I think the proposal will be agreeable to you, I have acceded to his request," etc.

His Majesty answered in writing that he accepted me for the service of his son, and, in consequence, I was taken to the Temple. There, I was searched; they gave me advice as to the manner in which, they said, I must conduct myself; and the same day, August 26, at eight in the evening, I entered the Tower of the Temple.

It would be difficult for me to describe the impression made upon me by the sight of that august and unfortunate family. The queen was the one who spoke to me. After a few words of kindness, she added: "You will serve my son, and you will arrange with M. Huë in all that concerns us." I was so oppressed with feelings that I could scarcely answer her.

During the supper, the queen and the princesses, who had been a week without their women, asked me if I could comb their hair; I replied that I would do whatever they desired of me. A municipal officer thereupon came up to me, and told me to be more circumspect in my answers. I was frightened at such a beginning.

During the first eight days that I passed in the Temple, I had no communication with the exterior. M. Huë was alone charged with asking for and receiving the things necessary for the royal family; I served conjointly and indiscriminately with him. My service to the king was confined to dressing his hair in the morning and rolling it at night; I noticed that I was watched incessantly by the municipal officers; a mere nothing displeased them; I kept on my guard to avoid any imprudence, which would infallibly have ruined me.

On the 2d of September, there was much disturbance around the Temple. The king and his family went down as usual to walk in the garden; a municipal who followed the king said to one of his colleagues: "We did wrong to consent to let them walk this afternoon." I had noticed all that morning the uneasiness of the commissioners. They now hurried the royal family into the building; but they were scarcely assembled in the queen's room before two municipal officers who were not on duty at the Tower entered. One of them, Matthieu, an ex-capucin friar, said to the king: "You are ignorant of what is going on; the country is in the greatest danger; the enemy has entered Champagne; the King of Prussia is marching on Châlons; you are answerable for all the harm that will come of it. We, our wives and children, may perish, but you first, before us; the people will be avenged." — "I have done all for the people," said the king; "I have nothing to reproach myself with."

This same Matthieu said to M. Huë: "The Council has ordered me to put you under arrest." "Who?" asked the king. "Your *valet de chambre.*" The king wished to know of what crime he was accused, but could learn nothing, which made him very uneasy as to M. Huë's fate; he recommended him earnestly to the two municipal officers.

They put the seals on the little room he had occupied, and he went away with them at six o'clock in the evening after having passed twenty days in the Temple. As he went out, Matthieu said to me: "Take care how you behave, or the same thing may happen to you."

The king called me a moment after, and gave me some papers which M. Huë had returned to him; they were accounts of expenditures. The uneasy air of the municipals, the clamour of the people in the neighbourhood of the Tower, agitated his heart cruelly. After he had gone to bed, he told me to pass the night beside him; I placed a bed beside that of His Majesty.

On the 3d of September, while I was dressing the king, he asked me if I had heard anything of M. Huë, and if I knew any news of Paris. I answered that during the night I had heard a municipal say that the people were attacking the prisons, and that I would try to get more information. "Take care not to compromise yourself," said the king, "for then we should be left alone, and I fear their intention is to surround us with strangers."

At eleven o'clock that morning, the king being with his family in the queen's room, a municipal told me to go into that of the king, where I should find Manuel and several members of the Commune. Manuel asked me what the king had said about M. Huë's removal. I answered that His Majesty was uneasy at it. "Nothing will happen to him," he said, "but I am ordered to inform the king that he will not return, and that the Council will put some one in his place. You can warn the king of this." I begged him to excuse me from doing so; I added that the king desired to see him in regard to many things, of which the royal family was in the greatest need. Manuel, with difficulty, made up his mind to go into the room where His Majesty was; he then told him of the decision of the Council, in relation to M. Huë, and warned him that another person would be sent. "I thank you," replied the king, "but I shall use the services of my son's *valet de chambre*, and if the Council opposes it, I shall serve myself. I am resolved on this." Manuel said he would speak of it to the Council, and retired. I asked him, as I showed him out, if the disturbances in Paris continued. He made me fear by his answers that the people would attack the Temple. "You are charged with a difficult duty," he added. "I exhort you to courage."

At one o'clock the king and his family expressed a wish to take their walk; it was refused. During dinner the noise of drums and the shouts of the populace were heard. The royal family left the dinner table in a state of anxiety, and again collected in the queen's room. I went down to dine with Tison and his wife, who were employed as servants in the Tower.

We were hardly seated before a head at the end of a pike was presented at the window. Tison's wife screamed loudly; the murderers thought it was the queen's voice, and we heard the frantic laughs of those barbarians. Thinking that Her Majesty was still at table, they had raised the victim's head so that it could not escape her sight; it was that of the Princesse de Lamballe. Though bloody, it was not disfigured; her blond hair, still curling, floated around the pike.

I ran at once to the king. Terror had so changed my face that the queen noticed it; it was important to hide the cause from her; I meant to warn the king and Madame Élisabeth; but the two municipals were present. "Why do you not go to dinner?" asked the queen. "Madame," I answered, "I do not feel well." At that moment a municipal entered the room and spoke mysteriously with his colleagues. The king asked if his family were in safety. "There is a

Mme Vigée Le Brun

The Princesse de Lamballe

rumour going," they replied, "that you and your family are no longer in the Tower; the people want you to appear at the window, but we shall not allow it; the people ought to show more confidence in their magistrates."

The cries and shouts outside increased; we heard, very distinctly, insults addressed to the queen. Another municipal came in, followed by four men deputed by the people to make sure that the king and his family were in the Tower. One of them, in the uniform of the National Guard, wearing two epaulets and carrying a large sabre, insisted that the prisoners should show themselves at the window. The municipals opposed it. The man then said to the queen in the coarsest tone: "They want to prevent your seeing the Lamballe's head, which has been brought here to show you how the people avenge themselves on tyrants; I advise you to appear." The queen fainted; I ran to her support; Madame Élisabeth helped me to place her in an arm-chair; her children burst into tears and tried by their caresses to bring her to. The man did not go away; the king said to him firmly: "We expect everything, monsieur; but you might have refrained from telling the queen of that dreadful thing." The man then went out with his comrades; their object was accomplished.

The queen, recovering her senses, wept with her children, and passed with the family into the room of Madame Élisabeth, where less was heard of the clamours of the populace. I remained a moment longer in the queen's room, and, looking out of the window through the blinds, I saw the head of Madame de Lamballe a second time; the man who carried it had mounted a pile of rubbish, fallen from the houses they were demolishing to isolate the Tower; another man beside him carried the bloody heart of the unfortunate princess. They wanted to force in the door of the Tower; a municipal, named Daujeon, harangued them, and I very distinctly heard him say: "The head of Antoinette does not belong to you; the department has rights; France confided the keeping of these great criminals to the city of Paris; it is for you to help us to keep them until national justice avenges the people." It was only after one hour's resistance that he succeeded in making them go away.

On the evening of the same day one of the commissioners told me that the populace had attempted to enter with the deputation, and to carry into the tower the naked and bloody corpse of Madame de Lamballe, which they had dragged from the prison of La Force to the Temple; he said that the municipals, after struggling for some time with the mob, finally opposed them by tying a tri-colour ribbon across the principal entrance to the Tower; that they had vainly requested the help of the Commune of Paris, of General Santerre, and of the National Assembly, to stop designs which were not concealed, and that for six hours it was uncertain whether the royal family would or would not be massacred. The truth is the factious were not yet all-powerful; the leaders, though agreed as to the regicide, were not agreed as to the method of executing it, and perhaps the Assembly desired that other hands than its own should be the instrument of the conspiracy. A circumstance sufficiently remarkable is that the municipal made me pay him forty sous which the tri-colour ribbon had cost him.

By eight o'clock that evening all was quiet in the neighbourhood of the Tower, but the same tranquillity was very far from reigning in Paris, where the massacres continued for four or five days. I had an opportunity while undressing the king to tell him what I had seen and give him the details I had heard. He asked me which were the municipals who had shown the greatest firmness in defending the

The Tower of the Temple

lives of his family. I told him of Daujeon, who had checked the impetuosity of the people, though he was far from being in favour of the king. That municipal did not return to the Tower until four months later, but the king remembered his conduct and thanked him then.

The scenes of horror of which I have just spoken were followed by some tranquillity, so that the royal family continued the uniform system of life which they had adopted on entering the Temple. That the reader may follow its details easily, I think I ought to place here a description of the *small* tower in which the king was then confined.

It backed upon the large Tower, without any interior communication between the two, and it formed an oblong square flanked by two small, corner towers [*tourelles*]. In one of these small towers was a little staircase that started from the second floor and led up to a gallery along the eaves; in the other were little cabinets which were alike on each floor of the tower.

The building had four floors. The first was composed of an antechamber, a dining-room, and a cabinet made in one of the *tourelles*, in which was a library of some twelve to fifteen hundred volumes.

The second floor was divided in about the same manner. The largest room was made the bed-chamber of the queen and the dauphin; the second room, separated from the first by a small and dark antechamber, was the bedroom of Madame Élisabeth and Madame Royale. It was necessary to cross this room to enter the cabinet made in the *tourelle*, and that cabinet, which served as a privy to the entire main building, was common to the royal family, the municipal officers, and the soldiers.

The king lived on the third floor, and slept in the large room. The cabinet made in the *tourelle* was used by him as a reading-room. On one side was a kitchen, separated from the king's bedchamber by a small dark room, occupied at first by MM. de Chamilly and Huë and now sealed up. The fourth floor was closed and locked. On the ground-floor were kitchens of which no use was made.

The king rose usually at six in the morning; he shaved himself, and I arranged his hair and dressed him. He went at once into his reading-room. That room being very small the municipal guarding the king sat in the bedroom, the door being half-open in order that he might not lose sight of the person of the king. His Majesty prayed on his knees for five or six minutes, and then read till nine o'clock. During that time, and after having done his room and prepared the table for breakfast, I went down to the queen. She never opened her door until I came, so as to prevent the municipal from entering her bedroom. I then dressed the young prince and arranged the queen's hair; after which I went to perform the same service to Madame Élisabeth and Madame Royale. This moment of their toilet was one of those in which I could tell the queen and the princess what I heard and what I knew. A sign told them I had something to say, and one of them would then talk to the municipal officer to distract his attention.

At nine o'clock the queen, her children and Madame Élisabeth went up to the king's room to breakfast; after having served them I did the bedrooms of the queen and the princesses; Tison and his wife helped me only in that sort of work. It was not for service only that they had been placed where they were; a more important rôle was confided to them, namely: to observe all that might escape the vigilance of the municipals, and also to denounce the municipals themselves. Crimes to be committed no doubt entered the plan of those who selected them, for the Tison woman, who seemed then of a rather gentle nature and who trembled before her husband, afterwards revealed herself by an infamous denunciation of the queen, which was followed by a fit of insanity. Tison himself, formerly a clerk in the customs, was an old man, hard and malignant by nature, incapable of an emotion of pity, and destitute of all feelings of humanity. Beside those who were the virtuous of the earth the conspirators had chosen to place those that were vilest.

At ten o'clock the king came down with his family into the queen's room and passed the day there. He occupied himself with the education of his son, made him recite passages from Corneille and Racine, gave him lessons in geography, and taught him to colour maps. The precocious intelligence of the young prince responded perfectly to the tender care of the king. His memory was so good that on a map covered with a sheet of paper he could point out the departments, districts, towns, and the course of the rivers; it was the new geography of France that the king was teaching him. The queen, on her side, was occupied with the education of her daughter, and these different lessons lasted till eleven o'clock. The rest of the morning she spent in sewing, knitting, and doing tapestry. At midday the three princesses went into Madame Élisabeth's room to change their morning gowns; no municipal went with them.

At one o'clock, if the weather was fine, the royal family were taken down into the garden; four municipal officers and a captain of the National Guard accompanied them. As there were quantities of workmen about the Temple, employed in pulling down houses and building new walls, the royal family were allowed to walk only in the horse-chestnut alley. I was permitted to share these walks, during which I made the young prince play either at quoits, or football, or running, or other games of exercise.

At two o'clock they returned to the Tower, where I served the dinner; and every day at the same hour Santerre, a brewer, general-commanding the National Guard of Paris, came to the Temple, accompanied by two aides-de-camp. He searched the different rooms. Sometimes the king spoke to him; the queen never. After the meal, the royal family returned to the queen's room where Their Majesties usually played games at piquet or backgammon. It was during that time that I dined.

At four o'clock the king took a short rest; the princesses sat by him, each with a book in her hand; the deepest silence reigned during that nap. What a spectacle! a king pursued by hatred and calumny, fallen from a throne to a prison, yet sustained by his conscience and sleeping peacefully the sleep of the just! his wife, his sister, his children contemplating with respect those august features, the serenity of which seemed increased by troubles, so that even then there could be read upon them the peace he enjoys to-day! No, that sight will never be effaced from my memory.

When the king awoke, conversation was resumed. He made me sit beside him. I gave, under his eyes, writing-lessons to the young prince; and I copied out, under his selection, passages from the works of Montesquieu and other celebrated authors. After this lesson, I took the little prince into Madame Élisabeth's chamber, where I made him play ball or battledore and shuttlecock.

At the close of the day the royal family sat round a table; the queen read aloud books of history or other well-chosen works suitable to instruct and amuse her children; sometimes unexpected scenes corresponding to her own situation occurred and gave rise to painful thoughts. Madame Élisabeth read also in turn, and the reading lasted till eight o'clock. I then served the supper of the young prince in

Madame Élisabeth's bedroom; the royal family were present; the king took pleasure in amusing his children by making them guess the answers to conundrums taken from a file of the "Mercure de France" which he had found in the library.

After the dauphin's supper, I undressed him; it was the queen who heard him say his prayers; he said one especially for the Princesse de Lamballe; and by another he asked God to protect the life of Mme. de Tourzel, his governess. If the municipals were very near, the little prince himself took the precaution to say these last two prayers in a low voice. I then made him go into the cabinet, and if I had anything to tell the queen, I seized that moment. I told her what the newspapers contained, for none were allowed to enter the Tower; but a street-crier, sent expressly, came every evening at seven o'clock and stood near the wall on the rotunda side within the Temple inclosure, where he cried, with several pauses, a summary of what was taking place in the National Assembly, the commune, and the armies. I stationed myself in the king's cabinet to listen; and there, in the silence, it was easy to remember what I heard.

At nine o'clock the king supped. The queen and Madame Élisabeth took turns to remain with the dauphin during this meal; I carried to them what they desired for supper; that was another opportunity to speak to them without witnesses.

After supper the king went up for a moment into the queen's room, gave her his hand in sign of adieu, also to his sister, and kissed his children; then he went to his own room, retired into his cabinet and read there till midnight. The queen and the princesses closed the doors of their rooms; one of the municipals remained all night in the little room between their two chambers; the other followed the king.

I then placed my bed beside that of the king; but His Majesty waited, before going to bed, till the municipals were changed and the new one came up, in order to know which one it was, and if he was one the king did not know, he always told me to ask his name. The municipals were relieved at eleven in the morning, at five in the afternoon, and at midnight. The above manner of life lasted the whole time that the king was in the little tower, that is to say, until September 30.

I now resume the course of events. September 4th Pétion's secretary came to the Tower to remit to the king a sum of two thousand francs in *assignats;* he exacted from the king a receipt. His Majesty requested him to pay M. Huë five hundred and twenty-six francs, which he had advanced in his service; the secretary promised that he would. That sum of two thousand francs was all that was ever paid, although the Legislative Assembly voted five hundred thousand francs for the expenses of the king in the Tower of the Temple; but this was before it perceived the real intentions of its leaders, or dared to share them.

Two days later, Madame Élisabeth made me collect a number of little articles belonging to the Princesse de Lamballe which she had left in the Tower when suddenly taken away from it. I made a package and addressed it, with a letter, to the princess's waiting-woman. I heard later that neither package nor letter reached her.

At this period, the character of most of the municipals chosen to come to the Temple shows what manner of men had been used by the leaders for the revolution of August 10, and for the massacres of the 2d of September.

A municipal named James, a teacher of the English language, chose, one day, to follow the king into his little reading-room, and sit beside him. The king told him in a mild way that his colleagues always left him alone there; that, the door remaining open, he could not escape his sight, and that the room was so small two persons could not remain in it. James insisted in a harsh and vulgar way, and the king was forced to yield; he gave up his reading for that day, and returned to his chamber, where the same municipal continued to torment him with the same tyrannical surveillance.

One day, when the king rose, he mistook the municipal on guard for the one of the night before, and he said with interest that he was sorry they had forgotten to relieve him; the municipal answered this impulse of kind feeling on the part of the king with insults. "I come here," he said, "to keep watch on your conduct, and not for you to take notice of mine." Then, coming close up to the king, his hat on his head, he added: "No one, and you less than any one, has the right to meddle with me." He was insolent for the rest of the day. I heard afterwards that his name was Meunier.

Another commissioner, named Le Clerc, a doctor by profession, was in the queen's room while I was giving a writing lesson to the dauphin. He affected to interrupt our work, with a dissertation on the republican education that ought to be given to the young prince; he wished to have the most revolutionary works substituted for the books the child read.

A fourth was present when the queen was reading to her children a volume of the history of France, at the period when the Connétable de Bourbon took arms against his country; he declared that the queen wished by that example to inspire her son with feelings of vengeance against France, and he made a formal denunciation to the Council. I warned the queen, who, after that, chose her subjects in a way that prevented any one from calumniating her intentions.

A man named Simon, a shoemaker and a municipal officer, was one of six commissioners charged with the duty of inspecting the works and expenditures of the Temple; but he was the only one who, under pretence of properly fulfilling his office, never quitted the Tower. This man affected the lowest insolence whenever he was in presence of the royal family; often he would say to me, close to the king, so that His Majesty might hear him: "Cléry, ask Capet if he wants anything, for I can't take the trouble to come up a second time." I was forced to answer, "He wants nothing." It was this Simon who, at a later period, was put in charge of the young Louis, and who, by a well-calculated barbarity, made that interesting child so wretched. There is reason to think that he was the tool of those who shortened the prince's life.

To teach the young prince how to reckon, I made, by order of the queen, a multiplication-table. A municipal declared that she was showing her son how to talk in cipher, and they made her renounce the lessons in arithmetic.

The same thing happened in regard to the tapestry at which the queen and the princesses worked when they were first imprisoned. Several chair-backs being finished, the queen directed me to have them sent to the Duchesse de Sérent. The municipals, from whom I asked permission, thought the designs represented hieroglyphics, destined to open a correspondence with the outside; consequently they obtained a decree by which it was forbidden to allow any work done by the princesses, to leave the Tower.

Some of the commissioners never spoke of the king and queen, the prince and the princesses, without adding the most insulting epithets to their names. A municipal, named Turlot, said one day before me, "If the executioner doesn't guillotine that s . . . family, I'll do it myself."

The king and his family, when going to walk, had to pass before a great many sentinels, some of whom, even at this time, were posted in the interior of the little tower. They presented arms to the municipals and officers of the National Guard, who accompanied the king, but when the king passed them, they grounded their muskets, or pointedly reversed them. One of these sentinels, posted inside the tower, wrote one day on the door of the king's chamber: "The guillotine is permanent, and is awaiting the tyrant, Louis XVI." The king read the words; I made a motion to efface them, but His Majesty opposed it.

One of the two porters of the Tower, named Rocher, a horrible object, dressed as a *Sapeur*, with long moustaches, a black fur cap on his head, a large sabre and a belt from which hung a bunch of big keys, presented himself at the door whenever the king wished to go out; he would never open it till the king was close beside it, and then, under pretence of choosing the right key from his enormous bunch, which he rattled with a frightful noise, he kept the royal family waiting, and drew back the bolt with a crash. Then he would hurry down the stairs, and stand by the last door, a long pipe in his mouth, and as each member of the royal family passed him he would puff the smoke in their faces, especially those of the princesses. Some of the National guards, who were amused by such insolence, would gather near him, and laugh loudly at each puff of smoke, permitting themselves to say the coarsest things; some, to enjoy the spectacle more at their ease, would even bring chairs from the guard-room, and, sitting down, obstructed the passage, already very narrow.

During the promenade of the family the artillery-men assembled to dance and sing songs, — always revolutionary, and sometimes obscene.

When the royal family returned to the Tower they were forced to endure the same insults; often the walls were covered with most indecent apostrophes, written in such large letters that they could not escape their eye, such as: "Madame Veto shall dance;" "We will put the fat pig on diet;" "Down with the *Cordon rouge*;" "Strangle the cubs;" etc. Once they drew a gibbet on which dangled a figure, and beneath it was written: "Louis taking an air bath." At another time it was a guillotine with these words: "Louis spitting into the basket."

Thus the little walk in the garden granted to the royal family became a torture. The king and queen might have escaped it by remaining in the Tower, but their children, the objects of their tenderness, needed the air; it was for them that Their Majesties endured daily without complaint these innumerable outrages.

Nevertheless, some signs of fidelity or pity came at times to soften the horror of these persecutions, and were all the more remarked because so rare.

A sentinel mounted guard one day at the queen's door; he belonged to the faubourgs, and was clean in his dress, which was that of a peasant. I was alone in the first room reading. He looked at me attentively and seemed much moved. I rose and passed before him. He presented arms and said in a trembling voice, "You cannot go out." "Why not?" "My orders are to keep you within sight." "You mistake me," I said. "What! monsieur, are you not the king?" "Then you do not know him?" "I have never seen him, and I would like to see him away from here." "Speak low;" I said, "I shall enter that room and leave the door half open; look in and you will see the king; he is sitting by the window with a book in his hand." I told the queen of the sentry's desire, and the king, whom she informed, had the kindness to go from one room to the other and walk before him. I then went back to the sentry. "Ah! monsieur," he said, "how good the king is! how he loves his children!" He was so moved that he could hardly speak. "No," he continued, striking his chest, "I cannot believe he has done us all that harm." I feared that his extreme agitation would compromise him, and I left him.

Another sentry, posted at the end of the alley where the royal family took their walk, still very young and with an interesting face, expressed by his looks the desire to give us some information. Madame Élisabeth, on the second turn of their walk, went near him to see if he would speak to her. Whether from fear or respect he did not dare to do so; but tears fell from his eyes, and he made a sign to indicate that he had laid a paper near him in a rubbish heap. I began to look for it, under pretence of finding quoits for the dauphin. But the municipal officers stopped me, and forbade me to go near the sentinels in future. I have never known the intentions of that young man.

This hour for their walk brought another kind of spectacle to the royal family which often rent their hearts. A number of faithful subjects daily profited by that brief hour to see their king and queen by placing themselves at the windows of houses which look into the garden of the Temple. It was impossible to be mistaken as to their sentiments and their prayers. Once I was sure I recognized the Marquise de Tourzel. I judged especially by the extreme attention with which she watched the movements of the little prince when he left his parents' side. I said this to Madame Élisabeth, who believed her a victim of September 2d. The tears came into her eyes on hearing the name. "Oh!" she said, "can she be living still!"

The next day I found means to get information. The Marquise de Tourzel was living on one of her estates. I also learned that the Princesse de Tarente and the Marquise de la Roche-Aymon, who were at the Tuileries on the 10th of August, had escaped the massacre. The safety of these persons, whose devotion was manifested on so many occasions, gave some moments of consolation to the royal family; but they heard soon after the awful news that the prisoners of the upper court of Orléans had all been massacred at Versailles on the 9th.

September 29, at nine in the evening, a man named Lubin, a municipal, arrived, surrounded by gendarmes on horseback and a numerous populace, to make a proclamation in front of the Tower. The trumpets sounded, and great silence succeeded. Lubin had the voice of Stentor. The royal family could hear distinctly the proclamation of the abolition of royalty, and the establishment of a republic. Hébert, so well-known under the name of Père Duchesne, and Destournelles, afterwards minister of public taxation, happened to be on guard that day over the royal family; they were seated at the moment near the door, and they stared at the king, smiling treacherously. The king noticed them; he had a book in his hand and continued to read; no change appeared upon his face. The queen showed equal firmness; not a word, not a motion that could add to the enjoyment of those two men. The proclamation ended, the trumpets sounded again. I went to the window; instantly all eyes turned to me; they took me for Louis XVI.; I was loaded with insults. The gendarmes made threatening motions towards me with their sabres, and I was obliged to retire in order to stop the tumult.

The same evening I informed the king that his son had need of curtains and covering for his bed, as the cold was beginning to be felt. The king told me to write the request and he would sign it. I used the same expressions I had hitherto employed: "The king requests for his son, etc." "You are very daring," said Destournelles, "to use a title abolished by the will of the people, as you have just heard." I replied that I had heard a proclamation, but I did not know its object. "It is," he said, "the abolition of royalty, and you can tell *monsieur* (pointing to the king) to cease to take a title the people no longer recognize." "I cannot," I said to him, "change this note, because it is already signed; the king would ask me the reason, and it is not for me to tell it to him." "You can do as you choose," he replied, "but I shall not certify your request." The next day Madame Élisabeth ordered me to write in future for such purposes as follows: "It is necessary for the service of Louis XVI. — or Marie-Antoinette — or Louis-Charles — or Marie-Thérèse — or Marie-Élisabeth."

Up to that time I had been forced to repeat these requests often. The small amount of linen the king and queen had was lent to them by persons of the Court during the time they were at the Feuillants. They could get none from the château of the Tuileries, where, on the 10th of August, everything had been pillaged. The royal family lacked clothing of every kind, and the princesses mended what they had daily. Often Madame Élisabeth was obliged to wait until the king went to bed, in order to darn his clothes. I obtained at last, after many requests, that a small amount of new linen should be made for them. Unfortunately, the work-people marked it with *crowned* letters, and the municipals insisted that the princesses should pick out the crowns; they were forced to obey.

CHAPTER II.

Continuation of their Life and Treatment. The King separated from his Family, and summoned for Trial before the Convention.

On the 26th of September, I learned from a municipal that it was proposed to separate the king from his family, that an apartment was being prepared for him in the great Tower, and that it was then nearly ready. It was not without precaution that I announced to the king this new tyranny; I showed him how much it cost me to distress him. "You could not give me a greater proof of attachment," said His Majesty. "I exact of your zeal that you will hide nothing from me; I expect everything; try to learn the day of this cruel separation and inform me of it."

On the 29th of September, at ten o'clock in the morning, five or six municipals entered the queen's room where the royal family was assembled. One of them, named Charbonnier, read to the king a decree of the council of the Commune which ordered "the removal of paper, pens, ink, pencils, and written papers, whether on the persons of the prisoners or in their rooms; also from the *valet de chambre*, and all other persons on service in the Tower." Charbonnier added: "If you have need of anything, Cléry will come down and write your requests on a register which will be kept in the council-chamber."

The king and his family, without making the slightest observation, searched their persons and gave up their papers, pencils, pocket-cases, etc. The commissioners then searched the rooms, the closets, and carried off the articles designated in the decree. I learned then, from a member of the deputation, that the king was to be transferred that very evening to the great Tower. I found means to inform the king by means of Madame Élisabeth.

True enough, after supper, as the king was leaving the queen's room to go up to his own, a municipal told him to wait, as the council had something to communicate to him. A quarter of an hour later, the six municipals who, in the morning, had carried away the papers, etc., entered, and read to the king a second decree of the Commune, which ordered his removal to the great Tower. Though already informed of that event, the king was greatly affected on being notified of it; his distressed family tried to read in the eyes of the commissioners to what length their projects went. The king, in bidding them adieu, left them in the utmost alarm and uncertainty, and this separation, forecasting as it did so many other misfortunes, was one of the most cruel moments Their Majesties had yet passed in the Temple. I followed the king to his new prison.

The apartment of the king in the great Tower was not ready; there was only one bed and no other furniture in it. The painters and paperers were still at work, which caused so intolerable a smell that I feared His Majesty would be made ill by it. They intended to give me a room very far from that of the king, but I insisted vehemently on being nearer to him. I passed the first night in a chair beside His Majesty; the next day the king, with great difficulty, obtained for me a room adjoining his own.

After His Majesty had risen, I wished to go into the small tower to dress the young prince. The municipals refused. One of them, named Véron, said: "You are to have no communication in future with the other prisoners, nor your master either; he is never to see his children again."

At nine o'clock the king asked to be taken to his family. "We have no orders for that," replied the commissioners. His Majesty made a few observations, to which they did not reply.

Half an hour later, two municipals entered, followed by a serving-man who brought the king a piece of bread and a bottle of lemonade for his breakfast. The king expressed his desire to dine with his family; they replied that they would inquire the orders of the Commune. "But," said the king, "my *valet de chambre* can surely go down; he has the care of my son, and nothing prevents him from continuing that service." "That does not depend on us," said the commissioners, and they retired.

I was then in a corner of the room, overcome with distress and filled with heart-rending fears for that august family. On one side, I saw the suffering of my master; on the other, I thought of the young prince, abandoned perhaps to strange hands. The municipals had already talked of separating him from his parents, and what fresh suffering that would cause to the queen!

I was full of these distressing ideas when the king came to me holding in his hand the bread they had brought him; he offered me half, saying: "They seem to have forgotten your breakfast; take this, the rest is enough for me." I refused, he insisted. I could not restrain my tears; the king saw them, and his own flowed.

At ten o'clock other municipals brought the workmen to continue their work in the apartment. One of them said to the king that he had just been present at the breakfast of his family, and they were all in good health. "I thank you," said the king, "and I beg you to give them news of me; tell them that I am well. Can I not," he continued, "have a few books which I left in the queen's room? You would do me a great pleasure if you would send them to me, for I have nothing to read here." His Majesty named the books he wanted. The municipal consented to the king's request; but, not knowing how to read, he proposed that I should go with him to get the books. I congratulated myself on the man's ignorance, and I blessed Providence for giving us that moment of consolation. The king charged me with certain orders, his eyes told me the rest.

I found the queen in her room, with her children and Madame Élisabeth. They were weeping, and their grief increased on seeing me. They asked a thousand questions about the king, to which I could only answer with reserve. The queen, addressing the municipals who accompanied me, eagerly urged her request to be with the king at least a few moments a day, and during meals. No longer complaints and tears, it was cries and sobs of grief. "Well, they shall dine together to-day at least," said a municipal officer, "but as our conduct is subordinate to the decrees of the Commune we must do to-morrow what they prescribe." His colleagues consented.

At the mere idea of being again with the king, a sentiment that was almost joy came to soothe the afflicted family. The queen holding her children in her arms, and Madame Élisabeth, raising her eyes to heaven and thanking God for the unexpected mercy, presented a very touching sight. Some of the municipals could not restrain their tears (the only ones I ever saw them shed in that dreadful place). One of them, the shoemaker Simon, said aloud: "I believe those b . . . of women will make me cry." Then turning to the queen he added: "When you murdered the people on the 10th of August *you* did not cry." — "The people are greatly deceived about our sentiments," answered the queen.

I then took the books the king asked for and carried them

to him; the municipals went with me to inform His Majesty that he might see his family. I said to these commissioners that I supposed I could without doubt continue to serve the young prince and the princesses; they consented. I thus had an opportunity to inform the queen of what had taken place, also of how much the king had suffered in being parted from her. They served the dinner in the king's room where his family joined him; nothing more was said about the decree of the Commune, and the royal family continued to meet at their meals, and also when walking in the garden.

After dinner they showed the queen the apartment that was being prepared for her in the great Tower, above that of the king. She begged the workmen to finish it quickly, but it was three weeks before it was ready.

During that interval I continued my services towards Their Majesties as well as towards the young prince and the princesses. Their occupations remained the same. The care the king gave to the education of his son was not interrupted; but this abode of the royal family in two separate towers made the watchfulness of the municipals more difficult and rendered them very uneasy. The number of commissioners was increased, and their distrust left me but little means to gain information of what was passing outside. Here are the ways I made use of: —

Under pretext of getting my linen and other necessaries brought to me, I obtained permission for my wife to come once a week to the Temple. She was always accompanied by a lady, a friend of hers, who passed for one of her relatives. No one proved more attachment to the royal family than this lady, by the steps she took and the risks she ran on various occasions. On their arrival, they were taken into the council chamber, but I could only speak to them in presence of the municipals. We were closely watched, and the first visits brought no results; but I managed to make them understand that they must come at one o'clock in the afternoon, the hour of the king's walk, during which time most of the municipals followed the royal family; only one was left in the council chamber, and if he was a kindly man he gave us some liberty, without, however, losing us from sight.

Getting thus a chance to speak without being overheard, I obtained from them news of the persons in whom the royal family took interest, and I heard of what was going on in the Convention. It was my wife who engaged the crier whom I have already mentioned as coming every day near the walls of the Temple and crying the items in the newspapers several times at intervals.

To this information I added what I could pick up from some of the municipals, but especially from a faithful man named Turgy, serving in the king's kitchen, who, out of devotion to His Majesty, had contrived to get himself employed in the Temple with two of his comrades, Marchand and Chrétien. They brought to the Tower the meals of the royal family, prepared in the kitchen of the palace of the Temple; they were also in charge of the business of provisioning, and Turgy, who was thus able to leave the precincts of the Temple two or three times a week, obtained information of what was happening. The difficulty was to convey that information to me. He was forbidden to speak to me except about the service of the table, and always in presence of the municipals. When he wanted to tell me something, he made a sign we had agreed upon, and I made different pretexts to approach him. Sometimes I asked him to do my hair; then Madame Élisabeth, who knew of my relations with Turgy, would speak to the municipals, and so give me time to exchange a few words unobserved; at other times I would make occasions for him to enter my chamber, and he seized the moment to put newspapers and other printed documents into my bed.

When the king or queen desired some particular information from the outside, and the day of my wife's visit was far off, I employed Turgy. If it was not his day for going out I would pretend to be in need of something for the royal family. "It must be for another day," he would answer. "Very good," I then said, with an indifferent air, "the king can wait." By speaking thus I expected to induce the municipals to give him an order to go out. Often they did give it and he brought me the details the king wanted that night or the next morning. We had agreed together as to this system of communicating, but we had to be careful not to employ the same means twice before the same commissioners.

Other obstacles were in the way of my informing the king of what I had learned. I could only speak to His Majesty in the evening at the moment when they changed the guard and as he went to bed. Sometimes I could say a word to him in the mornings when his watchers were not yet in a state to appear. I affected to wait until they were, letting them see, however, that the king was waiting for me. If they let me enter, I immediately opened the curtains of the king's bed, and while I put on his shoes and stockings I was able to speak to him without being heard. More often, however, my hopes miscarried, and the municipals made me wait for the end of their own toilet before they would let me attend to that of his Majesty. Several among them treated me roughly; some ordered me in the morning to take away their flock-beds and obliged me to replace them in the evening; others constantly made insulting remarks to me; but such conduct gave me additional means of being useful to

Their Majesties; by showing only gentleness and compliance to the commissioners, I ended by getting their good-will almost in spite of themselves; I inspired them with confidence without their being aware of it; and I thus succeeded in learning from themselves what I wanted to know.

Such was the plan that I was following with great care ever since my entrance to the Temple, when a singular and unexpected event made me fear I should be separated forever from the royal family.

One evening, towards six o'clock, — it was on the 6th of October, — after having accompanied the queen to her apartment, I was going back to the king with the two municipal officers, when a sentinel placed at the door of the large guardroom stopping me by the arm and calling me by name, asked how I was and said, with an air of mystery, that he had something he wished to speak about. "Monsieur," I answered, "speak out loud; I am not permitted to whisper with any one." "I am told," said the man, "that the king has been put in a dungeon for the last few days, and that you are with him." "You see it is not so," I replied, leaving him. One of the municipals was walking before me, the other followed me; the first stopped and listened to what was said.

The next morning two commissioners waited for me at the door of the queen's room. They took me to the council-chamber, and the municipals who were there assembled, questioned me. I reported the conversation with the sentinel just as it had taken place; the municipal who had listened to it confirmed my account; the other maintained that the sentinel had given me a paper, that it was a letter to the king and he had heard it rustle. I denied the fact, and invited the municipals to search me and make other inquiries. They drew up a *procès-verbal* of my examination, and I was confronted with the sentinel, who was sentenced to twenty-four hours imprisonment.

I thought the affair ended when, on the 26th of October, while the royal family were dining, a municipal entered, followed by six gendarmes, sabre in hand, a clerk, and a sheriff, both in uniform. I was in terror, thinking they had come to seize the king. The royal family rose; the king asked what was wanted of him; but the municipal, without replying to him, called me into the next room; the gendarmes followed, and the clerk having read to me a warrant of arrest they seized me to take me before the Tribunal. I asked permission to inform the king, and was told that from that moment I should not be allowed to speak to him. "Take nothing but a shirt," added the municipal, "it will not be long."

I believed I understood him and took nothing but my hat. I passed beside the king and his family who were standing and seemed in consternation at the manner in which I was carried off. The populace collected round the Temple assailed me with insults and demanded my head. An officer of the National Guard said it was necessary to preserve my life until I had revealed secrets of which I was the sole depositary. The same vociferations continued the whole way.

As soon as I reached the Palais-de-Justice I was put in solitary confinement. There I remained six hours, vainly endeavouring to imagine what could be the motives for my arrest. I could only remember that on the morning of the 10th of August, during the attack on the château of the Tuileries, a few persons who were caught there and were trying to get away, asked me to hide in a bureau that belonged to me several precious articles, and even papers by which they might be recognized. I thought that perhaps those papers had been seized and might be my ruin.

At eight o'clock I was taken before judges, who were unknown to me. This was a revolutionary tribunal, established August 10, to make a selection among those who had escaped the fury of the people on that occassion and put them to death. What was my astonishment when I saw on the prisoner's bench the same young man who was suspected of giving me a letter three weeks earlier, and when I recognized in my accuser the municipal officer who had denounced me to the council of the Temple. They questioned me, and witnesses were heard. The municipal renewed his accusation; I retorted that he was not worthy to be a magistrate of the people, because, if he had heard the rustle of a paper and saw the man give me a letter he ought to have had me searched at once, instead of waiting eighteen hours to denounce me to the council of the Temple. After the debate, the jury voted, and on their declaration I was acquitted. The president ordered four of the municipals present to take me back to the Temple; it was then midnight. I arrived at the moment when the king was going to bed, and I was allowed to inform him of my return. The royal family had taken the keenest interest in my fate, and thought I was already condemned.

It was at this time that the queen came to live in the apartment prepared for her in the great Tower; but that day so earnestly desired, and which seemed to promise Their Majesties some consolation, was marked, on the part of the municipal officers, with a fresh proof of animosity against the queen. Since her arrival at the Temple they saw her devoting her existence to the care of her son and finding some relief to her troubles in his affection and his caresses; they now separated the two without warning her; her distress was extreme. The young prince being placed with his father, I had sole charge of his service. With what tenderness the queen begged me to watch incessantly over his life.

The events of which I shall henceforth have to speak having happened in a different locality from that I have already described, I think I ought to make known the new habitation of Their Majesties.

The great Tower, about one hundred and fifty feet high, had four storeys, all vaulted and supported up the middle from base to roof by a huge shaft [what was called the little tower flanked it, but without communication, on one side]. The interior is about thirty feet square.

The second and third floors allotted to the king and queen, being, like the other floors, of one room each, were divided by board partitions into four rooms. The ground-floor was used by the municipals, the floor above was the guardroom, the next was that of the king.

The first room of his floor (divided as above stated) was an antechamber from which three doors led into the other three rooms. Opposite to the entrance was the king's bedroom, in which a bed was now placed for the dauphin; my room was on the left, so was the dining-room, which was separated from the antechamber by a glass partition. In the king's room was a chimney; a great stove in the antechamber heated the other rooms. Each of these rooms was lighted by a window; but thick iron bars and shutters on the outside prevented the air from circulating freely. The embrasures of these windows were nine feet deep.

The floors of the great tower communicated by a staircase placed in one of the *tourelles* at the corner of it. This staircase went up to the battlements, and wickets were placed upon it at intervals, to the number of seven. From this staircase each floor was entered through two doors, one of oak, very thick and studded with nails, the other of iron. The other *tourelle*, opening into the king's chamber, was made into a reading-room; on the floor above, it was turned into a privy, and above that the firewood was stored in it and during the day the flock beds of the municipals who guarded the king at night were placed there.

The four rooms on the king's floor had canvas ceilings; the partitions were covered with paper; that of the antechamber represented the interior of a prison, and on one of the panels hung, in very large type, "The Declaration of the Rights of Man" framed in a border of the three colours. A washstand, a small bureau, four covered chairs, one arm-chair, four straw chairs, a mirror on the fireplace, and a bed of green damask composed the furniture; these articles, together with those used in the other chambers were taken from the palace of the Temple. The king's bed was the one used by the captain of the guards of the Comte d'Artois.

The Duc d'Angoulême, in his capacity of grand-prior of France, was proprietor of the palace of the Temple. The Comte d'Artois had furnished it and made it his residence whenever he came to Paris. The Tower, separated from the palace by about two hundred feet and standing in the middle of the garden, was the storehouse of the archives of the Knights of Malta.

The queen lodged on the third floor, above the king, the distribution of the rooms being nearly the same as that of the king's apartment. The bedroom of the queen and Madame Royale was over that of the king and dauphin; Madame Élisabeth occupied the room above mine; the municipal sat in the antechamber all day and slept there. Tison and his wife lodged in the room above the dining-room of the king's apartment.

The upper (fourth) floor was unoccupied; a gallery ran round the inside of the battlements and was sometimes used as a promenade; but blinds had been placed between the battlements to prevent the royal family from seeing and being seen.

After the reunion of Their Majesties in the great Tower there was little change in the hours of meals, readings, walks, or in the time given by the king and queen to the education of their children. After the king rose, he read the service of the Knights of the Saint-Esprit, and as they had refused to allow mass to be said in the Temple, even on feast-days, he ordered me to buy for him the breviary that was used by the diocese of Paris. Louis XVI. was truly religious, but his pure and enlightened religion never caused him to neglect his other duties. Books of travel, the works of Montesquieu, those of the Comte de Buffon, "The Spectacle of Nature" by Pluche, Hume's History of England, the Imitation of Jesus Christ in Latin, Tasso in Italian, the drama of our different schools, were his habitual reading from the time he entered the Temple. He always gave four hours a day to Latin authors.

Madame Élisabeth and the queen desiring to have the same books of devotion as those of the king, His Majesty ordered me to obtain permission to buy them. How often have I seen Madame Élisabeth on her knees at her bedside praying fervently!

At nine o'clock they came to fetch the king and his son to breakfast in the queen's room; I accompanied them. I then did the hair of the three princesses, and, by order of the queen, I showed Madame Royale how to dress hair. During this time the king played chess or dominoes with the queen or with Madame Élisabeth.

After dinner the young prince and his sister played in the antechamber at battledore and shuttlecock, at *Siam*, or other games. Madame Élisabeth was always present, sitting near a table, with a book in her hand. I remained in the room, sometimes reading; and I then sat down, to obey the orders of the princess. This dispersal of the royal family often made the municipals very uneasy; unwilling to leave the king and queen alone, they were still more unwilling to separate from one another, so much did each distrust his fellow. This was the moment that Madame Élisabeth snatched to ask me questions or give me orders. I listened to her and answered without turning my eyes from the book which I held in my hand, so as not to be detected by the municipals. The dauphin and Madame Royale, in collusion with their aunt, facilitated these conversations by their noisy games, and often warned her by certain signs of the entrance of the municipals into the room. I was distrustful above all of Tison, suspected by the Commissioners themselves, whom he had more than once denounced; it was in vain that the king and queen treated him kindly; nothing could conquer his natural malignity.

In the evening, at bed-time, the municipals placed their beds in the antechamber so as to barricade the room in which His Majesty slept. They then locked the door leading from my room into that of the king and took away the key. I was obliged therefore to pass through the antechamber whenever His Majesty called me during the night, bear the ill-humour of the commissioners, and wait till one of them chose to get up and let me pass.

On the 7th of October, at six in the evening, I was made to go down to the council-chamber, where I found some twenty of the municipals assembled, presided over by Manuel, who, from being a prosecutor for the Commune of Paris had risen to be a member of the National Convention. His presence surprised me and made me anxious. They ordered me to take from the king, that very evening, the orders with which he was still decorated, such as those of Saint-Louis and the Golden Fleece; His Majesty no longer wore that of the Holy-Spirit, which had been suppressed by the first Assembly.

I represented that I could not obey; that it was not my place to make known to the king the decrees of the council. I made this answer in order to gain time to warn His Majesty, and I then saw by the embarrassment of the municipals that they were acting this time, at least, without being authorized by any decree, either of the Commune or the Convention. The commissioners refused at first to go up to the king; but Manuel induced them to do so by offering to accompany them. The king was seated, reading; Manuel addressed him, and the conversation that ensued was as remarkable for the indecent familiarity of Manuel as for the calmness and moderation of the king.

"How are you?" asked Manuel; "have you all that is necessary?"—"I am content with what I have," replied His Majesty.—"You are informed no doubt of the victories of our armies, of the taking of Spire, and of Nice, and the conquest of Savoie?"—"I heard them mentioned a few days ago by one of those *messieurs*, who was reading an evening journal"—"What! do not you see the newspapers which are now so interesting?"—"I receive none."—"*Messieurs*," said Manuel, addressing the municipals "give all the newspapers to monsieur (pointing to the king); it is well that he should be informed of our successes." Then, addressing His Majesty again, "Democratic principles are propagating themselves; you know, of course, that the people have abolished royalty and adopted a republican government?"—"I have heard it said, and I hope that Frenchmen will find the happiness that I always wished to give them."—"Do you also know that the National Assembly has suppressed all orders of knighthood? They ought to have told you to take off those decorations. Relegated to the class of other citizens you must be treated in the same manner as they. As for the rest, ask for what is necessary and they will hasten to procure it." — "I thank you," said the king, "I have need of nothing;" and he resumed his reading. Manuel had hoped to discover regrets or provoke impatience; he found a great resignation and an unalterable serenity.

The deputation retired; one of the municipals told me to follow it to the council-room, where I was again ordered to remove from the king his decorations. Manuel added: "You will do well to send to the Convention the crosses and ribbons. I ought to warn you," he continued, "that the imprisonment of Louis XVI., may last long, and if your intention is not to remain here, you had better say so now. It is intended, in order to make the surveillance easier, to lessen the number of persons employed in the Tower. If you remain with the *cidevant* king you will be absolutely alone, and your work will become much heavier. Wood and water for one week will be brought to you; but you will have to clean the apartment and do all the other work." I replied that being determined not to leave the king I would submit to everything. They then took me back to the apartment of His Majesty, who said to me: "You heard what was said; you will take my decorations off my coats this evening."

The next day, when dressing the king, I told him I had locked up the crosses and the cordons, though Manuel had told me it was proper to send them to the Convention. "You did right," said His Majesty.

The tale has been spread that Manuel came to the Temple in the month of September to request His Majesty to write to the King of Prussia at the time of his entrance into Champagne. I can assure every one that Manuel appeared in the Temple only twice during the time that I was there, on the 3d of September and the 7th of October; that each time he was accompanied by a large number of municipals, and that he never spoke to the king in private.

On the 9th of October, they brought to the king the journal of the debates in the Convention; but a few days later, a municipal, named Michel, a perfumer, obtained an order which again forbade the entrance of all public prints to the Tower; he called me into the council-chamber and asked me by whose order journals were sent to my address. It was true that, without being myself informed how or why, four newspapers were daily brought to the Tower, bearing this printed address: "To the valet de chambre of Louis XVI., in the Tower of the Temple." I have always been ignorant, and still am, of the name of the person who paid the subscription. Michel wanted to force me to point it out to him, and he made me write to editors and publishers and get an explanation from them; but their answers, if they made any, were not communicated to me.

This rule of not permitting newspapers to enter the Tower had exceptions, however, when they gave an opportunity for fresh outrage. If they contained insulting remarks about the king or queen, atrocious threats, infamous calumnies, certain of the municipals had the deliberate wickedness to leave them on the mantel or the washstand in the king's room, in order that they might fall into his hands.

Once he read in one of those sheets the speech of an artillery-man who demanded "the head of the tyrant, Louis XVI., that he might load his cannon with it and send it to the enemy." Another paper, speaking of Madame Élisabeth and seeking to destroy the admiration which her devotion to the king and queen inspired in the public mind, tried to destroy her virtue by the most absurd calumnies. A third said they ought to strangle the two little wolflings in the Tower, meaning thereby the dauphin and Madame Royale.

The king was not affected by such articles, except on

account of the people. "The French," he said, "are most unfortunate in letting themselves be thus deceived." I took care to abstract those journals if I chanced to be the first to see them; but they were often laid there when my duties took me out of his room, and there were very few of these articles, written for the purpose of outraging the royal family, either to provoke to regicide or to prepare the people to let it be committed, which were not read by the king. Those who know the insolent writings published in those days can alone form an idea of this intolerable form of torture.

The influence of those sanguinary writings could be seen in the conduct of most of the municipal officers, who, until then, had not shown themselves so harsh or so malignant.

One day, after dinner, I wrote a memorial of expenditures in the council-chamber and locked it up in a desk of which they had given me the key. I had hardly left the room before Marino, a municipal officer, said to his colleagues (though he was not on duty) that the desk must be opened and examined to prove whether or not I was in correspondence with the enemies of the people. "I know him well," he added, "and I know that he receives letters for the king." Then accusing his colleagues of connivance, he loaded them with insults, threatened to denounce them as accomplices, and went off to execute that purpose. The others immediately drew up a *procès-verbal* of all the papers contained in my desk and sent it to the Commune before whom Marino had already made his denunciation.

This same man declared, another day, that a back-gammon-board, which I had had mended with the consent of his colleagues, contained a correspondence; he took it entirely apart and finding nothing he had it glued together again in his presence.

One Thursday, my wife and her friend having come to the Temple as usual, I talked with them in the council-chamber; the royal family, who were walking in the garden, saw us, and the queen and Madame Élisabeth gave us a little nod. That motion, one of simple interest, was noticed by Marino; nothing more was needed to make him arrest my wife and her friend the moment they left the council-chamber. They were questioned separately; they asked my wife who the lady was who accompanied her. "My sister," she replied. The other, being asked the same question, said she was her cousin. This contradiction served as the matter of a long *procès-verbal* and the gravest suspicions,— Marino declaring that the lady was a page of the queen disguised. At last, after three hours of the most painful and insulting examination, they were set at liberty.

They were allowed to return to the Temple, but we redoubled our prudence and precautions. I often managed, in our short interviews, to give them notes which Madame Élisabeth had contrived to secrete from the searches of the municipals; these notes usually related to information desired by Their Majesties. Luckily, I had not given any on that occasion; had one of those notes been found upon them we should all three have run the greatest danger.

Other municipals made themselves remarkable by ridiculous actions. One broke up all the macaroons to see if they contained writings; another, for the same purpose, ordered the peaches cut in two before him, and their stones cracked. A third forced me one day to drink some essence of soap with which the king shaved himself, affecting to fear there was poison in it. After each meal Madame Élisabeth used to give me a little knife with a gold blade to clean; often the commissioners would snatch it from my hands to see if a note had been slipped into the sheath.

Madame Élisabeth ordered me one day to send back to the Duchesse de Sérent a book of devotions; the municipals cut off the margins of every page, fearing she had written something on them with invisible ink.

One of them forbade me one day to go up into the queen's room to do her hair. Her Majesty was forced to come down into the king's room, and bring with her all that was required for her toilet.

Another wanted to follow her when, according to her custom, she went into Madame Élisabeth's room to change her morning dress. I represented to him the indecency of that proceeding. He insisted; Her Majesty then left the room and renounced dressing herself.

When I received the linen from the wash, the municipals made me unfold every piece and examine it in broad daylight. The washerwoman's book and all other papers were held to the fire to see if there was secret writing on them. The linen the king and the princesses took off was subjected to the same examination.

Some municipals, however, did not take part in the harshness of their colleagues; but most of these, becoming suspected by the Committee of Public Safety, died victims of their humanity; those who still live have languished long in prison.

A young man named Toulan, whom I thought, from his talk, to be one of the worst enemies of the royal family, came one day close to me and said, with mystery, "I cannot speak to the queen to-day on account of my comrades; tell her that the commission she gave me is done, and that in a few days I shall be on duty, and then I will bring her the answer." Astonished to hear him speak thus, and fearing that he was laying a trap, I replied, "Monsieur, you are mistaken in addressing yourself to me for such commissions."

'No, I am not mistaken," he replied, grasping my hand as he left me. I related the conversation to the queen. "You can trust Toulan," she said. This young man was afterwards implicated in the queen's trial, with nine other municipal officers accused of wishing to favour the escape of the queen from the Temple. Toulan perished in the last executions.

Their Majesties, shut up in the Tower for three months, had so far seen none but the municipal officers, when, on the 1st of November, a deputation from the National Convention was announced to them. It was composed of Drouet, post-master at Varennes, Chabot, an ex-capuchin, Dubois-Crancé, Duprat, and two others whose names I forget. This deputation asked the king how he was treated and whether they gave him all necessary things. "I complain of nothing," answered His Majesty. "I merely request that the commissioners will remit to my valet de chambre, or deposit with the council, the sum of two thousand francs for small current expenses; also, that we may receive linen and other clothing of which we are greatly in need." The deputies promised all this, but nothing was sent.

Some days later the king had quite a considerable swelling of his face; I asked urgently that his dentist, M. Dubois, might be sent for. They deliberated three days, and then refused the request. Fever set in, and then, at last, they permitted His Majesty to consult his head physician, M. le Monnier. It would be difficult to picture the distress of that respectable old man when he saw his master.

The queen and her children almost never left the king during the day; they nursed him with me, and often helped me in making his bed. I passed the nights alone beside him. M. le Monnier came twice a day, accompanied by a large number of municipals. His person was searched, and he was not allowed to speak except in a loud voice. One day when the king had taken medicine, M. le Monnier asked to be allowed to remain a few hours. As he remained standing, — the municipals being seated with their hats on their heads, — the king asked him to take a seat; he refused, out of respect, and the commissioners murmured loudly.

The king's illness lasted ten days. A few days later the young prince, who slept in His Majesty's room, the municipals refusing to transfer him to that of the queen, had fever. The queen felt all the more anxiety because she could not obtain permission, though she urged it eagerly, to stay during the night with her son. She gave him the most tender care during the hours she was allowed to be with him. The same illness was communicated to the queen, to Madame Royale, and to Madame Élisabeth. M. le Monnier obtained permission to continue his visits.

I fell ill in my turn. The room I occupied was damp and without a chimney; the shutter of the window intercepted what little air there was. I was attacked by rheumatic fever with severe pains in the side which forced me to keep my bed. The first day I rose to dress the king, but His Majesty, seeing my state, refused my care, ordered me to go to bed, and himself dressed his son.

During that first day the dauphin hardly left me; that august child gave me drink; in the evening, the king took advantage of a moment when he seemed to be less watched, to enter my room; he gave me a glass of some drink, and said, with a kindness that made me shed tears: "I should like to take care of you myself, but you know how we are watched; take courage; to-morrow you shall see my doctor." At supper-time, the royal family came into my room and Madame Élisabeth gave me, without the municipals observing it, a bottle containing syrup of squills; the princess, although she had a heavy cold, deprived herself of that remedy for me. I wanted to refuse it, but she insisted. After supper, the queen undressed the dauphin and put him to bed; and Madame Élisabeth rolled the king's hair.

The next morning M. le Monnier ordered me to be bled; but the consent of the Commune had to be obtained to the entrance of a surgeon. They talked of transferring me to the palace of the Temple. Fearing that I should never get back into the Tower if I once went out of it, I pretended to feel much better. That evening new municipals arrived and there was no further question of transferring me.

Turgy asked to pass the night with me. The request was granted, also to his two comrades who took turns in sitting up with me. I was six days in bed, and each day the royal family came to see me; Madame Élisabeth often brought me things she used for herself. So much kindness restored a portion of my strength, for instead of the feeling of my sufferings, I had that of gratitude and admiration. Who would not have been touched to see that august family suspend, as it were, the thought of its great misfortunes, to busy itself with those of its servant?

I ought not to forget here a trait of the dauphin which proves the goodness of his heart and how much he profited by the examples of virtue he had always before his eyes.

One night, after putting him to bed, I retired to make way for the queen and the princesses, who always came to kiss him for good-night in his bed. Madame Élisabeth, with whom the close watchfulness of the municipals had that day prevented me from speaking, took advantage of that moment to give him a little box of ipecacuanha tablets, telling him to give them to me when I returned. The princesses went up to their rooms, the king passed into his cabinet, and I went to supper. I returned about eleven o'clock to prepare the king's bed; I was alone; the little prince called me in a low voice. Much surprised at finding him awake and fearing he was ill, I went to him. "My aunt gave me this little box for you," he said, "and I would not go to sleep without giving it to you; it was high time you came, for my eyes have shut up several times." Mine filled with tears; he saw them and kissed me, and in two minutes more he was sound asleep.

To this sensibility the young prince added many graces and the lovability of his age. Often by his naïveté, the gaiety of his nature, and his little rogueries he made his parents forget for a moment their cruel situation. But he felt it himself; although so young, he knew he was in a prison and watched by enemies. His behaviour and his talk acquired that reserve which instinct, in presence of a danger inspires perhaps at any age. Never did I hear him mention the Tuileries, or Versailles, or any subject that might remind the queen or the king of painful memories. When he saw some municipal kinder than his colleagues on guard, he would run to his mother and say with an expression of great satisfaction: "Mamma, it is Monsieur Such-a-one to-day."

Once he fixed his eyes so long on a municipal, seeming to recognize him, that the man asked where he had seen him. The little prince refused for sometime to answer; at last, leaning towards the queen, he said to her in a whisper, "It was when we went to Varennes."

Here is still another proof of his sensitive feelings. A mason was employed in making holes in the wall of the antechamber so as to put enormous bolts to the door. While the man ate his breakfast the little prince amused himself with his tools; the king took the hammer and chisel from his son's hands and showed him how to use them. The mason, touched at seeing the king work, said to His Majesty:

"When you get out of here you can say that you worked yourself at your prison."—"Ah!" said the king, "when and how shall I get out?" The little prince burst into tears; the king let fall the hammer and chisel and went back to his room, where he walked up and down with hasty strides.

December 2d, the municipality of the 10th of August was replaced by another, under the title of Provisional Municipality. Many of the former members were re-elected. I thought, at first, that the new set were better than the old, and I hoped for some favourable changes in the system of the prison. I was mistaken. Many of the new commissioners gave me reason to regret their predecessors; the latter were coarser, it is true, but it was easy to take advantage of their natural indiscretion to find out all they knew. I had to study the commissioners of the new municipality to judge of their conduct and their character; their malignity was much more premeditated.

Until this time only one municipal was constantly on guard over the king, and one over the queen. The new municipality ordered two, and henceforth it was much more difficult for me to speak with the king and the princesses. On the other hand, the council, which until then had been held in one of the halls of the Temple palace, was transferred to a room on the ground-floor of the Tower. The new municipals wished to surpass the former ones in zeal, and this zeal was emulation of tyranny.

December 7, a municipal, at the head of a deputation from the Commune, came to read to the king a decree which ordered him to take from the prisoners "knives, razors, scissors, penknives, and all other sharp instruments of which prisoners presumed criminal are deprived; and to make a most minute search of their persons and of their apartments."

During the reading, the municipal's voice shook, and it

was easy to see the violence he was putting upon himself; and he afterwards proved by his conduct that he had allowed himself to be sent to the Temple solely to endeavour to be useful to the royal family. The king took from his pockets a knife and a little case of red morocco, from which he drew scissors and a penknife. The municipals made the most careful search through the apartments, taking razors, a ruler for rolling hair, a toilet-knife, little instruments for cleaning the teeth, and other articles in gold and silver. The same search was made in my room, and I was ordered to give up whatever was on my person.

The municipals then went up to the queen: they read the same decree to the three princesses and took away from them even the little articles that were necessary for their work.

An hour later, I was made to go down into the council-chamber, and they asked me if I knew what articles remained in the red morocco case the king had put back into his pocket. "I order you," said a municipal named Sermaize, "to take that case away from him to-night." "It is not my place," I said, "to execute the decrees of the Convention, nor to search the king's pockets." "Cléry is right," said another municipal; "it was your place," addressing Sermaize, "to make that search."

They then drew up a *procès-verbal* of all the articles taken from the royal family, and sorted them into packets, which they sealed up; they next ordered me to sign my name at the bottom of a decree which enjoined me to report to the council if I discovered on the king or the princesses, or in their apartments, any sharp instruments; these different documents were sent to the Commune.

On looking through the registers of the Temple it will be seen that I was often forced to sign decrees of which I was very far from approving either the object or the wording. I never signed anything, never said anything, never did anything, except by the special order of the king or of the queen. A refusal on my part would have caused my separation from Their Majesties, to whom I had consecrated my existence; my signature at the foot of certain decrees had no other meaning than to admit that those documents had been read to me.

This Sermaize of whom I have just spoken took me back to the apartment of His Majesty. The king was sitting near the fireplace, tongs in hand. Sermaize asked him, in the name of the council, to show what remained in the red morocco case. The king drew it from his pocket; in it was a screw-driver, a corkscrew, and a flint. Sermaize took possession of them. "Are not these tongs which I have in my hand sharp instruments?" said the king, turning his back upon him.

At dinner-time an argument arose among the commissioners. Some were opposed to the use by the royal family of knives and forks; others consented to allow forks; at last it was decided to make no change; but to take away the knives and forks at the conclusion of each meal.

This deprivation of their little articles was all the more trying to the queen and the princesses because it obliged them to give up various kinds of work which until then had served to occupy and amuse those long days in prison. One day, when Madame Élisabeth was mending the king's clothes, she broke off the thread with her teeth, having no scissors. "What a contrast!" said the king, looking at her fixedly and tenderly; "you lacked for nothing in your pretty house at Montreuil." "Ah! brother," she replied, "can I have regrets when I share your sorrow?"[1]

---

[1] Madame Élisabeth was always *notable* and clever at work of all kinds. One of her ladies, watching her one day, said what a pity it was that such

Day after day brought new decrees each of which was a fresh tyranny. The roughness and harshness of the municipals towards me was greater than ever. The three men from the kitchen were forbidden to speak to me; this, and other things made me fear some fresh catastrophe. The queen and Madame Élisabeth, struck by the same presentiment, asked me constantly for news, which I could not give them.

At last, on Thursday, my wife and her friend arrived. I was taken down to the council-chamber. She talked, as usual, in a loud voice to disarm the suspicions of our new jailers; and while she was giving me details of our domestic affairs her friend said: "Next Tuesday, they take the king to the Convention; his trial will begin; he may get counsel; all this is certain."

I did not know how to announce this dreadful news to the king; I wanted to inform the queen or Madame Élisabeth of it first; but I was in great alarm; time was passing, and the king had forbidden me to conceal anything from him. That night, as I undressed him, I told him what I had heard; I made him foresee that they would certainly during his trial separate him from his family; and I added that there were but four days in which to concert with the queen some method of communication between them. I assured him that I was determined to undertake everything that would facilitate that object. The entrance of a municipal did not allow me to say more and prevented His Majesty from replying to me.

The next day, when he rose, I could not find a chance to speak to him. He went up with his son to breakfast

---

a faculty was wasted on one who did not need it. "Ah!" exclaimed Madame Élisabeth, " it is good to do everything as well as one can; and, besides, who knows ? I may have to get my living in this way."—Tr.

with the princesses and I followed him. After breakfast he talked some time with the queen and I saw by her look of sorrow that he was telling her what I had said to him. I found, in the course of the day, an opportunity to talk with Madame Élisabeth; I explained to her how much it had cost me to inform the king of his coming trial and thus increase his troubles. She reassured me, saying that the king was much touched by that mark of my attachment. "What troubles him most," she added, "is the fear of being separated from us; try to get more information."

That evening the king told me how glad he was to have heard in advance that he was to appear before the Convention. "Continue," he said, "to try to discover what they mean to do with me; do not fear to distress me. I have agreed with my family not to seem informed, in order not to compromise you."

The nearer the day of the trial approached, the more distrust was shown to me; the municipals would not reply to any of my questions. I had already employed, in vain, various pretexts to go down into the council-chamber, where I might have picked up some new details to communicate to the king, when the commission appointed to audit the expenses of the royal family came to the Temple. They were obliged then to let me go down to give information, and I heard from a well-intentioned municipal that the separation of the king from his family, though decreed by the Commune, was not yet decided in the National Assembly. That same day Turgy brought me a newspaper in which I found the decree, which ordered that the king be brought before the bar of the Convention; he also gave me a memorial on the king's trial, published by M. Necker. I had no other means of conveying the paper and memorial to the king than to place them under one of the articles of furniture in the privy, telling the king and the princesses that they were there.

December 11, 1792, at five o'clock in the morning, we heard the *générale* beaten throughout Paris, and cavalry and cannon were brought into the garden of the Temple. This uproar would have cruelly alarmed the royal family if they had not already known its cause. Nevertheless, they feigned to be ignorant of it, and asked an explanation of the commissioners on duty, who refused to reply.

At nine o'clock the king and the dauphin went up to breakfast in the queen's apartment. Their Majesties remained about an hour together; always under the gaze of the municipals. This continual torture for all the family of never being able to show any emotion, any effusion of feeling at a moment when so many fears agitated them, was one of the most refined cruelties of their tyrants and the one in which those tyrants took most delight. The time came to separate. The king quitted the queen, Madame Élisabeth, and his daughter; their looks expressed what they could not say. The dauphin went down, as usual, with the king.

The little prince, who often persuaded his father to play a game of *Siam* with him, was so urgent that day that the king, in spite of his situation, could not refuse. The dauphin lost all the games, and twice could not go higher than sixteen. "Every time I get to that point *Seize* I lose the game," he said with some vexation. The king made no reply; but I thought I saw that the sound of that word made a certain impression on him.

At eleven o'clock, while the king was giving his son a reading-lesson, two municipals entered and told His Majesty that they had come to fetch young Louis and take him to his mother. The king wished to know the reason of this removal; the commissioners replied that they executed the orders of the council of the Commune. His Majesty kissed his son tenderly, and charged me to go with him. When I returned to the king, I told him I had left the young prince in his mother's arms, and that seemed to tranquillize His Majesty. One of the commissioners entered to inform him that Chambon, mayor of Paris, was in the council-chamber and was coming up to see him. "What does he want of me?" asked the king. "I do not know," replied the municipal.

His Majesty walked hastily up and down his room for some moments; then he seated himself in an arm-chair close to the head of his bed; the door was half closed and the municipal dared not enter, to avoid, as he told me, questions. Half an hour passed thus in the deepest silence. The commissioner became uneasy at not hearing the king; he entered softly, and found him with his head on one of his hands, apparently deeply absorbed. "What do you want?" asked the king, in a loud voice. "I feared you were ill," replied the municipal. "I am obliged to you," said the king, in a tone of the keenest sorrow, "but the manner in which my son has been taken from me is infinitely painful to me." The municipal said nothing and withdrew.

The mayor did not appear for an hour. He was accompanied by Chaumette, public prosecutor of the Commune, Colombeau, secretary, several municipal officers, and Santerre, commander of the National Guard, who brought his aides-de-camp with him.

The mayor told the king that he had come to fetch him to take him before the Convention, in virtue of a decree which the secretary of the Commune would read to him. This decree stated that "Louis Capet would be arraigned before the bar of the National Convention." "Capet is not my name," said the king; "it is the name of one of my ancestors. I could have wished, monsieur," he added, "that the commissioners had left me my son during the two hours I have passed in waiting for you. This treatment is but the sequel of all that I have borne here for the past four months; I shall now follow you, not to obey the Convention, but because my enemies have the power to force me." I gave His Majesty his overcoat and his hat, and he followed the mayor of Paris. A numerous escort awaited him at the gate of the Temple.

Left alone in the room with a municipal I learned from him that the king would never see his family again, but that the mayor was to consult with some of the deputies about the separation. I asked the commissioner to take me to the dauphin, who was with the queen, which he did. I did not leave the little prince until six o'clock, when the king returned from the Convention. The municipals informed the queen of the king's departure for the Assembly, but they would not enter into any details. The princesses and the dauphin went down as usual to dine in the king's room, and returned to their own immediately.

After dinner a single municipal remained in the queen's room; he was a young man about twenty-four years of age, belonging to the section of the Temple; he was on guard at the Tower for the first time, and seemed to be less suspicious and more civil than most of his colleagues. The queen began a conversation with him, asked him about his profession, his parents, etc. Madame Élisabeth seized the moment to pass into her own room, and made me a sign to follow her.

Once there, I told her that the Commune had decreed the separation of the king from his family, that I feared it would take place that very evening, for although the Convention had not determined on it, the mayor had gone there to make the request, which would, no doubt, be granted.

"The queen and I," answered Madame Élisabeth, "expect the worst; we make ourselves no illusions as to the fate they are preparing for the king. He will die a victim to his kindness and his love for his people, for whose happiness he has never ceased to work since he ascended the throne. How cruelly that people is deceived! The king's religion and his great confidence in Providence will sustain him in this cruel adversity. "And now, Cléry," added the virtuous princess, her eyes filling with tears, "you will be alone with my brother; redouble, if possible, your care of him, and neglect no means of making news of him reach us; but for any other purpose do not expose yourself, for if you do we shall be left with no one in whom we can trust." I assured Madame Élisabeth of my devotion to the king, and we agreed upon the means to employ to keep up a correspondence.

Turgy was the only one whom I could put into the secret; but I could seldom speak to him, and then with precaution. It was agreed that I should continue to take care of the linen and clothes of the dauphin; that every two days I should send him what was necessary, and that I should use that opportunity to convey to them news of what was happening with the king. This suggested to Madame Élisabeth the idea of giving me one of her handkerchiefs. "Keep it," she said, "as long as my brother is well; if he should be ill send it to me in my nephew's linen." The manner of folding it was to indicate the sort of illness.

The grief of the princess in speaking to me of the king, her indifference as to her personal situation, the value she deigned to set on my poor services to His Majesty affected me deeply. "Have you heard anything said of the queen?" she asked with a species of terror. "Alas! what can they bring against her?" "No, Madame," I replied, "but what can they bring against the king?" "Oh, nothing, nothing," she said, "but perhaps they regard the king as a victim necessary to their safety. The queen, on the contrary, and her children cannot be obstacles to their ambition." I took the liberty of remarking that probably the king would be sentenced only to transportation; that I had heard it spoken of, and that Spain, being the only country that had not declared war, it was likely that the king and his family would be taken there. "I have no hope," she said, "that the king will be saved."

I thought I ought to add that the foreign Powers were consulting as to the means of drawing the king out of prison; that *Monsieur* and the Comte d'Artois were again assembling the *émigrés* around them, and would unite them with the Austrian and Prussian troops; that Spain and England would take steps; that all Europe was interested in preventing the death of the king, and therefore that the Convention would have to reflect very seriously before deciding his fate.

This conversation lasted an hour, and then Madame Élisabeth (to whom I had never before spoken at such length), fearing the entrance of the new municipals, left me to return to the queen's apartment. Tison and his wife, who watched me incessantly, remarked that I had stayed a long time with Madame Élisabeth, and they were afraid that the commissioner would notice it. I told them that the princess had been talking to me about her nephew, who would probably be in future with his mother.

At six o'clock the commissioners sent for me into the council-room. They read me a decree of the Commune which ordered me to have no further communication with the three princesses and the little prince, because I was to serve the king only. It was also decreed, in order to put the king into more solitary confinement, that I should no longer sleep in his apartment, but in the small tower, and be conducted to the king at such times only as he had need of me.

At half-past six o'clock the king returned from the Convention. He seemed fatigued, and his first desire was to be taken to his family. The request was refused under pretext of having no orders; he insisted that the queen should at least be told of his return, and this was promised to him. He ordered me to ask for his supper at half-past eight o'clock; and he employed the interval in his usual reading, surrounded by four municipals.

At half-past eight I went to inform His Majesty that his supper was served; he asked the commissioners if his family were not coming down; they made him no answer. "But at least," said the king, "my son will pass the night with me, his bed and clothes being here." Same silence. After supper the king again insisted on his desire to see his family. They answered that he must await the decision of the Convention. I then gave out what was necessary for the young prince's bedtime.

That evening, while I was undressing the king, he said: "I was very far from expecting the questions that were put to me." He went to bed tranquilly. The decree of the Commune relating to my removal during the night was not executed; it would have been too troublesome to the municipals to have fetched me every time the king needed me.

The next day, 12th, the king no sooner saw the municipals than he asked if a decision had been made on his request to see his family. They told him they were still awaiting orders. The king commanded me to have the young prince's bed taken up to the queen's room, where he had passed the night on one of her mattresses. I begged His Majesty to wait for the decision of the Convention. " I do not expect any justice, any consideration," replied the king, " but I will wait."

The same day a deputation of four members of the Convention brought to the king a decree authorizing him to obtain counsel. He declared that he chose M. Target, and failing him, M. Tronchet, or both of them if the National Convention consented. The deputies made the king sign his request, and signed it themselves after him. The king added that it would be necessary to furnish him with paper, pens, and ink.

On the 13th, in the morning, the same deputation returned and told the king that M. Target refused to be his counsel; that M. Tronchet had been sent for and would doubtless appear during the day. They also read to him several letters addressed to the Convention by MM. Sourdat, Huet-Guillaume, and Lamoignon de Malesherbes, formerly president of the *cour des aides* and afterwards minister of the king's house. Malesherbes' letter was as follows: —

Paris, December 11, 1792.

CITIZEN PRESIDENT, — I do not know whether the Convention will give Louis XVI. counsel to defend him, or whether it will leave the selection to him. In the latter case, I desire that Louis XVI. should know that if he chooses me for that function I am ready to devote myself to it. I do not ask you to lay my offer before the Convention, because I am far from thinking myself of enough importance to occupy its time; but I have twice been called to the counsel of him who was once my master, in days when every one was ambitious of that function; I owe him the same service when that function is one which many persons would think dangerous. If I knew any possible means of letting him know my inclinations, I would not take the liberty of addressing you. I think that in the position you occupy, you will have better means than any one to convey to him this suggestion. I am, with respect, etc.,

LAMOIGNON DE MALESHERBES.

His Majesty replied as follows to the deputation: "I am sensible of the offers that so many persons have made, asking to serve me as counsel, and I beg you to express to them my gratitude. I accept M. de Malesherbes as my counsel; if M. Tronchet cannot lend me his services, I will consult M. de Malesherbes and choose some one to fill his place."

CHAPTER III.

The King's Trial — His Will — The Decree of the Convention condemning the King to Death — Last Meeting with his Family — Leaves the Temple for his Execution.

DECEMBER 14, M. Tronchet had, as the decree permitted, a conference with His Majesty. The same day M. de Malesherbes was brought to the Tower. The king ran forward to meet that respected old man, whom he tenderly pressed in his arms. The former minister burst into tears on seeing his master, whether because he recalled the past years of his reign, or, more probably, because he faced at that moment a virtuous man in the grasp of misfortune.[1]

As the king had permission to confer with his counsel in private, I closed the door of his room that he might speak more freely with M. de Malesherbes. A municipal blamed me, ordered the door to be opened, and forbade me to shut it again; I opened the door, but the king was already in the *tourelle*.

On the 15th, the king received the reply regarding his family, which was, in substance, as follows: the queen and Madame Élisabeth could not communicate with the king during the course of his trial; his children might go to him if he desired it, but on condition that they should not see their mother or their aunt until the trial was over. As soon as it was possible to speak to the king freely, I asked his orders. "You see," he said, "the cruel alternative in which they place me; I cannot resolve to have my children with

[1] Lamoignon de Malesherbes, aged 78, was guillotined just before the 9th thermidor (July 27, 1794), the end of the Reign of Terror. — TR.

me; as for my daughter, it is impossible; as for my son, I feel the grief it would occasion to the queen; I must consent to this fresh sacrifice." His Majesty then ordered me for the second time to have the dauphin's bed sent up to the queen's room, which I did immediately. I kept his linen and his clothes, and every second day I sent up what was necessary as agreed upon with Madame Élisabeth.

On the 16th, at four in the afternoon, came another deputation of four members of the Convention, accompanied by a secretary, a sheriff, and an officer of the Gardes. They brought the king his arraignment, and certain documents on which the accusations were based; most of them found at the Tuileries in a secret closet of His Majesty's apartment, called by the minister Roland "the iron closet."

The reading of these documents, one hundred and seven in all, lasted from four o'clock till midnight; all were read to and signed by the king, and copies of each were left in his hands. The king was seated at a large table; M. Tronchet beside him, the deputies opposite. His Majesty interrupted the long session by asking the deputies if they would sup; they accepted, and I served them a cold chicken and some fruit in the dining-room. M. Tronchet would take nothing, and remained alone with the king in his room.

A municipal, named Merceraut, then a stone-cutter and lately president of the Commune of Paris, though a porter of sedan chairs at Versailles before the Revolution, was on guard that day in the Tower for the first time. He wore his working-clothes in tatters, with a very old round hat, a leather apron, and his three-coloured scarf. The man affected to stretch himself out in an arm-chair beside the king, who was in a common chair; he thee'd and thou'd, with his hat on his head, all who spoke to him. The members of the Convention were amazed, and while they supped, one of them asked me several questions as to how the king was treated. I was about to answer when a commissioner told the conventional it was forbidden to speak to me, and that they would give him in the council-chamber all the details he could require. The deputy, fearing no doubt to compromise himself, said no more.

Among the bundles of documents were plans for the Constitution, annotated by the king's own hand, sometimes in ink, sometimes in pencil. There were also police registers in which were denunciations made and signed by the king's own servants; this ingratitude seemed to affect him much; these accusers rendered an account of what occurred in the king's room and the queen's room at the Tuileries in order to give a more truthful air to their calumnies.

From the 14th to the 26th of December, the king saw his counsel regularly. They came at five in the evening and retired at nine. M. de Sèze was added to them. Every morning M. de Malesherbes brought the newspapers to his Majesty with the printed opinions of the deputies relating to his trial. He prepared the work for the evening, and remained with the king for one or two hours. His Majesty deigned to sometimes let me read those opinions; once he asked: "What do you think of that man's opinion?" adding, "I have learned how far the malignancy of men can go; I did not believe that there were such men." His Majesty never went to bed without reading all the different papers, and, in order not to compromise M. de Malesherbes, he took the precaution to burn them himself in the stove in his cabinet.

By this time I had found a favourable moment to speak to Turgy and send news to Madame Élisabeth about the king. The next day he told me that in giving him her napkin after dinner she had slipped in a little note in pinpricks asking the king to write her a line himself. The day after, I took the note to Turgy, who brought me the answer inside a ball of cotton, which he threw on my bed as he passed it. His Majesty took great comfort in the success of this means of communicating with his family. The wax-candles which the commissioners gave me came tied up with twine in bundles. As soon as I had twine enough I told the king that we could give greater activity than before to the correspondence, by sending up a part of it to Madame Élisabeth whose room was directly over mine, with its window perpendicularly above that of a little corridor upon which my room opened. During the night the princess could attach letters to the string and lower them down to the passage window. The same means would serve to send answers to the princess, also paper and ink, of which she was deprived. "That is a good project," the king said to me; "we will use it if the other means become impracticable." In point of fact, he soon used it exclusively. He always waited till eight in the evening; I then shut the door of my room and that of the corridor, and went to talk to the commissioners or get them to play cards, which diverted their attention.

After his separation from his family the king refused to go into the garden, and when it was proposed to him to do so he answered: "I cannot resolve to go out alone; walking was only agreeable to me when I enjoyed it with my family." But, in spite of being thus parted from objects so dear to his heart, no complaints or murmurs escaped him; he had already pardoned his oppressors. Each day he gathered in his reading-room the strength that maintained his courage; when he left it he entered the details of a life always uniform yet embellished by him with little traits of kindness. He deigned to treat me as if I were more than his servant;

he treated the municipals who guarded his person as if he had no reason to complain of them; he talked to them, as formerly with his subjects, on matters relating to their condition, their family, their children, the advantages and duties of their profession. Those who listened were astonished at the accuracy of his remarks, at the variety of his knowledge, and at the manner in which it was all classified in his memory. His conversations did not have as their object the distraction of his mind from his troubles; his sensibility was keen and deep, but his resignation rose superior to his sorrows.

On the 19th of December the king said to me while dining: "Fourteen years ago you got up earlier than you did to-day." I understood His Majesty at once. "That was the day my daughter was born," he continued tenderly, "and to-day, her birthday, I am deprived of seeing her!" A few tears rolled from his eyes, and a respectful silence reigned for a moment.

The day for his second appearance before the bar of the Convention was approaching. He had not been able to shave since they took away his razors; he suffered much in consequence, and was obliged to bathe his face in cold water several times a day. He asked me for scissors or a razor; but he was not willing to speak to the municipals about it himself. I took the liberty of remarking to him that if he appeared in his present condition before the Convention the people would see with what barbarity the council of the Commune had acted. "I ought not to try to interest persons in that way in my fate," replied the king; "I will address the commissioners." The following day the Commune decided to return the razors to the king, but for use only in presence of two municipals.[1]

During the three days that preceded Christmas, 1792, the

[1] See Appendix III.

king wrote more than usual. There was then a project of making him stay at the Feuillants for two or three days in order that he might be tried continuously. They had even given me orders to prepare to follow him and to get ready all that he might need; but that plan was changed.

It was on Christmas Day that the king wrote his will. I read it and copied it at the time it was handed over to the council of the Temple; it was written entirely by the king's own hand, with a few erasures. I think I ought to give here this monument, already celebrated, of his innocence and his piety:—

THE LAST WILL AND TESTAMENT OF LOUIS XVI., KING OF FRANCE.

In the name of the Holy Trinity, Father, Son, and Holy Spirit. This day, twenty-fifth of December, one thousand seven hundred and ninety-two, I, Louis, sixteenth of the name, King of France, being for the last four months shut up with my family in the Tower of the Temple by those who were my subjects, and deprived of all communication whatsoever since the eleventh of the present month with my family; involved moreover in a trial of which it is impossible to foresee the issue, because of the passions of men, and for which no pretext or means can be found in existing laws; having God as the sole witness of my thoughts and the only being to whom I can address myself, I here declare in his presence my last will and sentiments.

I leave my soul to God, my Creator; I pray him to receive it in his mercy; not to judge it according to its own merits, but by those of our Lord Jesus Christ, who offered himself a sacrifice to God, his Father, for us men, however unworthy we may be, and I first of any.

I die in the union of our Holy Mother, the Catholic, Apostolical, and Roman Church, which derives its powers by an uninterrupted succession from Saint Peter to whom Jesus Christ confided them.

I believe firmly and confess all that is contained in the symbol and the commandments of God and of the Church, the sacraments and the mysteries such as the Catholic Church teaches and has always taught them. I have never pretended to make myself a judge of the different manners of explaining the dogmas that rend the Church of Jesus Christ; but I have relied, and shall always rely, if God gives me life, on the decisions which the ecclesiastical superiors of the holy Catholic Church give and will give in conformity with the discipline of the Church, followed since Jesus Christ.

I pity with all my heart our brothers who may be in error; but I do not pretend to judge them, and I do not love them, one and all, less in Jesus Christ, following what Christian charity teaches.

I pray God to forgive me all my sins; I have scrupulously tried to know them, to detest them, and to humiliate myself in his presence. Not being able to have the ministry of a Catholic priest, I pray God to receive the confession which I have made to him, and, especially, the deep repentance which I feel for having put my name (though against my will) to acts which may have been contrary to the discipline and the belief of the Catholic Church, to which I have always remained sincerely united in heart. I pray God to receive the firm resolution in which I am to employ, if he grants me life, as soon as I can, the ministry of a Catholic priest to confess all my sins and to receive the sacrament of repentance.

I beg all those whom I may have injured through inadvertence (for I do not remember to have knowingly injured any one), and those to whom I may have set a bad example or caused offence, to forgive me the wrong they may think that I have done them; I beg all those who have charity to unite their prayers to mine to obtain of God the pardon of my sins.

I pardon with all my heart those who have made themselves my enemies without my having given them any cause, and I pray God to pardon them, as well as those who, from false zeal or misdirected zeal, have done me much harm.

I commend to God my wife and my children, my sister, my aunts, my brothers, and all those who are attached to me by ties of blood, or by any other manner whatsoever. I pray God especially to cast the eyes of his mercy on my wife, my children, and my sister, who have suffered so long with me; to support them by his grace if they lose me, and for as long as they remain in this perishable world.

I commend my children to my wife; I have never doubted her maternal tenderness for them; I entreat her, above all, to make good Christians and honest beings of them, to teach them to regard the grandeurs of this world (if they are condemned to experience them) as dangerous and perishable benefits, and to turn their eyes towards the only solid and durable glory of eternity. I beg my sister to continue her tenderness to my children, and to stand to them in place of a mother should they have the misfortune to lose theirs.

I beg my wife to forgive me for all the ills she has suffered for me, and the griefs I may have caused her in the course of our union; just as she may be sure that I keep nothing against her should she think she has anything for which to blame herself.

I request very earnestly of my children, after what they owe to God who comes before all, to remain united with each other, submissive and obedient to their mother and grateful

Mme Vigée Le Brun

The Dauphin and Madame Royale

for all the care and trouble she gives herself for them, and in memory of me. I beg them to regard my sister as a second mother.

I beg my son, if he has the misfortune to become king, to reflect that he owes himself wholly to the welfare of his co-citizens; that he ought to forget all hatred and all resentment, especially that which relates to the misfortunes and griefs that I have borne; that he cannot make the happiness of the people except by reigning according to the laws; but, at the same time, that a king cannot make the laws respected and do the good which is in his heart to do unless he has the necessary authority; otherwise, being fettered in his operations and inspiring no respect, he is more harmful than useful.

I commend to my son to take care of all the persons who have been attached to me, so far as the circumstances in which he may be placed will give him the ability; to remember that this is a sacred debt contracted by me towards the children and relatives of those who have perished for me, and towards those who are unfortunate for my sake.

I know that there are several persons among those who were attached to me who have not acted towards me as they should have done, and have even shown me ingratitude; but I pardon them (often in moments of trouble and excitement persons are not masters of themselves), and I beg my son, should the occasion come to him, to remember only their misfortunes.

I wish that I could manifest here my gratitude to those who have shown me a veritable and disinterested attachment; if, on the one hand, I have keenly felt the ingratitude and disloyalty of persons to whom I had never shown anything but kindness (to them, or their relatives, or to the friends of both), I have had the consolation of seeing the gratuitous attachment and interest that many persons have shown me; I beg those persons to receive my thanks. In the condition in which things now are, I should fear to compromise them if I spoke more explicitly, but I specially request my son to seek occasions of being able to recognize them.

Nevertheless, I think I should calumniate the sentiments of the nation if I did not commend openly to my son MM. de Chamilly and Hue, whose true attachment to me led them to shut themselves up in this sad place, and who came so near being also the unfortunate victims of it. I likewise recommend to him Cléry, whose care I have every reason to praise since he has been with me; as it is he who will remain with me to the end, I beg the gentlemen of the Commune to give him my clothes, my books, my watch, my purse, and whatever little property has been deposited with the council of the Commune.

I pardon once more, very willingly, those who guard me for the ill-treatment and the annoyances they have thought it their duty to practice towards me. I have met with some compassionate and feeling souls; may they enjoy in their hearts the tranquillity that their way of thinking will give them.

I beg MM. de Malesherbes, Tronchet, and de Sèze to receive here my thanks and the expression of my feelings for the cares and trouble they have taken for me.

I end by declaring before God, and about to appear before him, that I do not reproach myself with any of the crimes laid to my charge.

Done, in duplicate, at the Tower of the Temple, the twenty-fifth day of December, one thousand, seven hundred and ninety-two.

Louis.

On the 26th of December, the king was taken for the second time before the bar of the Convention. I had warned the queen, lest the noise of the drums and the movements of the troops should frighten her. His Majesty started at ten in the morning and returned at five in the afternoon. His counsel came that evening just as the king was finishing dinner; he asked them to take some refreshment; M. de Sèze was the only one who accepted the offer. The king thanked him for the pains he had taken in making his speech.

The next day His Majesty deigned to give me himself his printed defence, after asking the commissioners if he could do so without impropriety. Commissioner Vincent, a contractor for buildings, who had done the royal family all the services in his power, undertook to carry a copy secretly to the queen. He took advantage of the moment when the king thanked him for this little service to ask for the gift of something that had belonged to him. His Majesty unfastened his cravat and gave it to him. At another time he gave his gloves to a municipal, who desired to have them from the same motive. Even to the eyes of several of his guards, his remains were already sacred.

On the 1st of January, 1793, I went to the bedside of the king and asked him in a low voice to be allowed to offer my earnest wishes for the end of his troubles. "I receive those wishes," he said affectionately, holding out his hand, which I kissed and wet with my tears. As soon as he rose, he begged a municipal to go from him to inquire news of his family and give them his wishes for the new year. The municipals were much moved by the tone in which these words, so heart-rending in view of the king's situation, were said. "Why," said one of them to me after the king had gone into his cabinet, "why does he not ask to see his family? Now that the examinations are over there would be no difficulty; but it is to the Convention that he ought to make the request." The municipal who had gone to see the queen returned and announced to the king that his family thanked him for his good wishes and sent him their own. " What a New-Year's day!" exclaimed His Majesty.

That same evening I took the liberty of telling him I was almost certain of the consent of the Convention if he asked to be permitted to see his family. " In a few days," he replied, " they will not refuse me that consolation; I must wait."

The nearer the day for the verdict approached, — if one can use that term [*jugement*] for the proceedings the king was made to undergo, — the more my fears and anguish increased. I asked a hundred questions of the municipals, and everything I heard added to my terror. My wife came to see me every week, and gave me an exact account of what was going on in Paris. Public opinion seemed to be still favourable to the king; it was shown in a startling way at the Théâtre Français and at the Vaudeville. At the first, they were playing "L'Ami des Lois;" all the allusions to the trial of the king were seized and applauded vehemently. At the Vaudeville, one of the personages in " La Chaste Suzanne" says to the two old men, " How can you be accusers and judges both?" The audience insisted on the repetition of that speech many times. I gave the king a copy of "L'Ami des Lois." I often told him, and I also almost brought myself to believe it, that the members of the Convention, being opposed to one another, could pronounce only for the penalty of imprisonment or transportation. " May they have that moderation for my family," said the king; " it is only for them that I fear."

Certain persons sent me word through my wife that a considerable sum of money, deposited with M. Pariseau, editor of the "Feuille du jour," was at the king's disposal; they requested me to ask his orders and say that the money would be paid to M. de Malesherbes if the king wished it. "Thank those persons much, for me," he replied. "I cannot accept their generous offer, it would be to expose them." I begged him at least to mention the matter to M. de Malesherbes, and he promised to do so.

The correspondence between Their Majesties continued. The king, informed of Madame Royale's illness, was very uneasy for some days. The queen, after much entreaty, obtained permission for M. Brunier, her children's physician, to come to the Temple; this seemed to tranquillize him.

On the 16th of January, at six in the evening, four municipals entered the king's chamber and read to him a decree of the Commune, the substance of which was "that he be guarded night and day by four municipals; two of whom were to pass the night beside his bed." The king asked if his sentence had been pronounced. One of them (Du Roure) began by sitting down in the arm-chair of the king, who was standing; he answered that he did not trouble himself to know what went on in the Convention, but he had heard some one say they were still calling the votes.

A few moments later M. de Malesherbes arrived and told the king that the call of the votes [*l'appel nominal*] was not yet ended. While he was there the chimney of a room in the palace of the Temple took fire. A considerable crowd of people entered the courtyard. A commissioner came in alarm to tell M. de Malesherbes that he must go away immediately. M. de Malesherbes withdrew, after promising the king he would return to inform him of his sentence. "Why are you so alarmed?" I asked the commissioner. "They have set fire to the Temple," he said, "in order to rescue Capet in the tumult; but I have surrounded the walls with a strong guard." The fire was soon out, and it was shown to have been a mere accident.

Thursday, January 17th, M. de Malesherbes came at nine in the morning; I went to meet him. "All is lost," he said; "the king is condemned to death." The king, who saw him coming, rose to receive him. The minister threw himself at his feet, his sobs choked him, and it was some time before he could speak. The king raised him and pressed him against his bosom with affection. M. de Malesherbes told him of his condemnation to death; the king made no movement that showed either surprise or emotion; he seemed to be affected only by the grief of the old man, and tried to comfort him.

M. de Malesherbes gave an account to the king of the voting. Denouncers, relatives, personal enemies, laymen, ecclesiastics, absent deputies, all had voted, and, in spite of this violation of the forms, those who had voted for death — some as a political measure, others on pretence that the king was guilty — carried it by a majority of *only five votes*. Several deputies voted for death with respite [*sursis*]. A second vote was taken on this latter point, and it is to be presumed that the votes of those who wished to retard the commission of the regicide, joined to the votes of those who were against the death penalty, would have formed a majority. But, at the doors of the Convention, assassins devoted to the Duc d'Orléans and to the deputation of the Paris Commune, terrified by their cries and threatened with their knives whoever refused to listen to them; and whether it was stupor, indifference, or fear, no one dared to undertake anything further to save the king.

His Majesty obtained permission to see M. de Malesherbes in private. He took him into his cabinet, shut the door, and was alone with him for about an hour. His Majesty then conducted him to the entrance door, and asked him to come early that evening, and not to abandon him in his last moments. "The sorrow of that good old man has deeply affected me," said the king, returning to the room where I waited for him.

From the moment of M. de Malesherbes' entrance a great trembling had seized me; nevertheless I prepared what was necessary for the king to shave himself. He himself put the soap on his face, standing before me while I held the basin. Forced to control my grief, I had not yet dared to raise my eyes to my unfortunate master; by chance I looked at him and my tears flowed in spite of myself. I do not know if the state in which I was reminded the king of his position, but a sudden paleness overspread his face; his nose and his ears blanched suddenly. At that sight my knees gave way under me; the king, who noticed my fainting state, took me by both hands, pressed them hard, and said in a low voice, "Come, more courage." He was watched; a mute reply showed him my affection; he seemed to feel it; his face recovered its tone, he went on shaving tranquilly, and then I dressed him.

His Majesty remained in his chamber till dinner-time reading or walking up and down. In the evening I saw him go towards his cabinet, and I followed him, under pretext that he might need my services. "Have you read the report of my sentence?" asked the king. "Ah, Sire!" I said, "let us hope for a respite. M. de Malesherbes thinks it cannot be refused." "I seek for no hope," replied the king; "but I am much grieved that M. d'Orléans, my relative, should have voted for my death. Read that list." He gave me the list of the call of the House [*appel nominal*] which he held in his hand. "The public are murmuring loudly," I said to him. "Dumouriez is in Paris ; they say he is the bearer of a request from his army against the trial that has just taken place. The people revolt against the infamous conduct of the Duc d'Orléans. There is a rumour that the ambassadors of the foreign Powers are to assemble and go before the Convention. They say that the members are in fear of a popular uprising." "I should be very sorry if it took place," said the king; "there would be more victims. I do not fear death," he added, "but I cannot contemplate without a shudder the cruel fate that I leave behind me for my family, for the queen, for my unfortunate children!— and those faithful servants who never abandoned me, those old men who have no other means of subsistence than the modest pensions that I gave them, who will help them? I see the people given over to anarchy, becoming the victim of all the factions, crimes succeeding one another, perpetual dissensions rending France!" Then after a short silence: "O my God! is that the price I must receive for all my sacrifices? Did I not do all to procure the happiness of Frenchmen?" As he said those words he clasped my hand. Filled with a sacred respect I watered his with my tears. I was obliged to leave him in that state.

The king waited vainly all that evening for M. de Malesherbes. At night he asked me if he had come. I had asked the same question of the commissioners, and they answered no.

Wednesday, 18th, the king, hearing nothing of M. de Malesherbes, became very uneasy. An old "Mercure de France" falling into his hands, he there read a riddle which he gave me to guess. I tried in vain to make it out. "What! you cannot find it out?" he said; "yet it is very applicable to me at this moment. The word is *Sacrifice.*" He ordered me to look in the library for the volume of the History of England that contained an account of the death of Charles I.

On this occasion, I discovered that the king had read two hundred and fifty volumes since his imprisonment in the Temple. That evening I took the liberty of saying to him that he could not be deprived of his counsel, except by a decree of the Convention, and that he ought to ask for their admission to the Tower. "I will wait till to-morrow," replied the king.

Saturday, 19th, at nine in the morning, a municipal named Gobeau entered, a paper in his hand. He was accompanied by the porter of the Tower, named Mathey, who carried an inkstand. The municipal told the king he had orders to make an inventory of all his property and effects. His Majesty left me with him and retired into the *tourelle*. Then, under pretence of the inventory, the municipal began to rummage with the most minute care, to be certain, he said, that no weapon or dangerous instrument had been hidden in the king's room. Presently nothing was left to search but a little bureau in which were papers. The king was obliged to come and open all the drawers, to unfold and show every paper one after the other. There were three rolls of coin at the back of one drawer; they wished to examine them. "That money," said the king, "is not mine; it belongs to M. de Malesherbes." I had prepared it to return to him. The three rolls contained three thousand francs in gold; on the paper that wrapped each roll the king had written with his own hand, "Belonging to M. de Malesherbes."

While the same search was made in the *tourelle* the king returned to his chamber and wanted to warm himself. The porter, Mathey, was at that moment before the fire, holding his coat-tails up with his back to the fire. The king could not warm himself on either side of the man, and the insolent porter not moving, the king told him with some asperity to stand a little aside. Mathey withdrew, and the municipals went out soon after, having failed in their search.

That evening the king told the commissioners to ask the Commune the reason why his counsel were denied admission to the Tower, saying that he desired at least to consult with M. de Malesherbes. They promised to speak of it, but one of them said they were forbidden to take any communication from the king to the council of the Commune unless it were written and signed by his own hand. "Then why," replied the king, "have I been left for two days in ignorance of that change?" He wrote the request and gave it to the municipals; but they did not take it to the Commune until the next day. The king asked to see his counsel freely, and complained of the decree which ordered the municipals to keep him in sight day and night. "They ought to feel," he wrote to the Commune, "that in the position I am in it is very painful not to have the tranquillity necessary to enable me to collect myself."

Sunday, January 20, the king, as soon as he rose, inquired of the municipals if they had taken his request to the Commune. They assured him that they had taken it immediately. Towards ten o'clock I entered the king's room; he said to me: "M. de Malesherbes has not yet come." "Sire," I replied, "I have just learned that he has been here several times, but his entrance to the Tower is always refused." "I shall know the reason of that refusal," replied the king, "when the Commune decides upon my letter." He walked about his room and read and wrote, occupying himself thus the whole morning.

Two o'clock had just struck when the door was suddenly opened to admit the Executive council. Twelve or fifteen persons came in at once: Garat, minister of justice; Lebrun, minister of foreign affairs; Grouville, secretary of the council; the president and the prosecuting-syndic of the department; the mayor and public prosecutor of the Commune; the president and prosecuting attorney of the criminal tribunal.

Santerre, who advanced before the others, said to me: "Announce the Executive council." The king, who heard the noise of the arrival, had risen and made a few steps forward; but, on seeing this procession, he stopped in the doorway between his room and the antechamber, in a most noble and imposing attitude. I was beside him. Garat, his hat on his head, spoke and said: "Louis, the National Convention has ordered the Provisional Executive council to make known to you its decree of the 15th, 16th, 17th, 19th and 20th of January, 1793; the secretary of the council will now read it to you." Then Grouville, the secretary, unfolded the decree and read it in a weak and trembling voice:—

Decree of the National Convention of the 15th to the 20th of January.

ARTICLE I. The National Convention declares Louis Capet last King of the French, guilty of conspiracy against the liberty of the Nation, and of criminal attempts against the general safety of the State.

ARTICLE II. The National Convention declares that Louis Capet shall suffer the penalty of death.

ARTICLE III. The National Convention declares null the act of Louis Capet brought to the bar of the Convention by his counsel, called an appeal to the nation from the judgment rendered against him by the Convention; it forbids all persons from taking it up, under pain of being tried and punished as guilty of criminal attempts against the safety of the Republic.

Article IV. The Provisional Executive council will notify the present decree in the course of this day to Louis Capet, and take the necessary police and safety measures to carry out the execution within twenty-four hours from the time of its notification; rendering an account of all to the National Convention immediately after the execution.

During the reading of the decree not the slightest change appeared on the face of the king. I noticed only that in the first Article, when the word "conspiracy" was uttered, a smile of indignation came upon his lips; but at the words "suffer the penalty of death," a heavenly look which he cast on all those who surrounded him told them that death was without terrors for innocence.

The king made a step towards Grouville, the secretary, took the decree from his hand, folded it, drew his portfolio from his pocket, and put the paper into it. Then, taking another paper from the same portfolio, he said to Garat: "Monsieur the minister of justice, I beg you to send this letter at once to the National Convention." The minister seeming to hesitate, the king added, "I will read it to you," and without any change of tone he read what follows:—

"I ask for a delay of three days that I may prepare myself to appear before God. I demand for the same purpose to be able to see freely the person I shall name to the commissioners of the Commune, and that the said person shall be protected from all anxiety about the act of charity which he will do for me.

"I ask to be delivered from the incessant watching which the council of the Commune established recently.

"I ask to be able, during that interval, to see my family when I ask it, and without witnesses.

"I much desire that the National Convention shall at once concern itself with the fate of my family, and that it will permit them to retire freely wherever they may wish to go.

"I commend to the beneficence of the Nation all the persons who have been attached to me. Many have put their whole fortunes into their offices, and now, receiving no salaries, they must be in need; the same must also be the case with those who had only their salaries to support them; and among the pensionaries, there are many old men, women, and children who have nothing but their pensions to live upon.

"Done in the Tower of the Temple, January 20, one thousand seven hundred and ninety-three.   LOUIS."

Garat took the king's letter and assured him that he would take it to the Convention. As he was leaving, the king drew another paper from his pocket and said: "Monsieur, if the Convention grants my request for the person I desire, here is his address." That address, in another handwriting than that of the king[1] was as follows: "Monsieur Edgeworth de Firmont, No. 483 rue du Bac." The king then walked a few steps back; the minister and those who accompanied him went away.

His Majesty paced for a moment up and down his room; I stood leaning against the door as if deprived of all feeling. The king came to me and said, "Cléry, ask for my dinner." A few moments later, two municipals entered the dining-room; they read me an order which was as follows: "Louis is not to have knife or fork at his meals; a knife is to be given to his *valet de chambre* to cut his bread and meat in presence of two commissioners, and the knife will then be removed." The two municipals told me to inform the king. I refused.

On entering the dining-room the king saw the basket in

[1] Doubtless that of Madame Élisabeth. — TR.

which was the queen's dinner. He asked why they had made his family wait an hour; adding that the delay might have made them anxious. He sat down to table. "I have no knife," he said. The municipal Minier informed His Majesty of the order of the Commune. "Do they think me so cowardly as to take my own life?" said the king. "They impute to me crimes, but I am innocent and I can die without fear; I would that my death might make the welfare of Frenchmen and avert from them the evils I foresee." A great silence fell. The king cut his beef with a spoon, and broke his bread; he ate little, and his dinner lasted only a few minutes.

I was in my room, given over to frightful grief, when, about six in the evening, Garat returned to the Tower. I went to announce to the king the arrival of the minister of justice. Santerre, who preceded him, approached His Majesty and said in a low voice, with a smiling air, "Here is the Executive council." The minister, advancing, told the king that he had taken his letter to the Convention, which charged him to deliver the following answer: "Louis is at liberty to call for any minister of worship that he thinks proper; and to see his family freely and without witnesses; the nation, always grand and always just, will concern itself with the fate of his family; the creditors of his house will be granted just indemnities; as to the three days' respite, the National Convention passes to the order of the day."

The king listened to the reading of this reply without making any observation; he returned to his room, and said to me: "I thought, from Santerre's air, that the delay was granted." A young municipal, named Boston, seeing the king speak to me, came nearer. "You seem to feel what has happened to me," the king said to him; "receive my thanks." The man, surprised, did not know what to answer, and I was myself amazed at the expressions of His Majesty, for this municipal, not twenty-two years of age, with a sweet and interesting face, had said a few moments earlier: "I asked to come to the Temple that I might see the *grimaces* he will make to-morrow" (meaning the king). "And I, too," said Merceraut, the stone-cutter of whom I have already spoken. "Everybody refused to come; but I would not give up this day for a great deal of money." Such were the vile and ferocious men whom the Commune of Paris appointed to guard the king in his last moments.

For four days the king had not seen his counsel; those of the commissioners who had showed some feeling for his misfortunes, avoided coming near him; of all the subjects whose father he had been, of all the Frenchmen whom he had loaded with benefits, one single servant alone remained to him as confidant of his sorrows.

After the reading of the answer of the Convention, the commissioners addressed the minister of justice and asked him how the king was to see his family. "In private," replied Garat; "that is the intention of the Convention." The municipals then told him of the decree of the Commune ordering them not to lose sight of the king "day or night." It was agreed between the Commissioners and the minister that in order to combine these two opposing decrees, the king should receive his family in the dining-room where he could be seen through the glass partition, but that the door should be shut so that he could not be heard.

The king here recalled the minister of justice to ask if he had notified M. de Firmont. Garat replied that he had brought him in his carriage, that he was then in the council-room, and would come up immediately. His Majesty now, in the presence of Garat, gave to a municipal, named Beaudrais, who was talking with the minister, the sum of 3000 francs in gold, requesting him to return it to M. de Malesherbes to whom it belonged. The municipal promised to do so; but he took the money to the council-room, and it was never returned to M. de Malesherbes. M. de Firmont appeared; the king took him into the *tourelle* and closed the door. Garat having gone, no one remained in his Majesty's apartment but the four municipals. At eight o'clock the king came out of his cabinet and told the commissioners to take him to his family. They replied that that could not be done, but they would bring his family to him if he desired it. "Very well," said the king, "but I can, at least, see them alone in my room." "No," replied one of them, "we have arranged with the minister of justice that you shall see them in the dining-room." "You have heard the decree of the Convention," said His Majesty, "which permits me to see them without witnesses." "That is true," said the municipal, "you will be in private, the door will be shut, but we shall have our eyes upon you through the glass partition." "Bring down my family," said the king.

During this interval, His Majesty went to the dining-room; I followed him. I drew the table to one side and placed the chairs at the farther end of the room to give more space. "Bring some water and a glass," said the king. There was then on the table a bottle of iced water; I brought only a glass and placed it beside the water-bottle. "Bring water that is not iced," said the king. "If the queen drank the other it might make her ill. Tell M. de Firmont," added His Majesty, "not to leave my cabinet; I fear the sight of him would make my family too unhappy."

The commissioner who was sent to fetch the royal family was absent a quarter of an hour; during that time the king went back to his cabinet, returning several times to the entrance-door, with signs of the deepest emotion.

At half-past eight the door opened; the queen appeared first, holding her son by the hand; then Madame Royale and Madame Élisabeth; they ran to the arms of the king. A gloomy silence reigned for several minutes, interrupted only by sobs. The queen made a movement to draw the king into his room. "No," he said, "let us go into the dining-room, I can see you only there." They went there, and I closed the door, which was of glass, behind them. The king sat down, the queen on his left, Madame Élisabeth on his right, Madame Royale nearly opposite to him, and the little prince between his knees. All were bending towards him and held him half embraced. This scene of sorrow lasted seven quarters of an hour, during which it was impossible to hear anything; we could see only that after each sentence of the king the sobs of the princesses redoubled, lasting some minutes; then the king would resume what he was saying. It was easy to judge from their motions that the king himself was the first to tell them of his condemnation.

At a quarter past ten the king rose first; they all followed him; I opened the door; the queen held the king by the right arm; Their Majesties each gave a hand to the dauphin; Madame Royale on the left clasped the king's body; Madame Élisabeth, on the same side but a little behind the rest, had caught the left arm of her brother. They made a few steps towards the entrance, uttering the most sorrowful moans. "I assure you," said the king, "that I will see you to-morrow at eight o'clock." "You promise us?" they all cried. "Yes, I promise it." "Why not at seven o'clock?" said the queen. "Well, then, yes, at seven o'clock," replied the king. "*Adieu —*" He uttered that "adieu" in so expressive a manner that the sobs redoubled. Madame Royale fell fainting at the king's feet, which she clasped; I raised her and helped Madame Élisabeth to hold her. The king, wishing to put an end to this heart-rending scene, gave them all a most tender embrace, and then had the strength to tear himself from their arms. "Adieu — adieu," he said, and re-entered his chamber.

The princesses went up to theirs. I wished to go too to support Madame Royale; the municipals stopped me on the second stair and forced me to go back. Though the two doors were shut, we continued to hear the sobs and moans of the princesses on the staircase. The king rejoined his confessor in the *tourelle*.

Half an hour later he came out and I served the supper. The king ate little, but with appetite.

After supper, His Majesty having returned to his cabinet in the *tourelle*, his confessor came out an instant later and asked the commissioners to take him to the council-room. This was for the purpose of obtaining the sacerdotal robes, and other things necessary to say mass on the following morning. M. de Firmont obtained with difficulty the granting of this request. It was to the church of the Capuchins in the Marais, near the hôtel de Soubise, which had lately been made a parish church, that they sent for the articles required for divine service.

Returning from the council-room, M. de Firmont went back to the king. They both re-entered the *tourelle*, where they remained until half an hour after midnight. Then I undressed the king, and as I was about to roll his hair, he said to me, "It is not worth while." When I closed the curtains after he was in bed, he said, "Cléry, wake me at five o'clock."

He was hardly in bed before a deep sleep took possession of his senses; he slept until five o'clock without waking. M. de Firmont, whom His Majesty had urged to take a little rest, threw himself on my bed, and I passed the night on a chair in the king's room, praying God to preserve both his strength and his courage.

I heard five o'clock strike on the city clocks and I lit the fire. At the noise I made, the king awoke and said, opening his curtain," Is it five o'clock?" "Sire, it has struck five on several of the city clocks, but not here." The fire being lighted I went to his bedside. "I have slept well," he said; "I needed it, for yesterday tired me very much. Where is M. de Firmont?" "On my bed." "And you, where did you sleep?" "In this chair." "I am sorry," said the king. "Ah Sire! I exclaimed, "how can I think of myself at such a moment?" He held out his hand to me and pressed mine with affection.

I dressed the king and did his hair; while dressing, he took from his watch a seal, put it in the pocket of his waistcoat, and laid the watch upon the chimney-piece; then, taking from his finger a ring, which he looked at many times, he put it in the same pocket where the seal was. He changed his shirt, put on a white waistcoat which he had worn the night before, and I helped him on with his coat. He took from his pockets his portfolio, his eye-glass, his snuff-box, and some other articles; he laid them with his purse on the chimney-piece; all this in silence and before the municipals. His toilet completed, the king told me to inform M. de Firmont. I went to call him; he was already up, and he followed His Majesty into the *tourelle*.

I then placed a bureau in the middle of the room and prepared it, like an altar, for the mass. At two o'clock in the morning all the necessary articles had been brought. I took into my own room the priest's robe, and then, when everything was ready, I went to inform the king. He asked me if I could serve the mass. I answered yes, but that I did not know all the responses by heart. He had a book in his hand which he opened, found the place of the mass, and gave it to me, taking another book for himself.

During this time the priest robed himself. I had placed an arm-chair before the altar and a large cushion on the floor for His Majesty. The king made me take away the cushion, and went himself into his cabinet to fetch another, smaller and covered with horsehair, which he used daily to say his prayers. As soon as the priest entered, the municipals retired into the antechamber, and I closed one half of the door.

Mass began at six o'clock. During that august ceremony a great silence reigned. The king, always on his knees, listened to the mass with deep absorption, in a most noble attitude. His Majesty took the communion. After mass, he went into his cabinet, and the priest into my room to remove his sacerdotal garments.

I seized that moment to enter the king's cabinet. He took me by both hands and said in a touching voice: "Cléry, I am satisfied with your services." "Ah, Sire!" I cried, throwing myself at his feet. "Why can I not die to satisfy your murderers and save a life so precious to good Frenchmen! Hope, Sire,— they dare not strike you." "Death does not alarm me," he replied. "I am quite prepared; but you," he continued, "do not expose yourself; I shall ask that you be kept near my son; give him all your care in this dreadful place; remind him, tell him often, how I have grieved for the misfortunes he must bear: some day he may be able to reward your zeal." "Ah! my master, my king, if the most absolute devotion, if my zeal and my care have been agreeable to you, the only reward I ask is to receive your blessing — do not refuse it to the last Frenchman who remains beside you."

I was already at his feet, holding one of his hands; in

that position he granted my prayer and gave me his blessing; then he raised me, and pressing me to his bosom said: "Give it also to all who are attached to me; tell Turgy I am content with him. Now, go back," he added; "give no cause for complaint against you." Then, calling me back and taking a paper from the table, he said, "See, here is a letter Pétion wrote me at the time of your entrance to the Temple. It may be useful to you for remaining here." I caught his hand again and kissed it, and went out. "Adieu," he said to me again, "Adieu."

I returned to my chamber, where I found M. de Firmont praying on his knees beside my bed. "What a prince!" he said to me as he rose; "with what resignation, with what courage he looks at death! he was as tranquil as if he were hearing mass in his palace in the midst of his Court." "I have just received the most affecting farewell," I said to him. "He has deigned to promise me that he will ask to have me remain in the Tower to wait on his son. Monsieur, I beg of you to remind him, for I shall not have the happiness to speak to him in private again." "Be at ease about that," replied M. de Firmont as he turned to rejoin His Majesty.

At seven o'clock the king came out of his cabinet and called me; he took me into the embrasure of the window and said: "You will give this seal to my son — and this ring to the queen; tell her that I part from it with pain and only at the last moment. This little packet incloses the hair of all my family; you will give her that also. Say to the queen, to my dear children, to my sister, that although I promised to see them this morning, I wish to spare them the pain of so cruel a separation. — How much it costs me to go without receiving their last embraces!" He wiped away a few tears; then he added, with a most sorrowful accent,

"I charge you to take them my farewell." He immediately re-entered his cabinet.

The municipals who were close at hand had heard His Majesty, and had seen him give me the different articles which I still held in my hands. They told me to give them up to them; but one of their number proposed to leave them in my hands for a decision of the council about them, and this advice prevailed.[1]

A quarter of an hour later the king came out of his cabinet. "Ask," he said to me, "if I can have scissors;" and he went in again. I made the request of the commissioners. "Do you know what he wants to do with them?" I said I did not. "You must let us know." I knocked at the door of the cabinet. The king came out. A municipal who followed me said to him: "You have asked for scissors, but before we take your request to the council we must know what you wish to do with them." His Majesty replied, "I wish Cléry to cut my hair." The municipals retired; one of them went down to the council-chamber, where, after half an hour's deliberation, they refused the scissors. The municipals returned and announced that decision to the king. "I should not have touched the scissors," said His Majesty; "I should have requested Cléry to cut my hair in your presence; inquire again, monsieur; I beg you to take charge of my request." The municipal returned to the council, which persisted in its refusal.

It was then that I was told to be ready to accompany the king and undress him on the scaffold. At this announcement I was seized with terror; but collecting all my strength I was preparing to render this last duty to my master, to whom this service done by the executioner would be repugnant, when another municipal came to tell me that I was

[1] See Appendix V.

not to go; adding, "The executioner is good enough for him."

Paris was under arms from five o'clock in the morning; nothing was heard outside but the beating of the *générale*, the rattle of arms, the tramp of horses, the movement of cannon, which they placed and displaced incessantly. All this echoed through the Tower.

At nine o'clock the noise increased, the gates opened with a crash; Santerre, accompanied by seven or eight municipals, entered at the head of ten gendarmes, whom he ranged in two lines. At this disturbance the king came out of his cabinet. "Have you come to fetch me?" he said to Santerre "Yes." "I ask you for one minute." The king entered his cabinet and came out again immediately, his confessor with him. He held his will in his hand, and, addressing a municipal, Jacques Roux by name, a priest who had taken the oath, who was the man nearest to him, he said: "I beg you to give this paper to the queen, to my wife." "It is not my business," replied the priest, refusing to take the document. "I am here to conduct you to the scaffold." His Majesty then addressed Gobau, another municipal. "Give this paper, I beg you, to my wife. You can read it; it contains dispositions which I desire that the Commune should know." Gobau took the document.

I was behind the king, near the chimney; he turned to me and I offered him his overcoat. "I have no need of it," he said, "give me only my hat." I gave it to him. His hand touched mine, which he pressed for the last time. "Messieurs," he said, addressing the municipals, "I desire that Cléry should remain near my son, who is accustomed to his care; I hope that the Commune will accede to my request." Then, looking at Santerre, he said, "Let us go."

Those were the last words that he said in his apartment.

At the top of the staircase he met Mathey, porter of the Tower, and said to him: "I was a little hasty to you day before yesterday; do not bear me ill-will." Mathey made no answer; he even affected to turn away when the king spoke to him.

I remained alone in the room, my heart wrung with sorrow, and almost without sensation. The drums and the trumpets announced that His Majesty had left the Tower. An hour later salvos of artillery and cries of *Vive la nation! Vive la république!* were heard. The best of kings was no more!

NARRATIVE

OF MARIE-THÉRÈSE DE FRANCE,

DUCHESSE D'ANGOULÊME.

NARRATIVE

OF MADAME THÉRÈSE DE FRANCE.

Relating: I. Events from October 5, 1789, to August 10, 1792. II. Events taking place in the Tower of the Temple from August, 1792, to the Death of the Dauphin, June 9, 1795.

[THE latter part of this Narrative[1] was the part first written by Marie-Thérèse, Madame Royale de France, only surviving child of Louis XVI. and Marie-Antoinette. She wrote it in the Temple after the death of her brother in 1795, when her own captivity became less rigorous, and she was allowed the use of pencil and paper.

The first part of the Narrative, that which relates the various events taking place from October 5, 1789, to August 10, 1792, was written by her in 1799, during her exile and soon after her marriage to her cousin, the Duc d'Angoulême, son of the Comte d'Artois, subsequently Charles X. This manuscript was corrected and copied, in his own handwriting, by her uncle, *Monsieur*, Comte de Provence, subsequently Louis XVIII., with whom she lived during his two exiles and his two Restorations till his death. This copy, now in possession of the family of François Huë, a devoted attendant of the royal family of France, to whom the Duchesse d'Angoulême gave it, was first published by M. de Saint-Amand (Firmin Didot, Paris, no date). From that edition this translation is made. The additions by Louis XVIII. are placed in the text between brackets; his omissions, which are chiefly of words and brief sentences,

[1] Beginning on page 243. — TR.

made to correct his niece's French style, are, necessarily, not shown in the translation.]

First Uprising of the Populace on the 5th and 6th of October 1789. Removal of my Family to the Capital.

It was on the 5th of October, 1789, of a Monday, that the first disturbances which, in the end, convulsed all France, broke forth. In the morning of that too memorable day every one was still tranquil at Versailles. My father had gone to hunt at Meudon, a royal château midway to Paris; my mother had gone alone to her garden at Trianon; my uncle *Monsieur*, with *Madame*, remained at Versailles; my Aunt Élisabeth had ridden out on horseback to dine at her garden on the road to Paris; my brother and I had also gone out in the morning and returned towards half-past one to dine with my mother. Hardly had my Aunt Élisabeth reached Montreuil and begun her dinner when they came to tell her that all the women and all the rabble of Paris were coming, armed, to Versailles. A few moments later the news was confirmed; they were already very near Versailles, where my father had not yet returned. My aunt went back at once to Versailles accompanied by her two ladies-in-waiting. Going to my uncle's apartment, she asked if he knew what was happening; he said he had heard talk of all Paris coming out to Versailles armed, but he did not believe it; my aunt assured him that the thing was true, and together they went to my mother.

We had just finished dinner when it was announced that *Monsieur* and Mme. Élisabeth were there and wished to speak to the queen. My mother was surprised, because

Madame Élisabeth

it was not her usual hour for seeing them. She passed into another room [to speak with them], and returned almost immediately, much agitated by what she had heard and still more uneasy about my father; she was not aware that the moment the news of the insurrection reached Versailles two gentlemen, named Puymontbrun and La Devèze, had hastened on horseback to warn my father. He returned at five o'clock, and by six the whole troop of rioters were in Versailles; the iron gates of the château were closed and defended by the *Gardes du Corps*.

M. de la Fayette was at the head of this Parisian army. [None but the rabble came first; M. de la Fayette did not come, with troops little disciplined, until eleven at night.] They entered the hall of the Assembly, where they declaimed much against the king and the government. The president of the Assembly, M. Mounier, came several times to the château to speak to my father. The Duc d'Orléans was with la Fayette [they were not together], and it was said they intended to make him king. However that may be, the object of these rioters was not well known to themselves; none but the leaders were informed of their true purpose. Their [principal] purpose was to murder my mother, on whom the Duc d'Orléans wished to avenge himself for affronts he said she had put upon him; also to massacre the *Gardes du Corps*, the only ones who remained faithful to their king [they were then commanded by the Duc de Guiche].

Towards midnight the crowd retired, seeming to want rest; many of the women lay down on the benches of the National Assembly. M. de la Fayette himself went to bed, saying that everything was tranquil for the night; so that my father and mother, seeing that all was really quiet, retired to their rooms, and so did the rest of the family.

My mother knew that their chief object was to kill her; nevertheless, in spite of that, she made no sign, but retired to her room with all possible coolness and courage [after ordering all who had gathered there to retire also]. She went to bed, directing Mme. de Tourzel to take her son instantly to the king if she heard any noise during the night; she ordered all her servants to go to bed.

The rest of the night was quiet till five in the morning; but then the iron gates of the château were forced and the vagabonds, led, it was said, by the Duc d'Orléans himself, rushed straight to my mother's apartment. The Swiss Guard stationed at the foot of the staircase, which could have disputed their passage, gave way, so that the villains, without any hindrance, entered the hall of the *Gardes du Corps* wounding and killing those who tried to oppose their passage. Two of these guards, named Miomandre de Sainte-Marie and Durepaire, though grievously wounded, dragged themselves to my mother's door, crying out to her to fly and bolt the doors behind her. Their zeal was cruelly rewarded; the wretches flung themselves upon them and left them bathed in their blood, for dead. Meantime, my mother's women, wakened by the shouts of the insurgents and the *Gardes du Corps*, rushed to the door and bolted it. My mother sprang from her bed and, half-dressed, ran to my father's apartment; but the door of it was locked within, and those who were there, hearing the noise, would not open it, thinking it was the rioters trying to enter. Fortunately, a man on duty named Turgy (the same who afterwards served us in the Temple as waiter), having recognized my mother's voice, opened the door to her immediately.

At the same moment the wretches forced the door of my mother's room; so that one instant later she would have been taken without means of escape. As soon as she entered my father's rooms she looked for him, but could not find him; having heard she was in danger he had rushed to her apartment, but by another way. Fortunately, he met my brother, brought to him by Mme. de Tourzel, who urged him to return to his own rooms, where he found my mother awaiting him in mortal anxiety. Reassured about my father and brother, the queen came in search of me; I was already awakened by the noise in her rooms and in the garden under my windows; my mother told me to rise, and then took me with her to my father's apartment.

My great-aunts Adélaïde and Victoire arrived soon after. We were very uneasy about *Monsieur, Madame*, and my Aunt Élisabeth, of whom nothing had been heard. My father sent gentlemen to know where they were. They were found sleeping peacefully; the brigands not having gone to their side of the château, neither they nor their servants knew what was happening. They all came at once to my father. My Aunt Élisabeth was so troubled by the danger that the king and queen had run that she crossed the rooms inundated with the blood of the *Gardes du Corps* without even perceiving it. . . .

The courtyard of the château presented a horrible sight. A crowd of women, almost naked, and men armed with pikes threatened our windows with dreadful cries. M. de la Fayette and the Duc d'Orléans were at one of the windows, pretending to be in despair at the horrors which were being committed during that morning. I do not know who advised my mother to show herself on the balcony, but she went out upon it with my brother. The mob demanded that her son should be sent in; having taken him into the room my mother returned alone to the balcony [expecting to perish, but happily], this great courage awed the whole crowd of people, who confined themselves to loading her with insults without daring to attack her person.

M. de la Fayette, on his side, never ceased to harangue the rioters, but his words had no effect and the tumult still continued. He told them that my father consented to return with them to Paris; he said he could assure them of this as my father had given him his word. This promise calmed them a little, and while the Court carriages were being made ready to start, all the family returned to their rooms to make their toilet, for up to this time we still wore our night-caps.

All being arranged for the departure, there was fresh embarrassment about how to leave the château, because they wished to prevent my father from crossing the great guard-rooms which were inundated with blood. We therefore went down by a small staircase, crossed the Cour des Cerfs and got into a carriage for six persons; on the back seat were my father, mother and brother; on the front seat *Madame*, my Aunt Élisabeth and I, in the middle my uncle *Monsieur* and Mme. de Tourzel. My great-aunts, Adélaïde and Victoire started for their country-seat, Bellevue, at the same time.

The crowd was so great it was long before we could advance. In front of the cortège were carried the heads of the two *Gardes du Corps* who had been killed. Close to the carriage was M. de la Fayette on horseback surrounded by troops of the Flanders regiment on foot, and of the grenadiers of the French guard. [In the ranks of the latter and mingling with them, though with very different sentiments, were several of the *Gardes du Corps*, who gave to their king in these cruel moments the last mark of devotion which it was ever possible for their regiment to give.]

We started at one in the afternoon. Though the journey

from Versailles to Paris is usually done in two short hours we did not reach the barrier till six in the evening. Along the whole way the brigands never ceased firing their muskets, and it was useless for M. de la Fayette to oppose them; they shouted: *Vive la nation! À bas les Calotins! À bas les Prêtres!* M. Bailly, Mayor of Paris, in conformity with an ancient custom [so insolent and derisory at this moment], presented my father with the keys of the city on a gold plate, and made him a long speech in which he spoke of the pleasure the good city of Paris would have in possessing the king, whom he urgently requested to go at once to the Hôtel de Ville. My father was unwilling to consent, saying it would take too long and fatigue his children too much. Nevertheless, M. Bailly insisted, and M. de la Fayette being of the same opinion, — because he thought it better to go the same day rather than wait for the morrow when they would be forced to go, — my father decided to do so.

Having entered Paris, the shouts, the clamour, the insults increased with the mob of the populace; it took us two hours to reach the Hôtel de Ville. My father had ordered all persons in his suite who were in the other carriages to go straight to the Tuileries; he therefore went alone with his family to the Hôtel de Ville, where the municipality and M. Bailly received him, still civilly, and made him another speech on their joy at seeing that he wished to establish himself in Paris. My father answered in a few words, from which they could see that he felt his position much. They asked him to rest there a moment, as he had now been eight hours in the carriage. The People, who filled the square, shouted loudly and demanded to see the king; he placed himself therefore at a window of the Hôtel de Ville, and as it was now dark they brought torches in order to recognize him. Then we again got into the carriage and reached the Tuileries at ten o'clock.

Thus passed that fatal day, the opening epoch of the imprisonment of the royal family and the beginning of the outrages and cruelties it was to bear in the end. The rest of this year, and the year of 1790 were passed in a continual struggle between the Royal Power and that arrogated to itself by the Assembly, the latter always gaining the upper hand, although no very remarkable events happened during that time relating to the personal situation of my family.

Flight of my Father; Stoppage at Varennes; his Return to Paris.

On the 20th of June, 1790, my father and mother seemed to me greatly agitated during the whole day and much occupied, without my knowing the reason. After dinner they sent us, my brother and me, into another room, and shut themselves into their own, alone with my aunt. I knew later that this was the moment when they told the latter of their plan for escaping by flight from the durance under which they were living. At five o'clock my mother went to walk with my brother and me; during our walk my mother took me aside from her suite, and told me not to be uneasy at anything that I might see; that we might be separated, but not for long; I understood nothing of this confidence. Thereupon she kissed me and said that if the ladies of the suite questioned me as to this conversation I was to say that she had scolded me and forgiven me. We returned about seven o'clock and I went to my room very sad, not knowing what to think of what my mother had said to me. I passed the rest of the evening alone; my mother had induced

Mme. de Mackau, my subgoverness, to go and spend a few days in a convent of which she was very fond, and had also sent into the country a young girl who was usually with me; besides which she ordered me to send away all my servants except one woman.

I was hardly in bed before my mother came in; she told me we were to leave at once, and gave her orders for the arrangements; she said to Mme. Bruuyer, my waiting-woman, that she wished her to follow us, but that, having a husband, she was free to remain. That [good] woman replied immediately that they did right to go, and as for her she should not hesitate to leave her husband and follow us everywhere. My mother was touched by that mark of attachment. She then went down to bid good-night to *Monsieur* and *Madame*, who had supped with her as usual. *Monsieur* was already informed of the departure; on returning to his own apartment he went to bed, and then, having sent away all his people, he rose [without noise and, disguising himself as an English merchant] he started with one of his gentlemen, M. d'Avaray, who, by his intelligence and devotion enabled him to escape [or surmount] all the dangers of the route.

As for *Madame*, she was wholly ignorant of the intended journey, and it was not until after she was in bed that one of her women came and told her she was ordered by the king and *Monsieur* to take her without delay out of the kingdom. She started at once, and met *Monsieur* at the first post where they relayed, without appearing to know each other, and so arrived safely at Brussels.

My mother had already been to wake my brother, whom Mme. de Tourzel took down to her *entresol*. Having gone there with him we there found awaiting us one of the *Gardes du Corps* who was to be our guide. My mother came several times to cast an eye upon us while my brother was being dressed as a little girl; he was heavy with sleep, and did not know what was happening. At half-past ten we were ready; my mother took us herself to the carriage in the middle of the courtyard and put us into it, my brother and me and Mme. de Tourzel. M. de Fersen, a Swedish noble in the service of France, served us as coachman. To throw people off the scent we made several turns in Paris and returned to the little Carrousel near the Tuileries to wait for my father and mother. My brother was lying at the bottom of the carriage under Mme. de Tourzel's gown.

We saw M. de la Fayette pass close by us, going to the king's *coucher*. We waited there a full hour in the greatest impatience and uneasiness at my parents' long delay. During the journey Mme. de Tourzel was to pass for a Baronne de Korff; my mother as Mme. Bonnet, governess of the lady's children; my father, under the name of Durand, as *valet de chambre;* my aunt, named Rosalie, as the lady's companion, and my brother and I for the two daughters of Mme. de Korff, named Amélie and Aglaé. The two waiting-women followed us in a calèche. The three *Gardes du Corps* who accompanied us passed for servants; one was on horseback, one on the carriage, and the third went before us as courier.

After waiting one hour I saw a woman approach and walk round our carriage; it made me fear we were discovered, but I was soon reassured by seeing the coachman open the carriage door to admit my aunt; she had escaped alone with one other person. On entering the carriage she trod upon my brother, who was hidden at the bottom of it; he had the the courage not to utter a cry. She assured us that all was quiet at Court, and that my father and mother would soon come. In fact, the king came almost immediately, and then my mother with a member of the *Gardes du Corps*, who was to follow us. We then started. At first nothing happened until we reached the barrier, where we were to find the post-carriage which was there to take us on. M. de Fersen did not know precisely where it would be; we were obliged to wait a rather long time and my father got out, which made us uneasy. At last M. de Fersen came with the other carriage, into which we got; that done, he bade my father goodnight, mounted his horse, and disappeared.[1]

Nothing remarkable happened to us during the next morning. At Etoges we were on the point of being recognized, and at Châlons-sur-Marne, which we passed through at four in the afternoon, we were so completely. The inhabitants seemed well-intentioned; a great number of them were charmed to see their king and offered wishes for the success of his flight. At the post after Châlons, where we ought to have found troops on horseback to convoy the carriage to Montmédy, we found none; and we waited there, expecting them, till eight o'clock in the evening; then, going on, we reached Clermont, where we saw troops, but the rioters of the village would not allow them to mount their horses. One of their officers recognizing the king, approached the carriage and told him in a low voice that he was betrayed. We continued our way in agitation and anxiety, which, how-

---

[1] Footnote to the above, written by Louis XVIII. "I think that the last two words should be erased and the following substituted: 'and returned to Paris, where, having assured himself that all was quiet, he took the road to the Low Countries, arriving there without accident.' All that is true, and for a thousand reasons of which my niece is ignorant, and of which I hope she will always remain ignorant, it is proper that she should show interest in a man who on that day showed so much devotion."

As a matter of fact Count Fersen drove the party to Bondy, one hour and a half beyond the barrier, where he left them at the king's request; the royal family continuing along the post-road, and Count Fersen taking, on horseback, the cross-roads to Bonrget and thence to Mons. See "Diary and Correspondence of Count Axel Fersen" in the present Historical Series. — TR.

ever, did not prevent us from sleeping; but having been awakened by a violent jolt, they came and told us they were ignorant of what had become of the courier who preceded us. It can be imagined in what fear we were; we supposed he had been recognized and captured.

We arrived at the entrance to the village of Varennes, a very small place where there were scarcely a hundred houses and no post-house; so that travellers arriving there were obliged to get their horses from elsewhere. Those intended for us were really there, but at the château on the other side of the river, and none of our people knew it; besides which, our postilions protested that their horses were tired and could go no farther. Our courier then appeared, and with him a man whom he believed to be in our secret, but who was really, as we had reason to believe, a spy of M. de la Fayette. He came to the carriage in a night-cap and dressing-gown, put himself almost into it, and said he knew a secret but could not tell it. Mme. de Tourzel having asked him if he knew Mme. de Korff, he said no; except those words, said while he looked fixedly at my father, it was impossible to get anything from him.

They succeeded at last in persuading the postilions that the horses were at the château and that they must take us there; they therefore drove on; but very slowly. As we entered the village we were shocked by the dreadful cries around the carriage: "Stop! stop!" Then the horses' heads were seized and, in a moment, the carriage was surrounded by a number of armed men with torches; it was then eleven o'clock at night. They asked us who we were; we said: Mme. de Korff, and her family. They put their torches close to my father's face, and told us to get out; we refused, saying we were simple travellers and ought to be allowed to pass; they repeated loudly that we must get out or they would kill us all, and we saw their guns pointed at the carriage. We were therefore forced to get out. As we passed along the street we saw six dragoons on horseback; unfortunately there was no officer with them, for six determined men could have awed those people and saved the king. We were taken to the house of a man named Sauce, mayor of Varennes and a dealer in candles.

While the tocsin sounded and the people uttered cries, my father kept himself in the farthest corner of the room; but unfortunately his portrait was there, and the people gazed at him and the picture alternately. My mother and Mme. de Tourzel complained loudly of the injustice of our stoppage, saying that she was travelling quietly with her family under a government passport, and that the king was not with us. The crowd increased, but in spite of the dreadful noise, our three *Gardes du Corps* went to sleep. We were all packed together in a very small room, and many of the villagers were there with us. They sent for the judge, to examine my father and decide if he was the king. Having done so, he said nothing. My aunt asking impatiently if he believed it was my father, he still said nothing, but raised his eyes to heaven.

Meantime M. de Choiseul and Goguelat, officers appointed to bring troops to meet us, arrived, but without soldiers; they said they could not bring them because the bridge was blocked by a cart.[1]

[1] This, of course, is the narrative of a young girl, given, no doubt, with her natural conscientiousness. It ought to be compared with the Duc de Choiseul's own account, which seems to have satisfied Count Fersen, the man whose plan was ruined. See "Diary and Corr. of Count Axel Fersen," pp. 271-277.

The failure of the escape was due to four causes: (1) the carelessness of young Bouillé; (2) his father, the Marquis de Bouillé's error in waiting on the frontier; (3) the delay of four or five hours after leaving Châlons, for no real reason; (4) the king's want of character; it is plain that had he taken the situation by the horns and commanded it, he could easily have saved himself and family. — Tr.

At last, every one declaring himself convinced that my father was the king, he, seeing that he had no means of escape, took the course of disclosing himself; and having said he was the king, all present threw themselves at his feet and kissed his hands; among others, a major, named Rollin, who had insulted my father before he recognized him, now fell at his feet and protested all that a faithful subject could think or feel. He then rose as if furious, and retired. The whole family of the house also surrounded my father, and the tocsin still sounded. But in spite of these signs of devotion, they said he must not pass, for it was dreadful in him to abandon his people, and that he ought to return to Paris.

Things were thus when, at three in the morning, two agents of M. de la Fayette, sent in pursuit of my father, MM. Baillon and Romeuf, arrived, and they insisted vigorously on his return to Paris. M. Baillon let my father know that he came from the city of Paris to beg him to return, saying that they were in despair at his having quitted it as he had done, and that he ought necessarily to return.

Nevertheless, we tried on our side to delay as long as possible, to gain time, and wait to see if help would not arrive. On the other hand, those who had stopped us pressed us extremely to start, being in the greatest fear that in so small a place as Varennes and so near the frontier, the king might be carried off, which could very easily have happened if any one had been there who had any head.

On the other side of the river the son of M. de Bouillé was waiting, but as he had been three consecutive nights without sleep, fatigue overcame him, and he did not wake till the next morning, to hear of the stoppage of the king and his return to Paris. The other officers, who were on this side of the river, MM. de Damas and de Choiseul, got lost in the woods, having taken too long a road; their horses were exhausted, and they did not arrive until long after we were stopped; so that seeing the affair had failed, they were in despair and did not have the patience [the thought] or perhaps the means to go in search of the Marquis de Bouillé, who was waiting for us two posts beyond Varennes. At last, at six in the morning, seeing there was no remedy or help to be looked for, we were absolutely forced to take the road back to Paris.

During all this catastrophe we never saw the famous Drouet, who made so much talk about the part he was said to have played; it is true that, on leaving Clermont, we saw a man on horseback, who passed our carriage, and it may have been he. As for the other, named Guillaume, we saw him, but not until after my father had made himself known; and that man said he had not recognized him, but only my aunt, whom he saw at the Federation.

We therefore got into the carriage, but not without danger; they did not wish our three *Gardes du Corps* to accompany us, and it was with great difficulty that they at last permitted them to sit on the box of the carriage; the other officers were more exposed, and were afterwards imprisoned and taken to Orléans. . . . Arriving at Sainte-Menehould at half-past three o'clock, we were allowed to leave the carriage for the first time since six in the morning. They took us to the house of the mayor, named Farcy. This man had formerly served at Court, but was much dissatisfied with abuses he declared he had seen there. His wife came repeatedly to my father, saying, "But why did you wish to leave us?" In vain did they tell her, as they did to others, that my father did not mean to leave them, but only to go to Montmédy, which was really his project; but the people would listen to nothing and could not be pacified.

While we were at dinner a man named Bodand arrived, deputy of the Commune of Paris, to beg my father in the name of that city, to return to it as soon as possible; my father, being no longer master of doing otherwise, could only let himself be led. As soon as we had dined, we returned to the carriage, and an hour later met a gentleman of the neighbourhood named Dampierre, who, in despair at the king's being stopped, came to see him, but did not reach our carriage, only that of the waiting-women. The peasants knew him to be what they called an aristocrat, and showed themselves very ill-disposed towards him. Our women begged him to go away, but hardly had he spurred his horse before the people who surrounded the carriages fired at him; he was flung to the ground, and a man on horseback rode over him and struck him several blows with a sabre; others did the same, and soon killed him. The scene, which took place close to our carriage and under our eyes, was horrible for us; but more dreadful still was the fury of these wretches, who, not content with having killed him, wanted to drag his body to our carriage and show it to my father. He objected with all his strength; the postilions, however, would not advance! but at last one man, more humane than the others, went to the postilions pistol in hand, threatening to shoot them if they did not go on; so at last they started. In spite of that, these cannibals came on triumphantly, round the carriage, holding up the hat, coat, and clothing of the unfortunate Dampierre; and, paying no attention to my father's entreaties, they carried these horrible trophies beside us along the road. It was thus that we passed the rest of that day in the midst of insults and perils.

At last, at eleven at night we reached Châlons. There we heard of the arrest of M. de Briges, the king's equerry, who, hearing of my father's departure from Paris, had left his regiment to join him. He was met on the way by M. Baillon, M. de la Fayette's emissary, who, seeing that he had no posthorses, took him with him, brought him to Châlons, and there, with the cruellest treachery, denounced him, and had him arrested. Such was the reward of his love and attachment to his king. Hearing of our arrival at Châlons, M. de Briges asked to see my father, but in vain, and he had the pain of listening to the insults heaped upon him. We were taken to the Maison-Royale at Châlons, where we were well-lodged and well-treated. The inhabitants of the town seemed well-disposed, especially the mayor, M. Rose, and the military commander M. Reubel, a former *Garde du Corps*. My mother even found in her room a man who proposed to her to escape, which she refused, fearing treachery and seeing moreover countless difficulties.

We were all so fatigued at having passed two nights in uproar and terror that we slept soundly. The next day, we resumed the clothes belonging to our rank, and my brother was again dressed as a boy. Throughout that morning many persons came to see my father, and did so from interest and in no way with insult, as had been shown elsewhere. My brother, especially, enchanted every one by his amiability. This was the day of the *Fête-Dieu*, and they took us to mass at ten in the morning; but the Offertory had scarcely begun before we heard a great noise, and they came to tell my father that we must leave the mass at once, because the enemy was arriving. It was M. de Bouillé and his troops of whom they thus spoke. We were therefore taken to our rooms and shut up there, where we stayed quite a long time. They served us a dinner, but in the middle of it another alarm was sounded and they obliged us to start at once. Of all the places we passed through, Châlons was the one where we were best treated by the inhabitants. . . .

We reached Épernay at three in the afternoon. It was there that my father ran the greatest danger of the whole journey. Imagine the courtyard of the hotel where we were to get out filled with angry people armed with pikes, who surrounded the carriage in such crowds that it could not enter the courtyard. We were therefore absolutely obliged to leave it outside and cross that courtyard on foot amid the hoots of these people who said openly they wished to kill us. Of all the awful moments I have known, this was one of those which struck me most, and the horrible impression of it will never leave me.

Entering the house at last, they made us eat a miserable meal. In spite of all the threats of the ferocious populace to massacre every one, they did not go farther and we started from Épernay about six in the evening. Just then they came to tell us that deputies of the National Assembly were arriving. These were Pétion, Barnave, Maubourg, Dumas, commandant of the Garde of the Assembly, and his nephew La Rue. At the moment that the deputies approached our carriage, an unfortunate priest who had not taken the oath was close by it; the peasants, who wished to kill him, had thrown him on the ground, but a Garde on horseback picked him up, put him behind him and rode up to us. At that moment the murderers tried to seize him again under the very eyes of the deputies. My mother cried out to Barnave to save him, which he succeeded in doing through the ascendency he had over the people, and the poor priest escaped with only a wound.

The deputies, having approached the carriage, told my father that by order of the National Assembly they were charged to bring him back to Paris, blaming him at the same time for wishing to leave France. My father answered that he had never had any intention of leaving his kingdom, but only that of going to Montmédy. The deputies then, declaring they were ordered not to let us out of sight, said they must get into our carriage; but, as it could not hold so many persons, they arranged that my aunt and I should go in their carriage with Maubourg, and that Pétion and Barnave should sit with my father and mother. But my aunt and I absolutely refused to leave the carriage. In spite of that they entered it, and though there was no room, Pétion placed himself between my father and my mother, who was thus forced to take my brother on her knees. Barnave sat between my aunt, who placed me before her, and Mme. de Tourzel. These deputies talked much and disclosed openly their manner of thinking; to which my mother and my aunt replied rather energetically. This Pétion was a great rascal, as he proved later, and Barnave was a small lawyer of Dauphiné who wanted to play a part under the circumstances. Maubourg was [a man of another species, but] an insignificant being who had let himself be drawn into the Revolution without knowing why.

We reached Dormans in the evening, and slept at a little inn. The deputies were lodged side by side with us. Our windows looked on the street, which all night long was filled with the populace shouting, and wanting us to go on in the middle of the night; but the deputies no doubt wanted to rest themselves, and so we stayed. My brother was ill all night and almost had delirium, so shocked was he by the dreadful things he had seen on the preceding day.

The next day, June 24th, nothing happened of importance, except impertinent speeches from the deputies, yells and insults from the people, and the excessive heat which overcame us because we were, as I have said, eight persons in a carriage holding only four.

We stopped for dinner at Ferté-la-Jouarre; where my

father was well-received by the mayor, named Renard, who had the delicacy to prevent any one from entering his house or garden. We were told that our three *Gardes du Corps* must be left behind, because there was no safety for them in Paris. They remained, nevertheless, with us and nothing happened to them. . . . We slept at Meaux in the bishop's house, full of priests who had taken the oath, but otherwise civil enough; the bishop himself served us. They informed us that we must start the next day at five in the morning so as to reach Paris in good season.

We started at six, and though it is only ten leagues from Meaux to Paris, we did not reach Bondy, the last post, till midday nor the Tuileries till half-past seven at night. At Bondy the populace showed its desire to massacre our three *Gardes-du-Corps*, and my father did all he could to save them, in which, it must be owned, the deputies eagerly seconded him. The crowd we met along the road was innumerable, so that we could scarcely advance. The insults with which the people loaded us were our only food throughout the day. In the faubourgs of Paris the crowd was even greater, and among all those persons we saw but one woman fairly well-dressed who showed by her tears the interest she took in us.

On the Place Louis XV. was M. de la Fayette, apparently at the summit of joy at the success of the blow he had just struck; he was there, surrounded by a people submissive to his orders; he could have destroyed my father at once, but he preferred to save him longer in order that he might serve his own designs.

We were made to drive through the garden of the Tuileries, surrounded by weapons of all sorts, and muskets which almost touched us. When the deputies said anything to the people they were instantly obeyed, and it is no doubt to their intentions (good or bad) that my father owed his preservation at that moment; for had those deputies not been with us it is more than likely we should then have been murdered. It was they also who saved the *Gardes du Corps*.

On arriving at the Tuileries and getting out of the carriage, we were almost carried off our feet by the enormous crowd that filled the staircase. My father went up first, with my mother and my brother. As for me, I was to go with my aunt, and one of the deputies took me in his arms to carry me up. In vain did I cry for my aunt; the noise was so dreadful she could not hear me. At last we were all reunited in the king's room, where were nearly all the deputies of the National Assembly, who, however, seemed very civil and did not stay long. My father entered the inner rooms with his family, and seeing them all in safety, I left him and went to my own apartments, being quite worn out with fatigue and inanition. I did not know until the next morning what took place that evening. Guards were placed over the whole family, with orders not to let them out of sight, and to stay night and day in their chambers. My father had them in his room at night, but in the daytime they were stationed in the next room. My mother would not allow them to be in the room where she slept with a waiting-woman, but they stayed in the adjoining room with the doors open. My brother had them also, night and day; but my aunt and I had none. M. de la Fayette even proposed to my aunt to leave the Tuileries, if she wished to do so, but she replied that she would never separate from the king.

My father and mother could not leave their rooms, not even to go to church, and mass was said in their apartments. No one could enter the Tuileries unless by cards of permission, which M. de la Fayette granted to few.

Such was the state of my parents' captivity during more than two months until the acceptance by the king of the Constitution. After that, we had several months of respite and apparent tranquillity, but the king found himself in a constant struggle with the Assembly, which ulcerated all minds more and more, daily.

Assault on the Tuileries by the Populace June 20, 1792.

Under the circumstances of that time the people took a mania to place in all the public squares and gardens what were called "liberty trees;" these were little trees or tall poles, at the top of which they put the *bonnet rouge* with tricolour ribbons — that is to say, red, blue, and white. They expressed to my father a wish to plant one in the garden of the Tuileries, and he acquiesced. The day they planted this tree was made a species of revolutionary fête, somewhat like that formerly given at the planting of the May tree on the first of that month. They triumphed in having wrung this consent from my father, and to celebrate it they chose the 20th of June, the anniversary of our departure for Varennes, and the fête was to take place beneath our windows. From all these signs my parents could augur nothing good and expect nothing but fresh insults heaped upon them.

Previous to this, the Assembly had exacted that the king should sign their decree that all priests who had not taken the oath were to be sent out of France. My father would not acquiesce in that decree, and had put his veto upon it. This veto was a derisory right which the Assembly allowed the king to exercise when he would not acquiesce in their propositions. On this refusal, they exasperated all minds against my father, constantly seeking to force him in one way or another to give his consent to the decree. This, therefore, was the concealed object they wished to succeed in on the occasion of this fête.

On the 20th of June, about eleven o'clock in the morning, nearly all the inhabitants of the faubourgs Saint-Antoine and Saint-Marceau, where the populace chiefly lived, marched in a body to the National Assembly, to go from there to the garden and plant the liberty-tree. But as they were all armed, which gave reason to suspect bad intentions, my father ordered the gates of the Tuileries to be closed. The Assembly showed great dissatisfaction, and sent a deputation of four municipals to induce the king to order the gates to be opened. These deputies spoke very insolently; said they exacted the opening of the gates in order that those who had come to plant the tree, the sign of liberty, might return that way, inasmuch as the crowd in the rue Saint-Honoré was too great to allow them to pass. My father, however, persisted in his refusal, and they then went and opened themselves the gates of the garden, which was instantly inundated by the populace; the gates of the courtyards and the château still remained locked.

An hour later this armed procession began to defile before our windows, and no idea can be formed of the insults they said to us. Among others, they carried a banner on which were these words: " Tremble, tyrant; the people have risen;" and they held it before the windows of my father who, though he was not visible himself, could see all and hear their cries of " Down with Veto!" and other horrors. This lasted until three o'clock, when the garden was at last freed. The crowd then passed through the Place du Carrousel to the courtyards of the Tuileries, but quietly, and it was generally thought they were returning to their faubourgs.

During this time our family were in the rooms on the courtyard side, absolutely alone and observing all that went on; the gentlemen of the suite and the ladies dined on the other side. Suddenly we saw the populace forcing the gates of the courtyard and rushing to the staircase of the château. It was a horrible sight to see, and impossible to describe — that of these people, with fury in their faces, armed with pikes and sabres, and pell-mell with them women half unclothed, resembling Furies.

Two of the ushers wishing to run the bolts of my father's door, he prevented it and sprang himself into the next room to meet the rioters. My aunt followed him hastily, and hardly had she passed when the door was locked. My mother and I ran after her in vain; we could not pass, and at that moment several persons came to us, and finally, the guard. My mother cried out: "Save my son!" Immediately some one took him in his arms and carried him off. My mother and I, being determined to follow my brother, did all we could against the persons who prevented us from passing; prayers, efforts, all were useless, and we had to remain in our room in mortal anxiety. My mother kept her courage, but it almost abandoned her when, at last, entering my brother's room she could not find him. The persons who, on her own order, had carried him away lost their heads, and in the confusion, took him up higher in the château, where they thought him in greater safety. My mother then sent for him and had him brought back to his room. There we awaited, in the silence of profound anxiety, for news of what had happened to my father.

Returning to him, I must resume at the moment when he passed through the door which was then locked against us. As soon as he thought the danger passed the king dismissed his suite, so that no one was with him but my Aunt Élisabeth, [Maréchal de Mouchy (who in spite of his 77 years and my father's order persisted in remaining), two old ushers, the brave Acloque, commander of the division of the National Guard, an example of fidelity in the uniform of rebellion],[1] and M. d'Hervilly, lieutenant-colonel of the new King's-Guard, who, seeing the danger, ran to call the Guard and collected about twenty grenadiers, but on reaching the staircase he found only six had followed; the others had abandoned him. My father was therefore almost alone when the door was forced in by one *sapeur*, axe in hand raised to strike him, but [here] by his coolness and imperturbable courage my father so awed the assassin that the weapon fell from his hand,— an event almost incomprehensible. It is said that some one cried out: " Unhappy man, what are you about to do?" and that those words petrified him; for my part I think that what restrained that wretch was Divine Providence and the ascendancy that virtue always maintains over crime.

The blow having thus failed, the other accomplices, seeing that their leader had let himself be cowed, dared not execute their evil designs. Of all this mass of the populace, there were certainly very few who knew precisely what they were expected to do. To each had been given twenty sous and a musket; they were sent in drunk with orders to insult us in every imaginable way. Their leader, Santerre, had brought them as far as the courtyard, and there he awaited the success of his enterprise. He was desperate on learning that his stroke had missed, and he came near being killed himself by a man in the château, who aimed for him,

---

[1] This entire passage was rewritten, corrected, and the additions made by Louis XVIII.— FR. ED.

and was prevented from shooting only by remonstrances as to the danger to which he exposed my father; for if Santerre were sacrificed the brigands would surely avenge him.

My father was nevertheless obliged to allow all these wretches to go through the rooms of the château, and, standing himself in a window with my aunt, he watched them pass before him and heard the insults with which they overwhelmed him. It was on this horrible day that my father and my aunt each made a memorable speech. At the moment of the greatest danger a soldier came up to the king and said to him, "Sire, fear nothing." My father took his hand and laid it on his own heart. "Does it beat hard, grenadier?" he said. Shortly before, my Aunt Élisabeth, being mistaken for the queen, saw herself exposed to the utmost fury of the brigands; some one near was about to make her known. "Do not undeceive them," cried my aunt with sublime devotion.

This dreadful situation lasted from half-past three in the afternoon till eight at night. Pétion, mayor of Paris, arrived, pretending to be much astonished on hearing of the danger the king had run. In haranguing the people he had the impudence to say: "Return to your homes with the same dignity with which you came." The Assembly, seeing that the stroke had missed, changed its tone, pretended to have been ignorant of everything, and sent deputation after deputation to the king expressing the grief it feigned to feel for his danger.

Meantime my mother, who, as I said, could not rejoin the king, and was in her apartment with my brother and me, was a long time without hearing any news. At last, the minister of war came to tell her that my father was well; he urged her to leave the room where we then were, as it was not safe, and we therefore went into the king's little bedchamber. We were scarcely there before the rioters entered the apartment we had just left. The room in which we now were had three doors: one by which we had entered, another opening upon a private staircase, a third communicating with the Council Chamber. They were all three locked, but the first two were attacked, one by the wretches who were pursuing us, the other by men who came up the little staircase, where we heard their shouts and the blows of their axes.

In this close danger my mother was perfectly calm; she placed my brother behind every one and near the door of the Council Chamber, which was still safe, then she placed herself at the head of us all. Soon we heard some one at the door of the Council Chamber begging to enter. It was one of my brother's servants, pale as death, who said only these few words: "Madame, escape! the villains are following me." At the same instant, the other doors were forced in. In this crisis my mother hastily ordered the third door opened and passed into the Council Chamber, where there were, already, a number of the National Guard and a crowd of wretches.

My mother said to the soldiers that she came to take refuge with her son among them. The soldiers instantly surrounded us; a large table standing in the middle of the Chamber, served my mother to lean upon, my brother was seated on it, and the brigands defiled past it to look at us. We were separated from my father by only two rooms, and yet it was impossible to join him, so great was the crowd. We were therefore obliged to stay there and listen to all the insults that these wretches said to us as they passed. A half clothed woman dared to come to the table with a *bonnet rouge* in her hand and my mother was forced to let her place it on her son's head; as for us, we were obliged to put cockades on our heads. It was, as I have said, about eight o'clock when this dreadful procession of rioters ceased to pass and we were able to rejoin my father and aunt. No one can imagine our feelings at that reunion; they were such that even the deputies from the Assembly were touched. My brother was overcome with fatigue and they put him to bed. We stayed together for a time, the room being full of deputies. An hour later they went away, and about eleven o'clock, after having passed a most terrible day, we separated to get some rest. . . .

The next day Pétion came again to play the hypocrite, saying he had heard of more assemblings of the people and he had hastened to defend the king. My father ordered him to be silent; but as he still tried to protest his attachment, my father said: "Be silent, monsieur; I know your thoughts."

Massacre at the Tuileries; Dethronement of my Father. The Days from the 10th to the 13th of August, 1792.

After the fatal epoch of June 20, my family no longer enjoyed any tranquillity; every day there were fresh alarms, and rumours that the faubourgs Saint Antoine and Saint Marceau [together with those wretches who were called the Marseillais] were marching against the château. Sometimes they sounded the tocsin and beat the *générale*; sometimes, under pretext of a dinner of confraternity, they invited [and worked upon] the sections of opposite opinions to demand the dethronement of the king, which Danton, Robespierre, and their party wanted at all costs. After these many preludes, we heard with certainty on the 9th of August that the populace, armed, was assembling to attack the

Tuileries; it was already evening. The troops who remained faithful to my father were therefore hastily collected, among them the Swiss Guard; and a great number of the nobles who were [still] in Paris arrived [in haste]. Imagine the situation of my unhappy parents during that horrible night; they remained together [expecting only carnage and death], and my mother had ordered my brother and me to go to bed.

Pétion arrived about eleven o'clock, exclaiming loudly against this new tumult. My father treated him as he deserved and sent him away; nevertheless, malignant people spread the news that Pétion was kept prisoner in the Tuileries; [on which] minds grew [embittered and] inflamed even to fury, and at midnight the signal was given to begin the dreadful massacre. The first shot fired killed M. Clermont-Tonnerre, a member of the First Assembly. For a part of the night the tumult went on outside the Tuileries, where fresh reinforcements of the National Guard were successively arriving; unfortunately, [far] too many came, for most of them were already seduced and treacherously inclined.

At six in the morning it was suggested to my father to visit all the posts and encourage the troops to defend him; but only a few cries of *Vive le Roi!* were heard in the court-yards, and what was worse, when he wished to enter the garden, the artillery-men, most wicked of all, dared to turn their cannon against their king; a thing not believable if I did not declare that I saw it with my own eyes.

My father, having thus indubitably recognized the bad disposition of the National Guard, saw but too well that no faithful subjects remained about him, except a few nobles who had come to us, a part of the servants of the château, and the Swiss Guard; they all armed themselves. M. Mandat, commandant of the National Guard in the Tuileries [a man of little enterprise but faithful], was summoned by the mayor to the Hôtel de Ville; there he was murdered by order of the municipality, who immediately appointed Santerre to replace him. Towards seven in the morning Rœderer, head of the department, arrived. He asked to speak alone with the king; there, he threw himself at his feet and conjured him to save himself; he represented to him that furious brigands were arriving in masses, that he had too few persons to defend him, that he had no course left but to go, he and his family, and take refuge in the National Assembly. My father rejected the idea for a long time, but Rœderer insisting, and the peril becoming urgent and inevitable, he at last resolved to go to the Assembly with his family, Mme. de Lamballe, and Mme. de Tourzel. He left all the rest of his people in the château, not doubting that as soon as it was known that he had gone, the tumult would cease and there would be no longer any danger for those he left there.[1]

We crossed the garden of the Tuileries in the midst of a few National guards, who still remained faithful. On the way we were told that the Assembly would not receive my father. The terrace of the Feuillants, along which we had to pass, was full of wretches, who assailed us with insults; one of them cried out: "No women, or we will kill them all!" My mother was not frightened at the threat and continued her way. At last we entered the passage to the Assembly. Before being admitted [to the hall] we had to wait more than half an hour, a number of deputies still

[1] To this Louis XVIII. adds in a footnote: "After the words 'the rest of his people' [*son monde*] should be added: 'and the ladies, among whom were Mmes. de Tarente, de Duras, de la Rocheaymon, etc., who stayed there by his order.' I mention these ladies here all the more willingly because I am certain they were there. I add 'by his order,' 1st, because it is true; 2d, because it explains why so few persons followed the king and queen to the Assembly." — TR.

opposing our entrance. We were thus kept in a narrow corridor, so dark that we could see nothing, and hear nothing but the shouts of the furious mob. My father, my mother, and my brother were in front with Mme. de Tourzel; my aunt was with me, on the other side. I was held by a man whom I did not know. I have never thought myself so near death, not doubting that the decision was made to murder us all. In the darkness I could not see my parents, and I feared everything for them. We were left to this mortal agony more than half an hour.

At last we were allowed to enter the hall of the Assembly, and my father on entering said [in a loud voice] that he came to take refuge with his family in the bosom of the Assembly, to prevent the French nation from committing a great crime. We were placed at the bar, and they then discussed whether it was proper that my father should be present at their deliberations. They said, as to that, that it was impossible to let him stay at the bar without infringing on the inviolability of the sovereign people; and they declaimed speeches thereon which were full of horrors. After this they took us into the box of a journalist.

We had hardly entered this species of cage when we heard cannon, musket-shots, and the cries of those who were murdering in the Tuileries; but we were ignorant at the time of what was happening. We heard later how the massacre began. My father had hardly left the château before a party of wretches [already in the courtyards] began to attack with *armes blanches* [sabres and pikes] the Swiss Guard, who fired in self-defence. Nothing more was needed to push their fury to the highest point; those who were outside hearing the Swiss fire first, and taking them for the aggressors, spread the rumour that my father had ordered them to fire on the people. Soon, not only the courtyard gates but those of the château were forced, and these madmen rushed in, massacring all whom they found, especially the Swiss. [Then and there perished an immensity of faithful servitors of all ranks and all classes. Among the victims were MM. de Clermont d'Amboise and de Castéja, de Viomesnil and d'Hervilly; the Maréchal de Mailly, MM. de Maillardoz and de Bachmann died later. All the old officers of the Guard called "constitutional," the two battalions of the Filles-St.-Thomas and the Petits-Pères distinguished themselves by an unbounded devotion, though, unhappily, fruitless. What could they do against a multitude maddened with drink and blood and fury?] The Tuileries then became a spectacle of horror; blood ran everywhere, especially in the apartments of the king and queen. Nevertheless, in the midst of these abominations some traits of humanity were shown; among these monsters were some who saved several persons, taking them by the arm and making them pass for their friends or relatives. The carnage lasted all that day on one side or the other; the number of brigands who perished was considerable, for those wretches killed each other in their blind fury. At night, the château took fire; fortunately, the flames lasted but a little while, and so ended those awful and too memorable scenes.

Meantime our terrors increased as these dreadful noises went on; but it was even worse when we heard the same sort of cries close to the Assembly. The members themselves were frightened, and in their fear they tore out the iron railing of the box where we were and forced my father into the midst of them; but this tumult was soon appeased. It was occasioned by the approach of a number of the Swiss Guard who had escaped from the Tuileries and were trying to come to the support of the king; they had almost forced the door of the Assembly when an officer said to them:

"What are you doing? The king is in the midst of assassins; they will murder him if you advance." This reflection held them back and they surrendered; it was thus that these brave foreigners [ever faithful], to the number of about one hundred, escaped the massacre. As for those of their compatriots who did not perish in the Tuileries, they were taken to the Hôtel-de-Ville and there massacred with their principal officers. A forged order from the king was sent to summon the Swiss Guard from the barracks at Courbevoie; on their arrival in Paris they met the same fate.

Still kept in the box at the Assembly, we witnessed the horrors of all kinds which there took place. Sometimes they assailed my father and all his family with [the basest and most atrocious] insults, triumphing over him with cruel joy; sometimes they brought in gentlemen dying of their wounds; sometimes they brought my father's own servants, who, with the utmost impudence, gave false testimony against him; while others boasted of what they had done. At last, to complete the revolting scene, they brought in the Host and flung the sacred wafers on the ground. It was in the midst of these abominations that our entire day, from eight in the morning until midnight, passed [as one may say] through all gradations of whatever was most terrible, most awful.

The session ended by [a decree full of insults to my father, declaring the king suspended from his functions and ordering the convocation of a National Convention. They next wished to take up the fate of my brother; they proposed to appoint his governor, and even to make him king; but the latter motion was rejected, and that of giving him a governor was adjourned until the Convention should declare whether the Nation desired to still have a king]. At last they permitted us, about one at night to retire to one of the little rooms near-by, in the convent of the Feuillants; there we were left alone [without the slightest defence against the sanguinary rage of these wretches]. The next day, several persons belonging to my father's service came to us. We were forced to return again to the Assembly and spend the whole day there while they discussed what should be done with the king, and where he should be kept. The Place Vendôme, in which is the Chancellerie, was proposed for this purpose, on which Manuel, public prosecutor for the Commune of Paris, demanded, in the name of his constituents, to be intrusted with the responsibility of keeping my father and his family; and this being granted, he proposed the château of the Temple for our residence, which was decreed.

That day and the next were passed like the preceding day; we were forced to listen in the hall of the Assembly to the prowess of those who had distinguished themselves by their barbarities. At night we returned to our rooms, [where we were not allowed to enjoy in peace the hours consecrated to rest], a deputy of the Assembly coming an hour after midnight to search and see if we had men hidden there; none were found, for my father had been obliged to send away those who had come to him. On the 12th it was determined that we should be transferred to the Temple on the following day.

On the 13th we did not go to the Assembly. Towards three in the afternoon Pétion and Manuel came to take my father, and they made us all get into a carriage with eight seats, into which they got themselves [with their hats on their heads and shouting, *Vive la Nation!*]. We drove through the streets leading to the Temple in great peril and loaded with insults; our conductors themselves feared the people so much that they would not let the carriage stop for a moment; and yet it took two hours before we could reach the Temple through that immense throng. On the way they had the cruelty to point out to my parents things that would distress them, — the statues of the Kings of France thrown down, even that of Henri IV., before which the populace compelled us to stop, to make us look at him on the ground. We did not observe on our way any feeling souls touched by our condition, such terror was now inspired in those who still thought rightly. And yet, in the midst of so many sights which might well break down the strongest soul, my father and my mother preserved the tranquillity and courage that a good conscience can alone inspire.

Imprisonment of my Family in the Tower of the Temple, August 13, 1792, *followed by the Trial and Martyrdom of my Father, January* 21, 1793.[1]

On arriving at the Temple on Monday, August 13th, 1792, at six o'clock in the evening, the artillery-men under Santerre wished to take my father to the Tower and leave us in the château. Manuel had received on the way a decree of the Commune designating the Tower as our common prison. However, they calmed the artillery-men and we entered the château first, where the municipal guards kept my father and all of us within sight. An hour later, Pétion went away and my father supped with us. At eleven, my brother dying with sleep, Mme. de Tourzel took him to the Tower, where we were all to go, although nothing had been prepared to receive us. My father was surrounded by the municipal guards, drunk and insolent, who sat down beside him, and talked in a loud voice without the slightest regard to him. At one o'clock we were at last taken over to the Tower, where Manuel, as secretary-general of the

[1] Here begins the part she wrote in the Tower. — Tr.

Commune, committed us. He was ashamed himself, to find this lodging bare of everything, and such that my aunt was reduced to sleep in the kitchen for several nights.

The persons who were shut up with us in this fatal place were the Princesse de Lamballe, Mme. de Tourzel and her daughter Pauline, M. de Chamilly, my father's head *valet de chambre*, M. Huë, in the service of my brother, Mmes. Cimbris, Thibaut, Navarre, and Bazire, waiting-women to my brother, my mother, my aunt, and myself. My father was lodged above on the third floor of the building adjacent to the main body of the Tower; having a municipal guard in his room. My aunt occupied a kitchen with Mlle. de Tourzel and Mme. Navarre; my mother lodged below in a salon, with me and afterwards Mme. de Lamballe; and in a third room was my brother with Mme. de Tourzel his governess, and his maid, Mme. Cimbris; this was a billiard-room. Mmes. Thibaut and Bazire slept below. In the kitchen of the château, destined for our service, were Turgy, Chrétien, and Marchand, men long attached to the king's household, who brought the dishes for our meals to the Tower.

The next day my father came to breakfast at nine o'clock in my mother's room, and afterwards we all went together to look over the Tower, because they wanted to make bedchambers of the great rooms. We returned to dine on the first floor in a room adjoining the library. After dinner, Manuel and Santerre commander of the National Guard, came to the Tower, and my father went to walk with them in the garden. On our arrival the previous day they had demanded the departure of the women who were in our service, and we even found new women chosen by Pétion waiting to serve us, but they were not accepted. The day but one after, during our dinner, they brought us a decree of the Commune ordering that our women and even the ladies should be removed. My father opposed this vehemently and so did the municipal guards, which annoyed those who had brought the order. We were each asked privately if we did not wish for others; on which, having all responded no, things remained as they were.

From this time we were busy in regulating our hours. We passed the whole day together; my father taught my brother geography and history; my mother made him learn and recite verses; my aunt taught him arithmetic. Fortunately there was a Library adjoining our apartments [that of the guard of the Archives of Malta], where my father found an agreeable diversion; my mother, my aunt, and I often did worsted-work.

My father asked for a man and woman to do the rough work, and a few days later they sent a man named Tison and his wife. The guards became daily more uncivil and insolent, and they never left us one instant alone, either when we were together or separate. Mme. de Lamballe was allowed to write to the outside and ask for the things she needed, but always in open letters read by the municipals. At last, during the night of the 19th and 20th of August, they brought and read in all our rooms a decree of the Commune removing from the Tower all persons who were not of the royal family. They ordered Mme. de Lamballe to rise. My mother tried to oppose it by urging that she was her relative, but in vain; they replied that they had orders to take her away and question her. Obliged to submit, we all rose, with death in our hearts, to bid these ladies farewell [an eternal farewell to the Princesse de Lamballe, and it seemed as if we had a presentiment of her horrible fate. MM. de Chamilly and Huë were also taken away]; our waiting-women were prevented from taking leave of us.

Every one having gone, my brother was left alone in his room, and they brought him, still asleep, into that of my mother where two municipals were on guard. Unable to go to sleep again, even my brother who was awakened by the noise, we passed the night together; my father, though awakened, remained in his room with a municipal. The men who took away the ladies assured us they would return after their examination, but we learned the next day that they had been taken to the prison of La Force. M. Huë, however, returned at nine o'clock the next morning; the Council, having judged him innocent, sent him back to the Temple.

My mother, left thus alone, took charge of my brother, who slept in her room; I went to occupy the billiard-room with my aunt, and the municipal kept himself during the day in the queen's room and at night with the sentinel in the little room between us. My father remained above, where he slept; we went up to breakfast with him while they cleaned my mother's chamber, after which my father came down and spent the entire day with us.

The 24th, towards one in the morning, they came to search my father's room under pretence of looking for arms, and they took away his sword. The next day, the day of Saint-Louis, they shouted the "Ça ira" close by the Temple. We then heard that M. de la Fayette [having ended his rôle], had abandoned the army and quitted France, which news was confirmed to my father that evening by Manuel, who at the same time brought a letter, which had been opened, to my Aunt Élisabeth from my great-aunts in Rome; this was the last that my family received from without. Not only was my father no longer treated as king, but he was not even treated with simple respect; he was not called Sire or Your Majesty, but merely Monsieur, or Louis; the municipal guards sat down in his room, their hats on their heads. It was then that Pétion sent Cléry for the service of my brother, to which he already belonged; and he installed as jailers or turnkeys of the Tower two men named Risbey and Rocher. The latter was the horrible man who on the 20th of June had forced my father's door and tried to kill him. This monster roamed around us continually with dreadful glances; he never ceased torturing my father in every possible way; sometimes he sang the Carmagnole, and other such horrors; at other times he puffed the smoke of his pipe into my father's face as he passed, knowing that he disliked the smell of it; at night when we went to supper, as we were obliged to pass through his room, he was always in his bed, and sometimes he would be there at our dinner hour, pretending to sleep; in short there was no kind of insult and insolence he did not invent to torment us.

Meantime the king lacked everything; he therefore wrote to Pétion to obtain the money which was intended for him; but he received no answer and our discomforts were multiplied daily. The garden, the only place where my father could take the air, was full of workmen, who insulted us to such a point that one of them boasted he would knock off my mother's head, but Pétion had him arrested. Even at the windows on the street which looked into the garden, people came expressly to insult us. On the 2d of September, as we were walking there towards four in the afternoon, not knowing what was going on outside, a woman stood at one of those windows who loaded my father with insults and dared to assail him with stones which fell beside him; another of those windows offered us at the same moment a very touching contrast. How precious to the unfortunate is a mark of interest! A woman, not less feeling than courageous, having written on a large card the news of the taking of Verdun by the coalition army, held it towards us at a window long enough for us to read it, which my aunt did without the municipals perceiving it.

We had hardly rejoiced at the news when a new municipal arrived, named Matthieu [a former capuchin monk]. Inflamed with anger he came to my father and told him to follow him, which we all did, fearing that they meant to separate us. Going upstairs we met M. Huë, and Matthieu told him he arrested him; . . . then, turning to my father, he said all that fury could suggest, and especially these words: "The *générale* is beaten, the cannon of warning is fired, the tocsin is sounding, the enemies are at Verdun, if they come we shall all perish, but you the first." My father listened to his threats firmly, with the calm of innocence, but my brother, terrified, burst into tears and ran into the next room, where I followed him and did my best to console him, but in vain; he imagined he saw my father dead. Meantime, M. Huë having returned, Matthieu, continuing his insults, took him away with him and shut him up in the prison of the Mairie, instead of that of the Abbaye where he was to have gone, but the massacre of that day had already begun there . . . We heard that in the end he was set at liberty, but he never returned to the Temple.

The municipals all condemned the violent conduct of Matthieu, but they did not do better. They told my father they were certain the King of Prussia was on the march and killing all Frenchmen by an order signed Louis. There were no calumnies they did not invent, even the most ridiculous and the most incredible. My mother, who could not sleep, heard the *générale* beaten all night.

September 3d at eight in the morning, Manuel came to see my father, and assured him that Mme. dè Lamballe and the other persons taken from the Temple were well and all together, tranquilly, in La Force. At three in the afternoon we heard dreadful outcries; my father left the dinner-table and played backgammon with my mother, to control his countenance and be able to say a few words to her without being heard. The municipal guard in the room behaved well; he closed the door and window, also the curtains, so that they might see nothing. The workmen at the Temple and the jailer Rocher joined the murderers, which increased the noise. Several officers of the National Guard and some municipals arrived; the first desired that my father should show himself at the window. The municipals fortunately opposed this; but my father, having asked what was happening, a young officer replied: "Well, if you want to know, it is the head of Mme. de Lamballe they wish to show you." My mother was seized with horror; that was the sole moment when her firmness abandoned her. The municipals scolded the officer, but my father, with his usual kindness, excused him, saying it was not the officer's fault, but his own for having questioned him. The noise lasted till five o'clock.

We learned that the people had tried to force the gates; that the municipals had prevented it by tying across the door a tricolour scarf; and that finally they had allowed six of the murderers to enter and walk round our prison with the head of Mme. de Lamballe, but on condition that they left the body, which they wanted to drag round, at the gate. When this deputation entered, Rocher uttered shouts of joy on seeing the head of Mme. de Lamballe, and scolded a young man who was taken ill, so horrified was he at the sight.

The tumult was hardly over before Pétion, instead of exerting himself to stop the massacre, coldly sent his secretary to my father to reckon about money. This man was very ridiculous, and said many things which would have made us laugh at another moment; he thought my mother remained standing on his account; for since that awful scene she had continued standing, motionless, and seeing nothing that took place in the room. The municipal guard who had sacrificed his scarf at the door made my father pay for it. My aunt and I heard the *générale* beaten all night; my unhappy mother did not even try to sleep; we listened to her sobs. We did not suppose that the massacre was still going on; it was not until some time later that we learned it had lasted three days.

It is impossible to give all the scenes that took place, as much on the part of the municipals as on that of the National Guard; everything alarmed them, so guilty did they feel themselves. Once, during supper, there was a cry to arms; it was thought that the foreigners were arriving; the horrible Rocher took a sabre and said to my father, "If they come I will kill you." It was only some trouble with the patrols. Their severity increased daily. Nevertheless, we found two municipals who softened the misery of my parents by showing them kind feeling and giving them hope. I fear they are dead. There was also a sentinel who had a conversation with my aunt through the keyhole. That unfortunate man wept all the time he was near us in the Temple. I know not what became of him; may heaven have rewarded his attachment to his king.

When I took lessons and my mother prepared extracts for me, a municipal was always there, looking over my shoulder, believing that there must be conspiracy. The newspapers were not allowed us for fear we should know the foreign news; but one day they brought a copy to my father telling him he would find something interesting in it. Oh, horror! he there read that they would make a cannon-ball of his head. The calm and contemptuous silence of my father damped the joy they had shown in bringing him that infernal writing. One evening a municipal, on arriving, uttered many threats and insults, and repeated what we had already heard, that we should all perish if the enemy approached Paris; he added that my brother alone caused him pity, but, being the son of a tyrant, he must die. Such were the scenes that my family had to bear daily.

The Republic was established September 22, they told us joyfully; they also told us of the departure of the foreign army; we could not believe it, but it was true.

At the beginning of October, they took away from us pens, paper, ink, and pencils; they searched everywhere, and even harshly. This did not prevent my mother and me from hiding our pencils, which we kept; my father and aunt gave up theirs. The evening of the same day, as my father was finishing supper, they told him to wait; that he was going into another lodging in the Great Tower, and would in future be separated from us. At this dreadful news my mother lost her usual courage and firmness. We parted from him with many tears, still hoping, however, to see him again. The next day they brought our breakfast separately from his; my mother would eat nothing. The municipals, frightened and troubled by her gloomy grief, allowed us to see my father, but only at meals, forbidding us to speak in low tones or in foreign languages, but "aloud and in good French." We then went to dine with my father in great joy at seeing him again; but a municipal was there who perceived that my aunt spoke low to my father, and he made her a scene. At night, my brother being in bed, either my mother or my aunt stayed with him, while the other went with me to sup with my father. In the mornings we stayed with him after breakfast long enough for Cléry to comb our hair, because he was not allowed to come to my mother's room, and this gave us a short time longer to be with my father. We went to walk together daily at midday.

Manuel came to see my father and took away from him harshly his *cordon rouge* (order of Saint-Louis), and assured him that none of those who had been at the Temple, excepting Mme. de Lamballe, had perished. He made Cléry, Tison, and his wife take an oath to be faithful to the nation. A municipal, coming in one evening, woke my brother roughly to see if he was there; this was the only moment of anger which I saw my mother show. Another municipal told my mother that it was not Pétion's purpose to have my father die, but to shut him up for life with my brother in the castle of Chambord. I do not know what object that man had in giving us this information; we never saw him again. My mother was now lodged on the floor above my father's apartment in the great Tower, and my brother slept in my father's chamber, also Cléry and a municipal guard. The windows were secured by iron bars and shutters; the chimneys smoked much.

Here is how the days of my parents were passed. My father rose at seven o'clock and prayed to God till eight. Then he dressed, and so did my brother, till nine, when they came to breakfast with my mother. After breakfast, my father gave my brother lessons until eleven o'clock; the latter played till midday, when we all went to walk together, no matter what the weather was, because the guard, which was changed at that hour, wished to see us and be certain of our presence in the Tower; the walk lasted till two o'clock, when we dined. After dinner my father and mother played backgammon or piquet, or, to speak more correctly, pretended to play so as to be able to say a few words to each other. At four o'clock my mother went up with us to her own room and took my brother, because the king usually went to sleep at that hour. At six my brother went down. My father made him study and play till supper-time. At nine o'clock, after that meal, my mother undressed him quickly and put him to bed. We went up then to our room, but the king did not go to bed till eleven o'clock. My mother did a great deal of tapestry-work, and made me study and often read aloud. My aunt prayed to God; she read many books of piety; often the queen begged her to read them aloud.

The newspapers were now returned to us in order that we might see the departure of the foreigners and read the horrors about the king of which they were full. A municipal said to us one day: "Mesdames, I announce to you good news; many of the *émigrés*, those traitors, have been taken; if you are patriots you will rejoice." My mother, as usual, said not a word and did not even seem to hear him; often her contemptuous calmness and her dignified bearing awed these men; it was rarely to her that they addressed themselves.

The Convention came for the first time to see the king. The members who composed the deputation asked him if he had any complaints to make; he said no, he was satisfied, so long as he was with his family. Cléry complained that they did not pay the dealers who provided for the Temple. Chabot answered: "La nation n'est pas à un écu près." The deputies present were Chabot, Dupont, Drouet, and Lecointe-Puyraveau. They came back, after dinner, and asked the same questions. The next day Drouet came back alone and asked the queen if she had any complaints to make. My mother made him no answer. Some days later, as we were at dinner, the guards threw themselves roughly on Cléry and ordered him to follow them to the tribunal. Not long before, Cléry, coming down the staircase with a municipal, met a young man of his acquaintance who was on guard; they said good-day to each other and shook hands; the municipal thought that wrong and arrested the young man. It was to appear with him before the tribunal that Cléry was now taken. My father asked that he should return; the municipals assured him that he would not return; nevertheless he was back at midnight. He asked the king's pardon for his past conduct, which my father's manner, the exhortations of my aunt, and the sufferings of my relations made him change; after that he was very faithful.

My father fell ill with a heavy cold; they granted him a doctor and his apothecary. The Commune was uneasy; it had bulletins every day of his health, which was soon reestablished. The whole family were ill of this cold; but my father was more ill than the rest.

The Commune changed on the 2d of December. The new municipals came to inspect my father and his family at ten o'clock at night. Some days later they issued an order to turn Tison and Cléry out of our apartments and to take away from us knives, scissors, and all sharp instruments; they also ordered that our dishes should be tasted before they were served to us. The search was made for the sharp instruments, and my mother and I gave up our scissors.

December 11th we were made very anxious by the beating of drums and the arrival of a guard at the Temple. My father came with my brother to breakfast. At eleven o'clock Chambon and Chaumette, one the mayor, the other the public prosecutor of the Commune of Paris, and Colombeau their clerk, went to my father's apartment. There they informed him of a decree of the Convention which ordered him to be brought to its bar to be interrogated. They requested him to send my brother to my mother; but not having with them the decree of the Convention, they kept my father waiting two hours, so that he did not start till one o'clock, in the mayor's carriage, with Chaumette and Colombeau; the carriage was escorted by municipals on foot. My father observing that Colombeau bowed to many persons, asked him if they were all his friends; to which he answered: "They are the brave citizens of August 10th, whom I never see without joy."

I shall not speak of my father's conduct before the Convention; all the world knows it; his firmness, his gentleness, his kindness, his courage, amid assassins thirsting for his blood, are traits which will never be forgotten and which the most remote posterity will admire.

The king returned at six o'clock to the Tower of the Temple. We had been in a state of anxiety which it is impossible to express. My mother made every effort with the municipals who guarded her to learn what was happening; it was the first time that she deigned to question them. These men would tell her nothing, and it was only after my father's return that we heard the facts. As soon as he had returned she asked urgently to see him; she even sent to Chambon to ask it, but received no reply. My brother spent the night in her room; he had no bed, she gave him hers and remained up all night in a gloom so great that we did not like to leave her, but she forced us to go to bed, my aunt and me. The next day she again asked to see my father and to read the journals to learn about his trial; she insisted that at least, if she might not see my father, permission should be granted to my brother and me. This request was taken to the Council general; the newspapers were refused; they permitted my brother and me to see my father, but only on condition that we should be absolutely separated from my mother. They informed my father of this, and he said that, however great his pleasure might be in seeing his children, the great business in which he was now engaged would not allow him to occupy himself with his son, and that his daughter must not leave her mother. They then brought my brother's bed into my mother's room.

The Convention came to see my father; he asked for counsel, ink, paper, and razors with which to shave; all of which were granted to him. MM. de Malesherbes, Tronchet, and Desèze, his counsel, came to him; he was often obliged, in order to speak to them without being heard, to go with them into the little *tourelle*. He no longer went into the garden, neither did we; he heard no news of us, nor we of him, unless through the municipals, and then with difficulty. I had trouble in my foot, and my father, hearing of it, grieved about it with his customary kindness, and inquired carefully about my condition. My family found in this Commune a few charitable men, who, by their kind feeling, soothed our torture; they assured my mother that my father would not be put to death, that his case would be sent to the primary assemblies, which would certainly save him. Alas! they deceived themselves, or from pity endeavoured to deceive my mother. On the 26th of December, Saint-Stephen's day, my father made his will, because he expected to be murdered that day on his way to the bar of the Convention. He went there, nevertheless, with his usual calmness, and left to M. Desèze the care of his defence. He went at eleven and returned at three o'clock.

On the 18th of January, 1793, the day on which the verdict was given, the municipals entered the king's room at eleven o'clock, saying they had orders not to let him out of sight. He asked if his fate were decided; they answered no. The next morning M. de Malesherbes came to tell him that his sentence was pronounced. "But, sire," he added, "those wretches are not yet masters; all honest men will now come forward to save Your Majesty or perish at your feet." "M. de Malesherbes," said my father, "that would compromise many persons and bring civil war into France. I would rather die. I beg you to order them from me to make no movement to save me; the king does not die in France." After this last conference he was not allowed to see his counsel; he gave the municipals a note asking to see them, and complaining of the restraint he was under in being watched incessantly; no attention was paid to this.

Sunday, January 20, Garat, minister of justice, came to notify him that his sentence of death would be executed on the morrow; my father listened with courage and religion. He asked a respite of three days, to know what would become of his family, and to obtain a Catholic confessor. The respite was refused. Garat assured my father that there was no charge against his family and they would all be sent out of the country. He asked for a confessor, the Abbé Edgeworth de Firmont, whose address he gave. Garat brought him. The king dined as usual, which surprised the municipals, who expected that he would wish to kill himself.

We learned the sentence pronounced upon my father on that Sunday, the 20th, from the news criers, who came to shout it under our windows. At seven in the evening, a decree of the Convention arrived, permitting us to go to my father; we hurried there and found him much changed. He wept for sorrow over us, and not from fear of death; he related his trial to my mother, excusing the wretches who caused his death; he told her that it was proposed to appeal to the primary assemblies, but he opposed it, because that measure would bring trouble into the State. He then gave religious instruction to my brother, told him above all to pardon those who were putting him to death, and gave him his blessing; also to me. My mother ardently desired that we should pass the night with him; he refused, making her feel that he had need of tranquillity. She begged him at least to let us come the next morning; he granted that to her; but as soon as we were gone he told the guard not to let us come again, because our presence pained him too much. He remained after that with his confessor, went to bed at midnight, and slept till five o'clock, when he was wakened by the drums. At six o'clock, the Abbé Edgeworth said mass, at which my father took the Communion.

He started about nine o'clock; as he went down the stairway he gave his will to a municipal; he also gave him a sum of money which M. de Malesherbes had brought to him, and requested the man to return it; but the municipals kept it for themselves. He next met a jailer, whom he had reproved rather sharply the evening before, and said to him: "Matthieu, I am sorry to have hurt you." He read the prayers for the dying on the way. Arriving at the scaffold, he wished to speak to the people, but Santerre prevented it by making the drums beat; the few words he was able to say were heard by a few persons only. He then removed his clothing himself, his hands were bound by his own handkerchief, and not with a rope. At the moment when he was about to die the abbé said to him: *Fils de Saint-Louis, montez au ciel* — "Son of Saint-Louis, ascend to heaven."

He received the death-blow at ten minutes past ten in the morning of January 21, 1793. Thus perished Louis XVI. King of France, aged thirty-nine years, five months, and three days, having reigned eighteen years. He had been in prison five months and eight days.

Such was the life of the king, my father, during his rigorous captivity, in which nothing was seen but piety, grandeur of soul, kindness, gentleness, courage, patience in supporting the most infamous treatment, the most horrible calumnies; mercy in pardoning with all his heart his murderers; love of God, of his family, of his people — a love of which he gave proofs with his last breath and for which he has gone to receive his reward in the bosom of an all-powerful and merciful God.

Life in the Tower of the Temple from the Death of Louis XVI. to that of the Queen, October 16, 1793.

The morning of that terrible day [of the king's death] we rose at six o'clock. The evening before my mother had scarcely strength enough to undress my brother and put him to bed; she then threw herself, dressed as she was, upon her bed, and we heard her through the night trembling with cold and sorrow. At a quarter past six they opened our door to look for a prayer-book for my father's mass; we thought we were to go to him, and we still had that hope until the cries of joy of a frenzied populace came to inform us that the crime was consummated. In the afternoon my mother asked to see Cléry, who was with my father to his last moments, thinking that perhaps he had charged him with messages for her. We desired this shock, in order to cause an outflow of her gloomy sorrow and relieve the suffocated condition in which we saw her. My father had, in fact, ordered Cléry to return to my unhappy mother his wedding-ring, adding that he parted from it only in parting with life; he also gave him a packet of my mother's hair and ours, saying they had been so dear to him that he had kept them till the last instant. The municipals informed us that Cléry was in a dreadful state, and in despair because they refused to let him see us. My mother charged them to make her request to the council general; she also asked for mourning clothes. Cléry passed another month in the Temple and was then discharged.

We now had a little more liberty, the guards thinking we were about to be sent away. But nothing was able to calm the anguish of my mother; we could make no hope of any sort enter her heart; she was indifferent whether she lived or died. She looked at us sometimes with a pity that made us shudder. Happily, grief increased my illness, and that occupied her. My own doctor, Brunier, and the surgeon La Caze were brought, and they cured me in a month.[1]

We were allowed to see the persons who brought our mourning, but only in presence of the municipals. My mother would no longer go down into the garden, because that obliged her to pass the door of my father's room, which pained her too much; but fearing that want of air might harm my brother and myself, she asked, in February, to go up upon the Tower, which was granted to her.

It was discovered that a sealed package in the room of the municipals, which contained the king's seal, his ring, and several other things, had been opened, the seals broken, and the contents carried away. The municipals were very uneasy; but finally they believed it had been done by a thief who knew that the seal with the arms of France was set in gold. The person who took those things was rightly intentioned; he was not a thief; he did it for the right, because my mother wished the seal and ring to be saved for her son. I know who that brave man was; but alas! he is dead, not because of this affair, but in consequence of

---

[1] The close air and confinement had produced boils which covered the whole body of *la petite Madame* as she was called. Soon after her father's death she came near dying, and a rumour of her death was generally believed. — TR.

another good action. I cannot name him, hoping that he may have intrusted those precious objects to some one else before he perished.[1]

Dumouriez having left France, our imprisonment became more restricted. They built a wall which separated us from the garden; they put shutters to the top of the Tower; and plugged all holes with care. On the 25th of March the chimney caught fire. That evening Chaumette, prosecutor of the Commune, came for the first time to see my mother, and he asked her if she desired anything. My mother asked only for a door of communication between her room and that of my aunt. (The two terrible nights we had passed in her room we had slept, my aunt and I, on one of her mattresses placed on the floor.) The municipals opposed that request; but Chaumette said that in my mother's feeble state it might be necessary for her health, and he would speak of it to the Council general. The next day he came back at ten in the morning with Pache, the mayor, and that dreadful Santerre, commander of the National Guard. Chaumette told my mother he had spoken to the Council of her request for a door, which was refused. She made no answer. Pache asked her if she had any complaints to make. My mother said, "No," and paid no further heed to him.

Some time later we found certain municipal guards who soothed our griefs a little by their kind feeling. We knew after a while, those with whom we had to do; especially my mother, who saved us several times from trusting to a false show of interest. There was also another man who

[1] The man was one of the municipals, named Toulan, who gave the seal and ring to Turgy, who took them to *Monsieur*, afterwards Louis XVIII. (See Appendix V.) Toulan was one of the nine municipals guillotined soon after the queen, for having conspired to help her. — Tr.

did services to my family. I know all those who took an interest in us; I do not name them, for fear of compromising them as things now are, but the recollection of them is graven on my heart; and if I can never show them my gratitude, God will reward them; but if the day comes when I can name them they will be loved and esteemed by all virtuous persons.[1]

Precautions redoubled; Tison was not allowed to see his daughter, and he became ill-tempered. One evening a person brought some articles for my aunt; he was angry that this man should be allowed to enter, and not his daughter; he said things which led Pache, who was below, to send for him. They asked him why he was so displeased. "At not seeing my daughter," he replied, " and because some of these municipals are behaving badly." (He had seen them speaking low to my mother and aunt.) They asked their names; he gave them, and declared that we had correspondence with the outside. To furnish proofs he said that one day my mother, on taking out her handkerchief, had let fall a pencil; and another day he had found wafers and a pen in a box in my aunt's room. After this denunciation, which he signed, they sent for his wife, who repeated the same thing; she accused several of the municipals, declared that we had had correspondence with my father during his trial, and denounced my doctor, Brunier (who treated me for trouble in my foot), for having brought us news. She signed all that, being led away by her husband; but, in the end, she had great remorse for it. That denunciation was made April 19; the next day she saw her daughter.

On the 20th, at half-past ten at night, my mother and I had just gone to bed when Hébert arrived with several other

[1] These men were Toulan, Lepître, Beugneau, Vincent, Bruno, Michonis, and Merle. — Fr. Ed.

municipals; we rose hastily. They read us a decree of the Convention' ordering that we be carefully searched, even to the mattresses. My poor brother was asleep; they pulled him roughly out of his bed, to search it; my mother held him, all shivering with cold. They took from my mother the address of a shop she had always kept, a stick of sealing-wax from my aunt, and from me a Sacred Heart of Jesus and a prayer for France. Their search did not end till four in the morning. They wrote a *procès-verbal* of all they found, and obliged my mother and aunt to sign it, threatening to carry us off, my brother and me, if they refused. They were furious at having found nothing but trifles. Three days later they returned, and demanded to see my aunt in private. They then questioned her on a hat they had found in her room; they wished to know whence it came, and how long she had had it, and why she had kept it. She answered that it had belonged to my father at the beginning of his imprisonment in the Temple; that she had asked for it, to preserve it for love of her brother. The municipals said they should take it away as a suspicious thing; my aunt insisted on keeping it, but was not allowed to do so. They forced her to sign her answer and they carried away the hat.

Every day my mother went up on the Tower to have us take the air. For some time past my brother had complained of a stitch in his side [*point de côté*]. May 6th, at seven in the evening, a rather strong fever seized him, with headache and the pain in his side. At first he could not lie down, for it suffocated him. My mother was uneasy and asked the municipals for a doctor. They assured her the illness was nothing and that her motherly tenderness was needlessly frightened. Nevertheless, they spoke to the Council and asked in my mother's name for Dr. Brunier. The Council laughed at my brother's illness, because Hébert had seen him five hours earlier without fever. They positively refused Brunier, whom Tison had recently denounced. Nevertheless, the fever became very strong. My aunt had the goodness to take my place in my mother's room, that I might not sleep in a fever atmosphere, and also that she might assist in nursing my brother; she took my bed, and I went to hers. The fever lasted several days, the attacks being worse at night.

Though my mother asked for a doctor, it was several days before her request was granted. At last, on a Sunday, Thierry, the physician of prisons, was appointed by the Commune to take care of my brother. As he came in the morning he found little fever, but my mother asked him to return in the afternoon, when he found it very high, and he disabused the municipals of the idea they had that my mother was anxious about nothing; he told them that, on the contrary, the matter was more serious than she thought. He had the kindness to go and consult Brunier about my brother's illness and the remedies that should be given to him, because Brunier knew his constitution, he being our physician from infancy. He gave him some remedies, which did him good. Wednesday, he made him take medicine, and that night I returned to sleep in my mother's room. She felt much uneasiness on account of that medicine, because the last time that my brother had been purged he had frightful convulsions and she feared he might have them again. She did not sleep all night. My brother, however, took his medicine, and it did him good without causing him any accidents. He still had attacks of fever from time to time and the stitch in his side continued. His health began from this time to change, and it was never restored; the want of air and exercise did him much harm, also the sort of life the poor child lived, in the midst of tears and shocks, alarm and continual terrors, at eight years of age.

May 31st we heard the *générale* beaten and the tocsin rung, but no one would tell us the cause of the uproar. The guards were forbidden to let us go up on the Tower to take the air; an order always given when Paris was in disturbance. At the beginning of June, Chaumette came with Hébert and asked my mother if she desired anything. She answered no, and paid no further attention to them. My aunt asked Hébert for my father's hat which he had taken away; he replied that the Council general did not see fit to return it to her. My aunt, seeing that Chaumette did not go away, and knowing how much my mother suffered inwardly from his presence, asked him why he had come and why he remained. He answered that he visited all the prisons, they were all equal, and therefore he came to the Temple. My aunt replied no, because, in some, persons were justly imprisoned, and others unjustly. Chaumette and Hébert were both drunk.

Mme. Tison became insane; she was anxious about my brother's illness and had long been tortured by remorse; she languished and would not take the air. One day she began to talk to herself. Alas! it made me laugh, and my poor mother, also my aunt, looked at me with satisfaction, as if my laughter did them good. But Mme. Tison's insanity increased; she talked aloud of her wrong-doings, of her denunciations, of the prison, of the scaffold, of the queen, of her own family, and of our sorrows; admitting that because of her bad deeds she was unworthy to approach my family. She thought that those whom she had denounced had perished. Every day she watched for the municipals whom she had accused; not seeing them she went to bed gloomy; there she had frightful dreams and uttered cries, which we heard. The municipals allowed her to see her daughter, whom she loved. One day the porter, who did not know of this permission, refused entrance to the daughter. The municipals, finding the mother desperate, sent for her at ten at night. That late hour alarmed the woman still more; she was very unwilling to go down, and said to her husband: "They are going to take us to prison." She saw her daughter, but could not recognize her. She went back with a municipal, but on the middle of the stairway she would neither go up nor down. The municipal alarmed, called others to make her go up; when there, she would not go to bed, but talked and shouted, which prevented my family from sleeping. The next day, the doctor saw her and found her quite mad. She was always on her knees to my mother, begging her forgiveness. It is impossible to have more pity than my mother and my aunt had for this woman, to whom assuredly they had no reason to feel kindly. They took care of her and encouraged her all the time she remained in the Temple in this state. They tried to calm her by the sincere assurance of their pardon. The next day the guards took her from the Tower and put her in the château of the Temple, but, her madness increasing, they removed her to the Hôtel-Dieu and put a woman to spy upon her and report the things she might let drop.

On the 3d of July, they read us a decree of the Convention ordering that my brother be separated from us and lodged in a more secure room in the Tower. Hardly had he heard it when he flung himself into his mother's arms uttering loud cries, and imploring not to be parted from her. My mother, on her side, was struck down by the cruel order; she would not give up her son, and defended, against the municipals, the bed on which she placed him. They, absolutely determined to have him, threatened to employ violence and to call up the guard. My mother told them they would have to kill her before they could tear her child from her. An hour passed in resistance on her part, in threats and insults from the municipals, in tears and efforts from all of us. At last they threatened my mother so positively to kill him and us also that she had to yield for love of us. We rose, my aunt and I, for my poor mother no longer had any strength, but after we had dressed him she took him and gave him into the hands of the municipals herself, bathing him with tears and foreboding that she would never see him again. The poor little boy kissed us all very tenderly and went away in tears with the municipals. My mother charged them to ask permission of the Council general to let her see her son, if only at meals, and they promised her to do so. She was overcome by the separation; but her anguish was at its height when she learned that Simon, a shoemaker, whom she had seen as a municipal, was intrusted with the care of the unfortunate child. She asked incessantly to see him, but could not obtain it; my brother, on his side, wept for two whole days, never ceasing to ask to see us.

The municipals no longer remained in my mother's room; we were locked in night and day and under bolts. This was a comfort, as it relieved us of the presence of such persons. The guards came only three times a day, to bring our meals and examine the windows to make sure that the bars were not cut. We had no one to wait upon us, but we liked this best; my aunt and I made the beds, and served my mother. In the cabinet in the *tourelle* was a narrow opening through which we could see my brother when he went up to the battlements, and the sole pleasure my mother had was to see him through that little chink as he passed in the distance. She stayed there for hours, watching for the instant when she could see the child; it was her sole hope, her sole occupation. She rarely heard news of him, whether from the municipals or from Tison, who sometimes saw Simon. Tison, to repair his past conduct, behaved better, and sometimes gave news to us.

As for Simon, he maltreated my brother beyond what we could have imagined, and all the more because the child wept at being parted from us; but at last he frightened him so much that the poor boy dared not shed tears. My aunt entreated Tison, and those who in pity gave us news of him, to conceal these horrors from my mother; she knew or suspected enough. The rumour ran that my brother had been seen on the boulevard; the guards, vexed at not seeing him, declared he was no longer in the Temple. Alas! we hoped this for a moment; but the Convention ordered him to be taken down into the garden that people might see him. There my brother, whom they had not had time to change entirely, complained of being separated from my mother, and asked to see the law that ordered it; but they made him hold his tongue. The members of the Convention, who had come to make certain of my brother's presence, went up to my mother. She complained to them of the cruelty shown in taking her son from her; they answered that it was thought necessary to take that measure. A new prosecutor-general also came to see us; his manners astonished us, in spite of all we had learned to expect from our troubles. From the moment that man entered until he left he did nothing but swear.

On the 2d of August, at two in the morning' they woke us up to read to my mother the decree of the Convention which ordered that, on the requisition of the prosecutor of the Commune, she should be taken to the Conciergerie in preparation for her trial. She listened to the reading of the decree without emotion, and without saying a single word.

My aunt and I asked at once to go with my mother, but this mercy was not granted to us. While she was making up a parcel of her clothes the municipals never left her; she was obliged to even dress herself before them. They asked for her pockets, which she gave them; they searched them and took all that was in them although there was nothing of importance. They made a packet of these articles and said they should send it to the revolutionary tribunal, where it would be opened before her. They left her only a handkerchief and a smelling-bottle, in the fear that she might be taken faint.

My mother, after tenderly embracing me and telling me to have courage, to take good care of my aunt, and to obey her as a second mother, repeated to me the same instructions that my father had given me; then throwing herself into my aunt's arms she commended her children to her. I answered nothing, so terrified was I at the idea that I saw her for the last time; my aunt said a few words to her in a low voice. Then my mother went away without casting her eyes upon us, fearing no doubt that her firmness might abandon her. She stopped once at the foot of the Tower, because the municipals had to make a *procès-verbal* to discharge the concierge from the care of her person. As she went out, she struck her head against the lintel of the door, not thinking to lower it. They asked her if she was hurt. "Oh, no," she said; "nothing can hurt me now."

She was put into a carriage with a municipal and two gendarmes. On reaching the Conciergerie they placed her in the dirtiest, dampest, most unwholesome room in the building. She was kept in sight by a gendarme, who never left her day or night. My aunt and I were inconsolable and we passed many days and nights in tears. They had, however, assured my aunt, when my mother was taken, that no harm would happen to her. It was a great consolation for me not to be parted from my aunt, whom I loved much; but alas! all is now changed, and I have lost her too!

The day after my mother's departure, my aunt asked urgently, in her name and mine, to be reunited with her; but she could not obtain it, nor even get any news of her. As my mother, who never drank anything but water, could not endure that of the Seine, which made her ill, we begged the municipals to send her that of Ville d'Avray, which was brought daily past the Temple. They consented, and got a decree in consequence; but another of their colleagues arrived just then and opposed it. A few days later, my mother, in order to get news of us, tried to send for some necessary articles, among others her knitting, for she had begun a pair of stockings for my brother. We sent it, together with all we could find of silks and wools, for we knew how she liked to be busy; she had a habit in former days of always being at work, except in her hours of public appearance. In this way, she had covered a vast quantity of furniture and had even made a carpet and a great deal of coarse-wool knitting of all kinds. We therefore collected all we could; but we learned afterwards that nothing had been given to her, fearing, they said, that she might do herself a harm with the knitting-needles.

Sometimes we heard news of my brother from the municipals; but that did not last long. We could hear him every day singing, with Simon, the Carmagnole, the air of the Marseillais, and other horrors. Simon made him wear the *bonnet rouge*, and a carmagnole, and sing at the windows to be heard by the Garde; he taught him to swear dreadful oaths against God, his family, and aristocrats. My mother, happily, did not hear these horrors; oh! my God, what harm they would have done her! Before her depart-ire, they had come for my brother's clothes; she said she hoped they would not take off his mourning; but the first thing Simon did was to take away his black coat. The change of life and his bad treatment made my brother ill towards the end of August. Simon made him eat horribly and forced him to drink much wine, which he detested. All this gave him fever; he took medicine which did him harm, and his health became wholly out of order. He grew extremely fat but did not grow taller. Simon, however, still took him on the Tower to get air.

At the beginning of September I had an illness which had no other cause than my anxiety about my mother's fate. I could not hear the drums without fearing another September 2d. We went up on the Tower daily. The municipals paid their visits punctually three times a day; but their severity did not prevent us from hearing news from without, especially of my mother, which we cared for most. In spite of all their efforts, we always found some good souls in whom we inspired interest. We learned that my mother was accused of having correspondence with the outside. Immediately we threw away our writings, pencils, everything we still kept, fearing that they might make us undress before Simon's wife and that the things we had might compromise my mother; for we had always kept paper, ink, pens, and pencils, in spite of the closest search in our rooms and furniture. We heard also that my mother might have escaped, and that the wife of the concierge was kind and took great care of her.

The municipals came and asked us for my mother's linen, but they would give us no news of her health. They took away from us the pieces of tapestry which she had worked, and those on which we were then working, under pretext that there might be mysterious signs in that tapestry and a peculiar kind of writing.

September 21st at one o'clock in the morning, Hébert arrived with several municipals to execute a decree of the Commune, which ordered that we should be more closely confined, and have in future but one room; that Tison, who still did the heavy work, should be put in prison in the Tower; that we should be reduced to simple necessaries, and that we should have a grating at our entrance door through which our food should be passed, and finally, that no one should enter our room but the bearers of wood and water. This grating was not put in the door and the municipals continued to enter three times a day to bring our food and carefully examine the bars of our window, the closets, and bureaus. We made our beds, and were obliged to sweep our room, which took a long time from the little practice we had of it in the beginning. We had no one now to serve us. Hébert told my aunt that in the French republic equality was the first law, that the prisoners in other prisons had no one to serve them, and he should now take Tison from us.[1]

In order to treat us with still more harshness they deprived us of what were little comforts; for example, they took away the arm-chair in which my aunt always sat, and many other things; we were not even allowed what was necessary. We could no longer learn any news, unless from the street hawkers, and then indistinctly though we listened closely. They forbade us to go up on the Tower, and they

[1] Turgy, in his "Historical Fragments," thus relates how the captives were treated as to meals (he was on service in the kitchen and it was his duty to bring up the meals): "That day the commissioners ordered us to take up the dinner as usual, but they would not let us lay the table. They gave each princess a plate in which they put soup and a bit of beef, and a piece of coarse bread on the side of it; they gave them a pewter spoon, an iron fork, and a black-handled knife, and a bottle of wine from a tavern. The commissioners then made us serve to themselves the dinner prepared for the princesses." — FR. ED.

took away our large sheets, for fear that, in spite of the bars, we might escape through the windows; that was only a pretext. They gave us, in exchange, very coarse and dirty blankets.

I believe it was about that time that my mother's trial began. I heard, after her death, that friends had tried to rescue her from the Conciergerie. I was assured that the gendarmes who guarded her and the wife of the concierge had been bribed by one of our friends; that she had seen several very devoted persons in the prison, among them a priest who administered to her the sacraments, which she received with great piety. The opportunity to escape failed once because, having been told to speak to the second guard, she made a mistake and spoke to the first. Another time she was out of her room and had already passed the corridor, when a gendarme stopped her, although he was bribed, and forced her to go back to her room, which defeated the enterprise. Many persons took interest in my mother; indeed, unless they were monsters of the vilest species — and such, alas! many were — it was impossible to approach her and see her for even a few moments without being filled with respect, so much did kindness temper what was stately and dignified in her bearing. But we knew none of these details at that time; we knew only that my mother had seen a Chevalier de Saint-Louis who had given her a pink in which was a note; but we were now so closely confined we could not learn the result.[1]

Every day we were searched by the municipals. On the 4th of September they came at four in the morning to make a thorough visitation and take away the silver and the china. They took all that was left to us, and finding an

[1] This was M. de Rougeville; mention is made of his visit to the queen in the Conciergerie in Count Fersen's Diary. — TR.

article missing they had the baseness to accuse us of having stolen it, whereas it was one of their colleagues who had hidden it. They found behind the drawers of my aunt's wash-stand a roll of louis, which they seized with extraordinary avidity. They questioned my aunt closely to know who gave her that gold, how long she had had it, and for whom she was keeping it. She answered that the Princesse de Lamballe had given it to her after the 10th of August, and that, in spite of all the searches, she had preserved it. They asked her who had given it to Madame de Lamballe, and she said she did not know. The fact was that the Princesse de Lamballe's women had found means to send the money to her in the Temple, and she had shared it with my parents. They questioned me also, asked my name, as if they did not know it, and made me sign the *procès-verbal*.

October 8th at midday, as we were busy doing up our chamber and dressing ourselves, Pache, Chaumette, and David, members of the Convention, arrived with several municipals. My aunt would not open the door until she was dressed. Pache, turning to me, requested me to go down. My aunt wished to follow me; they refused her. She asked if I should return. Chaumette assured her that I should, saying: "You may rely on the word of a good republican." I kissed my aunt, who was trembling all over, and I went down. I was very embarrassed; it was the first time I was ever alone with men; I did not know what they wanted of me, but I commended myself to God. On the staircase Chaumette wished to do me civilities; I did not answer him. Entering my brother's room I kissed him tenderly; but they snatched him from my arms telling me to pass on into the next room. There Chaumette made me sit down; he placed himself in front of me. A municipal took a pen, and Chaumette asked me my name. After that Hébert questioned me; he began thus:—

"Tell the truth. This does not concern either you or your relations."

"Does it not concern my mother?"

"No; but persons who have not done their duty. Do you know the citizens Toulan, Lepître, Bruno, Bugnot, Merle, and Michonis?"

"No."

"What, you do not know them?"

"No, monsieur."

"That is false, especially as to Toulan, that small young man who often waited on you in the Temple."

"I did not know him any more than the others."

"You remember a day when you stayed alone with your brother on the tower?"

"Yes."

"Your relations sent you there that they might talk more at their ease with those men."

"No, monsieur, it was to accustom us to the cold."

"What did you do on the tower?"

"We talked, we played."

"And, on going out, did you see what those men brought to your relations?"

"I did not see anything."

Chaumette then questioned me on a great many vile things of which they accused my mother and my aunt. I was aghast at such horrors, and so indignant that, in spite of the fear I felt, I could not keep myself from saying it was an infamy. In spite of my tears they insisted long. There were things I did not understand, but what I did understand was so horrible that I wept with indignation. Then they questioned me on Varennes, and asked me many questions which I answered as best I could without compromising any one. I had always heard my parents say that it was better to die than to compromise any one, no matter who. At last my examination ended, at three o'clock; it began at midday. I asked Chaumette ardently to reunite me with my mother, telling him, with truth, that I had asked it a thousand times of my aunt. "I can do nothing about it," he said. "What! monsieur, cannot you obtain it from the Council general?" "I have no authority there," he replied. He then sent me back to my room with three municipals, telling me to say nothing to my aunt, who was now to be brought down. On arriving I threw myself into her arms, but they separated us and told her to go down.

They asked her the same questions that they asked me about the persons I have named. She denied all communication with the outside and replied with still greater contempt to the vile things about which they questioned her. She returned at four o'clock: her examination had lasted only one hour, mine three; this was because the deputies saw they could not intimidate her as they expected to do with one of my age; but the life I had led for four years, and the example of my relations had given me strength of soul.

Chaumette had assured us that our examination did not concern my mother or ourselves, and that she would not be tried. Alas! he deceived us, for my mother was tried and condemned soon after. I do not yet know the circumstances of her trial, of which we were ignorant, as we were of her death; therefore I can only say what I have since discovered.[1] She had two defenders, MM. Ducoudray and Chau-

[1] This part of the Narrative was written, it will be remembered, during the last solitary months of her life in the Tower. — TR.

veau-Lagarde. Many persons were brought up before her, among whom some, alas! were very estimable, others were not. Simon and Matthieu, the jailer at the Temple, appeared. I think of how my mother must have suffered when she saw those men whom she knew were near us. They summoned Dr. Brunier before the tribunal. They asked him if he knew my mother. "Yes." "Since when?" "Since 1788, when the queen confided to me the health of her children." "When you went to the Temple did you procure for the prisoners correspondence with the outside?" "No." My mother here said: "Dr. Brunier, as you know, never came to the Temple unless accompanied by a municipal, and never spoke to us except in his presence."

Finally, inconceivable fact! my mother's examination lasted three days and three nights without discontinuing. They questioned her on all the vile things about which Chaumette had questioned us — the mere idea could enter the minds of only such men. "I appeal to all mothers," was her answer to that infamous accusation. The people were touched. The judges, alarmed and fearing that her firmness, her dignity, her courage would inspire interest, hastened to condemn her. My mother heard her sentence with much calmness.

They gave her for her last moments a priest who had taken the oath. After gently refusing him, she took no further notice of what he said to her, and would not make use of his ministry. She knelt down, prayed to God alone for a long time, coughed a little, then went to bed and slept some hours. The next morning, knowing that the rector of Sainte-Marguerite was in prison opposite to her, she went to the window, looked at his window, and knelt down. I am told that he gave her absolution or his blessing. Then, having made the sacrifice of her life, she went to death with courage, amid curses which the unhappy, misguided people poured forth against her. Her courage did not abandon her in the cart, nor on the scaffold; she showed as much in death as she had shown in life.

Thus died, October 16, 1793, Marie-Antoinette-Jeanne-Josèphe de Lorraine, daughter of an emperor and wife of a king of France, aged thirty-seven years and eleven months, having been twenty-three years in France. She died eight months after her husband, Louis XVI.

Life in the Temple till the Martyrdom of Madame Élisabeth and the Death of the Dauphin, Louis XVII.

We were ignorant, my aunt and I, of the death of my mother, though we heard the hawkers crying her condemnation in the streets; but hope, so natural to the unhappy, made us think she had been saved. We refused to believe in a general abandonment.[1] But I do not yet know what things have happened outside, nor if I myself will ever leave this prison, though they give me hopes of it.

There were moments when, in spite of our hope in the Powers, we felt keen anxiety about my mother, when we saw the fury of the unhappy populace against us. I remained in this cruel uncertainty for one year and a half; then only, did I learn my misfortune, and the death of my honoured mother.

We learned from the hawkers the death of the Duc d'Orléans; this was the only news that reached us during

[1] They were abandoned virtually by all Europe. See the Diary and Correspondence of Count Fersen, the preceding volume of this Historical Series. — Tr.

Marie Antoinette leaving the Tribunal after her condemnation to death

Paul Delaroche

the winter [of 1793-94]. But the searches continued and they treated us with much severity. My aunt, who, since the Revolution, had an ulcer on her arm, had great difficulty in obtaining what was necessary to dress it; it was long refused to her. At last, one day, a municipal represented the inhumanity of such treatment, and an ointment was sent. They deprived me also of the means of making an herb-tea which my aunt made me take every morning for my health. Having no fish, she asked for eggs or other dishes on fast-days. They refused them, saying that in equality there was no difference of days; there were no weeks, only decades. They brought us a new almanac, but we did not look at it. Another time, when my aunt again asked for fast-day food they answered: "Why, *citoyenne*, don't you know what has taken place? none but fools believe all that." She made no further requests.

They continued to search us, especially in the month of November. An order was given to search us every day three times; one search lasted from four in the afternoon till half-past eight at night. The four municipals who made it were all drunk. No one could form an idea of their talk, their insults, their oaths during those four hours. They carried away mere trifles, such as our hats, cards having kings on them, books in which were coats of arms; and yet, they left religious books, after saying impurities and follies about them. Simon accused us of forging *assignats* and of having correspondence with the outside. He declared we had communicated with my father during his trial. He made a declaration in the name of my poor little brother, whom he had forced to sign it. A noise, that he said was the false money he accused us of making, was that of our backgammon, which my aunt, wishing to amuse me a little, had been kind enough to teach me. We played it in the evening during the winter, which passed rather quietly, in spite of the inquisition and searches. They gave us wood to burn, which they had hitherto refused us.

January 19th we heard a great noise in my brother's room, which made us conjecture that they were taking him from the Temple; we were convinced of it when, looking through the key-hole, we saw them carrying away packages. The following days as we heard his door open and persons walking in his room we were more than ever convinced that he was gone. We thought they had put some important personage in the lower room; but I have since learned that it was Simon who had gone away. Obliged to choose between his office as municipal and that of jailer to my brother, he preferred the former. I have since heard also that they had the cruelty to leave my poor brother alone; unheard-of barbarity which has surely no other example! that of abandoning a poor child only eight years old, already ill, and keeping him locked and bolted in, with no succour but a bell, which he did not ring, so afraid was he of the persons it would call; he preferred to want for all rather than ask anything of his persecutors.

He lay in a bed which had not been made for more than six months, and he now had no strength to make it; fleas and bugs covered him, his linen and his person were full of them. His shirt and stockings had not been changed for a year; his excrements remained in the room, no one had removed them during all that time. His window, the bars of which were secured by a padlock, was never opened; it was impossible to stay in his chamber on account of the foul odour. It is true that my brother neglected himself; he might have taken rather more care of his person; he could at least have washed himself, because they gave him a pitcher of water. But the unhappy child was half dead with fear, so much did

Simon and the others terrify him. He spent the day in doing nothing; they gave him no light; this condition did as much harm to him morally as it did physically. It is not surprising that he fell into a fearful marasmus; the time that his health remained good and was able to resist such cruelties proves the strength of his constitution.

They "thee'd and thou'd" us much during the winter; we despised all vexatious things, but this degree of coarseness always made my aunt and me blush. She performed her Lenten duties fully, though deprived of fast-day food. She took at dinner a bowl of coffee and milk (this was her breakfast which she kept over); in the evening she ate only a piece of bread. She ordered me to eat what was brought, not being old enough to bear abstinence, but as for her, nothing could be more edifying. From the time they refused her the fast-day food she never, on that account, neglected the duties prescribed by religion. When the spring began they took away our tallow candle and we went to bed when we could see no longer.

Until May 9th nothing remarkable happened. On that day, just as we were going to bed the bolts were withdrawn and some one knocked at our door. My aunt replied that she would put on her dress; they answered that she must not be so long, and they rapped so hard that we thought the door would burst in. She opened it when she was dressed. They said to her: "*Citoyenne,* you will please come down." "And my niece?" "We will attend to her later." My aunt kissed me and told me to be calm for she would soon return. "No, *citoyenne,* you will not return," they said to her; "take your cap and come down." They loaded her then with insults and coarse speeches; she bore it all with patience, took her cap, kissed me again, and told me to have courage and firmness, to hope always in God, to practise the good principles of religion given me by my parents, and not to fail in the last instructions given to me by my father and by my mother.

She went out; at the foot of the stairs they asked for her pockets; there was nothing in them; this lasted a long time because the municipals had to write a *procès-verbal* for the discharge of her person. At last, after countless insults, she went away with the clerk of the tribunal, in a hackney-coach, and was taken to the Conciergerie, where she passed the night. The next day they asked her three questions: —

"Your name?" "Élisabeth de France."

"Where were you on the 10th of August?" "In the château of the Tuileries with the king, my brother."

"What have you done with your diamonds?" "I do not know. But all these questions are useless; you want my death; I have made to God the sacrifice of my life, and I am ready to die — happy to rejoin my honoured relatives whom I loved so well on earth."

They condemned her to death.

She made them take her to the room of those who were to die with her; she exhorted all with a presence of mind, an elevation, an unction which strengthened them. On the cart she showed the same calmness, encouraging the women who were with her. At the foot of the scaffold they had the cruelty to make her wait and perish last. All the women on getting out of the cart asked permission to kiss her, which she gave, encouraging each of them with her usual kindness. Her strength did not abandon her at the last moment which she bore with a resignation full of religion. Her soul parted from her body to go and enjoy happiness in the bosom of the God she had loved.

Marie-Philippine-Élisabeth-Hélène, sister of King Louis XVI., died on the 10th of May 1794, aged thirty years, having always been a model of virtues. At the age of fifteen she gave herself to God and thought only of salvation. From 1790, when I became in a state to appreciate her I never saw anything in her but religion, love of God, horror of sin, gentleness, piety, modesty, and a great attachment to her family, for whom she sacrificed her life, being never willing to leave the king and queen. She was a princess worthy of the blood of which she came. I cannot say enough of the goodness that she showed to me, which ended only with her life. She considered me and cared for me as her daughter, and I, I honoured her as a second mother and vowed to her all those feelings. It was said that we resembled each other in face: I feel that I have her nature; would that I might have all her virtues and rejoin her some day, also my father and mother, in the bosom of God, where, I doubt not, they are now enjoying the reward of a death so meritorious.

I remained in great desolation when I felt myself parted from my aunt; I did not know what had become of her, and no one would tell me. I passed a very cruel night: and yet, though I was very uneasy about her fate, I was far from thinking I should lose her in a few hours. Sometimes I persuaded myself that they would send her out of France; then, when I recalled the manner in which they had taken her away, my fears revived. The next day I asked the municipals where she was; they said she had gone to take the air. I renewed my request to be taken to my mother, as I was parted from my aunt; they replied that they would speak of it. They came soon after and brought me the key of the closet in which my aunt kept her linen; I asked them to send some to her, because she had taken none with her; they told me they could not do so.

Seeing that when I asked the municipals to let me go to my mother, or tell me news of my aunt they always replied that they would speak of it, and remembering that my aunt had always told me that if I were left alone my duty was to ask for a woman, I did so, to obey her, but with great repugnance, feeling sure they would refuse me, or give me some vile woman. Accordingly, when I made this request, the municipals told me that I needed no one. They redoubled their severity and took away from me the knives, which had been returned to me, saying: "*Citoyenne*, tell us, how many knives have you?" "Only two, messieurs." "Have you none for your toilet, nor scissors?" "No, messieurs." Another time they took away my tinder-box, having found the stove warm. They said: "May we know why you made that fire?" "To put my feet in water." "How did you light it?" "With the tinder." "Who gave you that?" "I do not know." "As a precaution we shall take it away for your safety, for fear you should fall asleep and burn from that fire."

Searches and scenes like these were frequent, but unless I was positively questioned I never spoke, nor did I to those who brought my food. There came a man one day, whom I think was Robespierre; the municipals showed great respect for him. His visit was a secret to all the persons in the Tower, who either did not know who he was, or would not tell me. He looked at me insolently, cast his eyes over my books, and after searching the room with the municipals went away. The Guards were often drunk; nevertheless, we were left alone and tranquil, my brother and I, in our separate apartments, until the 9th thermidor.

My brother was still wallowing in filth; no one entered his room except at meal times; no one had any pity on that unfortunate child. There was but one guard whose manners were civil enough to induce me to commend my poor brother to him. He dared to speak of the harshness shown to the child, and he was dismissed the next day. As for me, I asked for only simple necessaries, which were often refused to me harshly; but at least I could keep myself clean, I had both soap and water. I swept the room every day. I finished doing it by nine o'clock when the Guards brought up my breakfast. I had no light, but when the days were long I suffered less from that privation. They would no longer give me books; I had none but those of piety and travels which I had read a hundred times. I had some knitting, but that ennuyéd me very much.

Such was our state when the 9th thermidor arrived. I heard the *générale* beaten and the tocsin rung; I was very uneasy. The municipals in the Temple did not stir out. When they brought my dinner I dared not ask what was happening. At last, on the 10th thermidor, at six o'clock in the morning, I heard a frightful noise in the Temple; the Guard cried to arms, the drums beat, the gates were opened and shut. All this uproar was occasioned by a visit from members of the National Assembly, who came to assure themselves that all was secure. I heard the bolts of my brother's door drawn back; I flung myself from my bed and was dressed before the members of the Convention arrived in my room. Barras was among them. They were all in full costume, which surprised me, not being accustomed to see them thus, and being always in fear of something. Barras spoke to me, called me by name, and seemed surprised to find me risen. They said to me several things to which I made no reply. They went away, and I heard them haranguing the Guards under the windows and exhorting them to be faithful to the National Convention. There were many cries of *Vive la Republique! Vive la Convention!* The guard was doubled; the three municipals who were in the Temple stayed there eight days. On the evening of the third day, at half-past nine o'clock, I was in my bed, having no light, but not asleep, so anxious was I about what was happening. They knocked at my door to show me Laurent, commissioner from the Convention, appointed to guard my brother and me. I rose; they made a long visit, showed everything to Laurent and then went away.

The next day at ten o'clock Laurent entered my room; he asked me politely if I wanted anything. He came daily three times to see me, always with civility, and did not "thee and thou" me. He never searched my bureaus and closets. At the end of another three days the Convention sent a deputation to report upon my brother's state; these men had pity upon him and ordered that he should be better treated. Laurent took down a bed which was in my room, because the one he had was full of bugs; he made him take baths, and removed the vermin with which he was covered. Nevertheless, they still left him alone in his room.

I soon asked Laurent about that which concerned me so keenly; I mean news of my relations, of whose death I was ignorant, and I begged to be reunited with my mother. He answered me with a very pained air that the matter did not concern him.

The next day came men in scarfs to whom I made the same appeal. They also answered that the matter did not concern them, and said they did not see why I wanted to leave that place, where I seemed to be very comfortable. "It is dreadful," I said, "to be parted from one's mother for over a year without knowing anything about her, and also one's aunt." "You are not ill?" "No, monsieur, but the cruellest illness is that of the heart." "I tell you that we can do nothing; I advise you to have patience, and to hope in the justice and goodness of Frenchmen." I said no nore. I was alarmed the next day by the explosion at Grenelle, which gave me a great fright.

During all this time my brother was still left alone. Laurent went to him three times a day, but, fearing to compromise himself as he was watched, he dared not do more. He took much care of me; and I had only to congratulate myself on his manners all the time he was on service. He often asked me if I needed nothing, and begged me to tell him what I wished and to ring if I wanted anything. He gave me back my match-box and candle.

Towards the end of October, at one o'clock in the morning, I was sleeping when they knocked at my door; I rose in haste, and, opened it, trembling with fear. I saw two men of the committee with Laurent; they looked at me, and went away without speaking.

At the beginning of November came the civil commissioners; that is to say, one man from each section, who passed twenty-four hours in the Temple to verify the existence of my brother. During the first days of this month another commissioner, named Gomier, arrived to be with Laurent. He took extreme care of my brother. For a long time that unhappy child had been left without lights; he was dying of fear. Gomier obtained permission that he might have them; he even passed several hours with him daily to amuse him. He soon perceived that my brother's knees and wrists were swelled; he feared he was growing rickety; he spoke to the committee and asked that the child might be taken to the garden for exercise. He first made him come down from his room into the little salon, which pleased my brother much because he liked a change of place. He soon perceived Gomier's attentions, was touched by them, and attached himself to him. The unhappy child had long been accustomed to none but the worst treatment — for I believe that no researches can show such barbarity to any other child.

On the 19th of December the committee-general came to the Temple in consequence of his illness. This deputation also came to me, but said nothing. The winter passed tranquilly enough. I was satisfied with the kindness of my jailers; they made my fire and gave me all the wood I needed, which pleased me. Also they brought me the books I asked for; Laurent had already procured me some. My greatest unhappiness was that I could not obtain from them any news of my mother and aunt; I dared not ask about my uncles and my great-aunts, but I thought of them incessantly.

During the winter my brother had several attacks of fever; he was always beside the fire. Laurent and Gomier induced him to go up on the Tower and get the air; but he was no sooner there than he wanted to come down; he would not walk, still less would he go upstairs. His illness increased, and his knees swelled much. Laurent went away, and in his place they put Lasne, a worthy man, who, with Gomier, took the greatest care of my brother.

At the opening of the spring they wanted me to go up on the Tower, which I did. My brother's illness grew worse and worse daily; his strength diminished; even his mind showed the effects of the harshness so long exercised towards him, and it gradually weakened. The Committee of Public Safety sent Dr. Desault to take care of him; he undertook to cure him, though he admitted that his illness was very dangerous. Desault died, and they sent as his successors Dumangin and the surgeon Pelletan. They saw no hope. They made him take medicines, which he swallowed with difficulty. Happily, his malady did not make him suffer much; it was debility and a total wasting away ather than acute pain. He had several distressing crises; ever seized him, his strength lessened daily, and he expired vithout a struggle.

Thus died, June 9, 1795, at three in the afternoon, Louis XVII., aged ten years and two months. The commissioners nourned him bitterly, so much had he made them love him or his gentle qualities. He had much intelligence; but mprisonment and the horrors of which he was the victim iad changed him much; and even, had he lived, it is o be feared that his mental faculties would have been iffected.

I do not think that he was poisoned, as was said, and is itill said: that is false, from the testimony of the physicians vho opened his body. The drugs he had taken in his last llness were analyzed and found to be safe. The only poison hat shortened his life was uncleanness, joined to the horible treatment, the unexampled harshness and cruelty exercised upon him.

Such were the lives and the end of my virtuous family luring their imprisonment in the Temple and elsewhere.

Written in the Tower of the Temple.

[Marie-Thérèse de France was exchanged in October, 1795, or the four commissioners of the Convention delivered up o Austria by Dumouriez in April, 1793. She left the Tower f the Temple during the night of December 18, 1795. That tragic building, — about which Marie-Antoinette exlaimed on hearing where she and her family were about to e imprisoned: "How often I begged the Comte d'Artois to iave that vile Tower of the Temple demolished! it was always horror to me," — that monument to anguish was razed o the ground by order of Napoleon in 1811. Until then ould be read, scratched upon the wall of the room where the child, Marie-Thérèse, lived her solitary life, these piteous words: —

"Marie-Thérèse is the most unhappy creature in the world. She can obtain no news of her mother; nor be reunited to her, though she has asked it a thousand times."

"Live, my good mother! whom I love well, but of whom I can hear no tidings."

"O my father! watch over me from heaven above."

"O my God! forgive those who have made my family die."

She went from the Temple to Vienna, where she lived, against her will, three years and a half, resisting all attempts to make her marry the Archduke Charles of Austria. At last, in 1799, she was allowed to go to her uncle the Comte de Provence (Louis XVIII.) at Mittau in Courlande, where she soon after married her cousin the Duc d'Angoulême, son of the Comte d'Artois (Charles X.). Driven from Courlande with Louis XVIII. by the Emperor Paul, she followed her uncle through all his exiles to Memel, Königsberg, Warsaw, again to Mittau, thence to Godsfield Hall and Hartwell in England. "She is the consoling angel of our master," wrote the Comte d'Avaray, "and a model of courage for us."

The portrait of her in this volume was painted by Danloux during the first months of her life in Vienna, when she was seventeen years of age. Its sorrowful expression deepened upon her face as the years went by until at last she became an ideal of Sorrow, and the courtiers of the Restoration reproached her for her sadness and turned from her! But her courage remained. She was absent from the side of Louis XVIII. when the first Restoration fell, but she made a gallant struggle to uphold the royal cause at Bordeaux where she then was. It was that struggle which led Napoleon to say of her that she was the only man of her family.

Later, she was at Vichy in 1830, when Charles X. signed the ordinances which cost him his throne. From that day until her death, a period of twenty-one years, she lived in exile, at Holyrood, Prague, Goritz, and Frohsdorf. Her husband's nephew, the Comte de Chambord, in whose behalf Charles X. and the Duc d'Angoulême abdicated, regarded her as a second mother, and she had a stronger influence over him than his own mother, the Duchesse de Berry. The last glimpse we have of her is at Frohsdorf in 1851, the year of her death, when the Comte de Falloux thus describes her:—

"Madame la Dauphine was, if I may so express it, pathos in person. Sadness was imprinted on her features and revealed in her attitude; but, in the same degree, there shone about her an unalterable resignation, an unalterable gentleness. Even when the tones of her voice were brusque, which often happened, the kindness of her intention remained transparent. She liked to pass in review the Frenchmen she had known; she kept herself closely informed about their family events; she remembered the slightest details with rare fidelity: 'How Madame loves France!' I said to her one day. 'That is not surprising,' she replied. 'I take it from my parents.' At Frohsdorf she was seated nearly the whole day in the embrasure of a certain window. She had chosen this window because of its outlook on copses which reminded her a little of the garden of the Tuileries; and if a visitor wished to be agreeable to her, he remarked upon this resemblance."

She died at Frohsdorf on the 18th of October, 1851, in the seventy-third year of her age, and the twenty-first year of her last exile. She was buried at Goritz, in the chapel of the Franciscans, between Charles X. and her husband, the Duc d'Angoulême. On her tombstone are carved these words: *O vos omnes qui transitis per viam, attendite et videte si est dolor sicut dolor meus.*

THE DUCHESSE D'ANGOULÊME.

BY C.-A. SAINTE-BEUVE.

November 3, 1851.

IN coming rather late and after all the other organs of publicity to render homage to a lofty virtue and a vast misfortune, I can only repeat, more or less, what has already been said and felt by all. There is one point of view, however, — if such an expression is permissible in presence of a figure so simple and true, so alien to all pompous attitude, — there is one point of view which we will here take especially for ours.

All suffers change; all dies or renews itself; the oldest and the most revered races have their end; nations themselves before they fall and end have their several ways of being successive, they take on divers forms of government in their diverse epochs; what was religion and fidelity in one age is only a monument and commemoration of the past in another; but through all (so long as vitiation does not come) something remains, namely: human nature and the natural sentiments that distinguish it, respect for virtue, for misfortune, especially if undeserved and innocent, and pity, which itself is piety towards God in so far as it turns towards human sorrow.

In speaking of Madame la Duchesse d'Angoulême it is to all those sentiments, apart from politics, that I address myself, — to the sensitive and durable side of our being.

The feature that stands out in this long life of suffering, of martyrdom in her early years and always of convulsion and vicissitudes, is perfect truth, perfect simplicity, and, it may be said, entire and unalterable consistency. That upright soul, just and noble, was early fixed and established, and at no moment later did it vacillate. It was fixed during the very years that are for youth the age of lightsomeness, of joy, of budding bloom, during those three years and four months of captivity in the Tower of the Temple when she saw die, one after another, her father, her mother, her aunt, her brother. She entered that place before she was fourteen years old, she left it the day she was seventeen. At that age she had not acquired the marked and rather strong features by which we have known her. The portrait we have of her soon after this period in the Temple, with the hair negligently knotted, has delicacy in its outline, and nobleness and gravity without excess. Misfortune, while weighing upon that forehead, has not yet drawn there the furrow which appeared a few years later and gave her, as she grew older, more and more resemblance to Louis XVI.

But at the close of this year, 1795, though the outward presence still retained much of its early youth, the soul was mature, it was formed and disciplined. In its depths that strong and healthy organization had been attacked. The liver suffered and was injured. This tender young slip of a long and illustrious race was blighted, perhaps withered even in its future shoots. If we may dare to form an idea of these mysteries of sorrow, it seems to me that on leaving the Temple both the life and the soul of Madame Royale were finished, completed in all essential things; they were closed to the future; all their sources, all their roots were henceforth in the past. Our heart, let it have had but one day in life, fixes or recalls the emotions of a certain hour that we hear strike for us whenever we re-enter our inner selves and dream there. The Duchesse d'Angoulême, who never dreamed but who prayed, when she retreated within herself (though she did not retreat, for she lived there), heard that hour strike on the clock of the Temple for the death-knell of her parents.

She has related the history of her captivity and the events happening in the Temple from the day she entered there until the day of her brother's death, and she has done it in a simple, correct, concise style, without one word too much, without one wrought-up phrase, as became an upright mind and a deep heart speaking in all sincerity of true sorrows, sorrows truly ineffable, which surpassed all that words could tell. She forgets herself as much as she can, and she stops her narrative at the death of her brother, — the last of the four immolated victims. Let us say more of her here than she has said of herself.

Marie-Thérèse-Charlotte de France, born December 19, 1778, was the first child of Louis XVI. and Queen Marie-Antoinette. Seven years had elapsed since the queen's marriage, when she one day informed the persons in her private circle of her first joy as a wife and her future hopes. About one year later she gave birth to Madame Royale. Although until then Louis XVI.'s timidity towards his young wife had been extreme, his passion from that moment was not less so, and this child, the first fruits of it, was to a great degree his image. Kindness, integrity, all the solid and virtuous qualities of her father were transmitted straight to Madame's heart, and Marie-Antoinette, with all her grace, could not hinder a little of that roughness of gesture and accent which covered the virtues of Louis XVI. from slipping into the wholly frank nature of his child. Also, she forgot to transmit to her that which women have so readily — a desire to please and the dawning charm of coquetry, even the most innocent and permissible. Of that, Madame Royale had no idea, and no conception. Or if, in the beginning, some trifle of it mingled in her blood, that little disappeared completely in the trials of a childhood and a youth so oppressed, so desolate. In order to comprehend the Duchesse d'Angoulême, we must never cease to remember that all that calls itself springtide joy and bloom, that joyous and bewitching aspect under which, on entering life, we so naturally see all things, was suppressed and early blighted in her. Her soul, scarcely in its first dawn, was suddenly reduced and worn, as it were, to its woof,— but a solid indestructible woof, which resisted and grew stronger under all assaults, fortifying itself by tears, by prayers, but casting far away from it, as if it were the equal of a lie, all that might have been grace and ornament. In truth, for her who had wept true tears, and never ceased to weep them, it would have been a lie.

Though she seems in her nature to have derived from her father more than from her mother, there is one virtue at least that she held through the latter, which was lacking in that poor Louis XVI. to save him: I mean firmness, the courage to act in decisive moments. In her august and modest life, in general so aloof from political questions, the Duchesse d'Angoulême found, once at least at Bordeaux, an opportunity to show that she had in her that courage of action which came to her from her mother and from her grandmother, Maria Theresa. And again, in 1830, when she rejoined the royal family at Rambouillet (after the faults were committed), her first impulsion was, as in 1815 at Bordeaux, to resist and fight.

She was not eleven years old when, with the terrible days of October, 1789, her public rôle beside her mother began. She was made to appear on a balcony and retire from it at the bidding of a furious populace; and in that flux and reflux of the popular storm, of which she strove to divine the meaning, she felt but one thing, — the clasp of her mother's hand, which pressed her against herself with the chill of death.

At that time, in the confines of the Tuileries to which the royal family was restricted, she received from her mother, now becoming more and more grave, from her noble Aunt Élisabeth, and from her father, the lessons of a practical and solid instruction and examples of an unalterable domestic religion. She was brought-up within that domesticity like a child of the most united and purest of noble families, but with mortal terrors added, and with agonies by day and night. It was in that long series of terrors, enigmas, and painful nightmares that the years and the dreams of girlhood, usually so lightsome, were passed.

On entering the Temple, there was no more enigma, the veil was rent away completely. Henceforth the world to her was sharply divided in two — the good and the wicked: the wicked, that is to say, all that human imagination in times of peace and social regularity scarcely dares to present nakedly to itself, — brutality in all its coarseness and degradation, vice and envy in all the ignoble drunkenness of their triumph; the good, that is to say, a few touched, pitying, timid souls, softening the evil secretly and concealing their deed.

That the young heart of Madame Royale did not take from that hour an undying hatred, a contempt unchangeable, for the human race, that she preserved her purity of soul, her faith, her trust in good, was owing to the divine examples and the help she had around her, especially in her Aunt Élisabeth, that celestial person; it was owing to religion, clearly defined and practical, at which no questioning mind can ever have the right to smile, because it alone has the power to sustain and to console under such sorrows. One day (April 20, 1793) the wretch Hébert with other municipals came to the Tower at ten at night, after the prisoners had gone to bed. "We rose hastily," says Madame Royale. . . . "My poor brother was asleep; they pulled him roughly from his bed to search it. . . . They took from my mother the address of a shop, from my Aunt Élisabeth a stick of sealing-wax, and from me a Sacred Heart of Jesus and a Prayer for France."

That Sacred Heart of Jesus and that Prayer for France were closer bound together than would seem at first; and perhaps she needed all her faith in the one to be able at that moment to pray for the other.

It has sometimes been said that the Duchesse d'Angoulême felt a rancour against France, and that when she returned in 1814, and again in 1815, she showed that feeling involuntarily in several of her remarks; as for acts, it would be impossible to find any for which to blame her. But the persons who knew her best, and who are most worthy of belief, declare that all such feelings were very far from being hers. She was frank and sincere; she was even a little harsh and brusque in manner, like her father. Incapable of an evil thought, but also of an insincerity, if she did not like you it was impossible for her to say to you or let you think the contrary. "She was a most loyal gentleman," some one said of her to me, "who was never false." She loved her friends, she forgave her enemies; but if, in the religion of her race and her misfortunes, she believed there were faithful and unfaithful, good men and wicked men, can we wonder?

The narrative she has given of the events of the Temple was written in it, during the last months of her imprisonment, when there was some relaxation of extreme severity. In this precise, methodical, sensible, and touching narrative Madame d'Angoulême gives the measure of her precocious reason, and of her good judgment in things of the soul. She shows herself greatly struck by the dignity of her mother, who, to the speeches of various kinds addressed to the noble captives, answered oftenest by silence. "My mother, as usual, said nothing," writes Madame, in regard to an insulting piece of news announced to them, which the queen had the air of not hearing; often her contemptuous calmness and her dignified bearing awed those men; it was rarely to her that they addressed themselves.

It was not until the first day of Louis XVI.'s trial, when she saw him taken away to be interrogated at the bar of the Convention, — it was not until that day that Marie-Antoinette succumbed to her anxiety and broke her noble silence: "My mother tried in every way to learn what was happening from the municipals who guarded her; it was the first time she had deigned to question them."

In this simple narrative, which no one can read without tears, there are touches that make a profound impression, of which the pen that wrote them had no suspicion. Madame has had a trouble in her foot (chilblains, as a result of the cold), complicated with some internal illness. During this time Louis XVI. is condemned. His family, who hoped to see him once more, to embrace him on the morning of his death, is left in a desolation we can well conceive.

"Nothing," writes Madame, "was able to calm my mother's anguish; we could make no hope of any sort enter her heart; she was indifferent whether she lived or died. She looked at us sometimes with a pity that made us shudder. Happily, grief increased my illness and that occupied her."

Happily! — that word slipping unconsciously into this picture of sorrow has an effect that no word of Bossuet's could equal.

It was in reflecting on these dolorous scenes of the Temple

that M. de Chateaubriand (not to confound him, however, as some too often do, with Bossuet) said in "Atala:" "The dweller in a cabin, and those in palaces, all suffer, and all moan here below; queens have been seen to weep like simple women, and men wonder at the quantity of tears that flow from the eyes of kings."

A popular poet alluding to that celebrated passage, but continuing to keep in opposition the classes, writes:—

"In the eye of a king the tears can be reckoned.
The eyes of the people are too full of tears for that."

The sense of opposition of that kind will never come, I am very certain, to whoso reads the simple, Christian, human narrative of Madame Royale in the Temple. All spirit of party disarms itself and dies as we read it; there is room for nothing but compassion and the deepest admiration. Gentleness, piety, and virgin modesty inspire these pages of the shocked and insulted young girl. She spent alone with her Aunt Élisabeth the winter of 93-94. "They *tutoyéd* us much during the winter," she says. "We despised all vexations, but this last coarseness always made my aunt and me blush."

The most cruel moment for her was that when, after the death of her father, after the disappearance of her mother and her aunt, ignorant of the actual fate of those dear heads, she heard in the distance, during the weeks that preceded the 9th thermidor, the voice of her brother, already a prey to the corrupters, singing the atrocious songs taught him by Simon, the shoemaker.

"As for me," she says, "I only asked for simple necessaries; often they were refused to me harshly. But at least I could keep myself clean; I had soap and water; I swept my room daily, and I finished by nine o'clock when the guard brought my breakfast. I had no light, but during the long days I suffered less from that privation. They would not give me books, I had only some of piety and travels which I had read a hundred times."

At last the Convention, after the 9th thermidor, softened in severity; public opinion made itself heard, and pity dared to murmur. One of the commissioners, whose duty it was to visit the young princess in the Temple, has left a representation of her in her seemly attitude, suffering and poverty-stricken, seated by the window knitting, and far from the fire (there was not light enough for her work near the chimney), her hands swollen with cold and covered with chilblains, for they did not give her wood enough to warm the room at any distance. This was the first time attention was shown to her or any desire to soften her fate. Her first impulse was to be incredulous, silent, and to refuse all offers. To a question which the commissioners put to her as to her books, which consisted of the "Imitation of Jesus Christ" and a few other books of devotion, saying that they were scarcely sufficient to amuse her, "Those books, monsieur," she replied, "are precisely the ones that suit my situation."

The period which came between the 9th thermidor, July 27, 1794, and the deliverance of the princess in the last days of 1795, was that in which a whole royalist literature attempted to burst forth around her. Sentimental songs were made and sung to her from a distance, the echoes of which told her that henceforth friends were watching over her fate. Odes were written on the goat and the dog she was allowed at the very last to have, and which, from neighbouring windows, were seen with her in the garden. The Duchesse d'Angoulême has been, or rather could have been, the centre of a whole contemporaneous literature, of which we can follow the trace, from the song of M. Lepitre, sung beneath the walls of the Temple, and the novel of "Irma, or the Sorrows of a Young Orphan" (published by Mme. Guénard in the year VIII.), to the "Antigone" of Ballanche, which more nobly crowned that allegorical and mythological literature in 1815. But one distinctive trait in her was to remain completely aloof from this rather tardy invasion of public sentimentality. It is to her honour that she never, in the slightest degree, suffered literature, romance, drama, to enter the sanctuary, veiled forever, of her sorrow. "I do not like scenes," she said one day, a little brusquely, to a woman who threw herself on her knees before her to thank her for some benefit.

Scenes! she had seen too many scenes, too awfully real, to endure the mere image of them. The deep sincerity of her mourning and of her filial affection had in this direction the same effect we should expect of the most enlightened and severe good taste. All this literature, more or less overpitched, and in the style of Mme. Cottin, which accumulated round the youth of Madame Royale, evidently never touched her; and the Narrative she wrote in 1795 of the events of the Temple will be the touchstone by which to judge of all these other narratives and false descriptions, could they even be brought into comparison. She proved her great good sense in her utmost sorrow.

When she leaves France, in Vienna, at Mittau, where they marry her to her cousin, everywhere, in the diverse exiles where fortune tosses her, she is still the same; the life of the Temple is there, like a background to her oratory, dominating each day and dictating to her the employment of it. Submissive to her uncle, in whom she sees both a king and a father, she thinks only of reuniting all her faiths, all her religions, and of practising them faithfully.

A most touching scene in her life is well related by one of her biographers (M. Nettement); it occurred at Mittau in

May, 1807, when she nursed and assisted till his end the Abbé Edgeworth de Firmont, the priest who had accompanied Louis XVI. to the scaffold. A contagious fever broke out among the French prisoners brought to Mittau by the events of the war. The Abbé Edgeworth, in taking care of them, contracted the disease, a species of typhus; and it was under these extreme circumstances that Madame d'Angoulême would not abandon him. "The less knowledge he has of his needs and his condition," she said, "the more the presence of a friend is necessary to him. . . . Nothing can prevent me from nursing the Abbé Edgeworth myself; I ask no one to accompany me." She wished to return to him, as much as it was in her to do so, that which he had carried of consolation and succour to Louis XVI. when dying. She lived and dwelt continually in that line of thought, without being distracted from it for a single day.

Did Madame d'Angoulême ever have a single day of real happiness after her issue from the Temple? Was there ever place in that heart, saturated with anguish in her tenderest years, for one unalloyed and veritable joy? It would be strange if, in spite of all, she did not feel one, like an unexpected, gushing spring, during the great moments of 1814,—that year which must have seemed to her at every step a startling testimony to the wonders of Providence. Nevertheless, this sort of exaltation, if she felt it, could not have survived the events of Bordeaux and the new and bitter proof she there obtained of human frailty and unfaithfulness.

She was, as every one knows, at Bordeaux at the moment when Napoleon's landing in Provence from Elba (March 1815) became known. Madame d'Angoulême, obeying the impulsion of her maternal blood, had the idea of resistance, and to organize it she did all that we should expect from so noble and virile a character. The opinion of the city was wholly favourable and devoted to her; but the troops in garrison seemed doubtful from the moment that the great captain and his eagles reappeared. Nevertheless, she (although warned by the generals), she could not believe that their fidelity was doubtful, because, only the evening before, she had received from these very men, whom she considered heroes, reiterated homage and oaths of fidelity.

The historians of the Restoration have very well related those scenes in which Madame d'Angoulême figures, and they all agree in praising her active courage and her bearing. She went through the barracks; she strove to electrify the soldiers, she piqued their honour — but it was all of no use; she found hearts closed against her, captured again by the old love. At the moment of leaving, after exhausting all efforts, she turned to the generals who had followed her, and said that she counted upon them to at least guarantee the inhabitants of Bordeaux against all reaction. "We swear it!" cried the generals, raising their hands. "I do not ask you for oaths," she said, with a gesture of disdainful pity; "enough have been made to me, I want no more." Those haughty words she had the right to say; surely few persons have seen with their eyes how far the malignancy or the instability of men can go.

Mirabeau said of Marie-Antoinette, "The king has but one man, and that is his wife." The Duchesse d'Angoulême deserves the speech of a like nature which Napoleon made about her conduct at Bordeaux. Such praises, even though they may be slightly exaggerated, serve as indications from afar and are registered in history.

The second Restoration could bring her no elation; on entering the Tuileries she saw Fouché, a regicide, made the king's minister. Her upright and inviolable conscience could not admit for a single moment such monstrous compromises, which policy itself finds it difficult to understand and which, most assuredly, it did not require. After that moment in 1815, we never meet Madame d'Angoulême again in any political action, properly so called; her whole after life was domestic and inward.

I have questioned, in regard to her, men who approached her constantly, and this is what they tell me. Each day was alike to her, except the funereal days of her sorrowful anniversaries. She rose very early, at half-past five o'clock for example; she heard mass for herself alone between six and seven. It is conjectured that she took the communion often, but she was never seen to do so, except on the great days occasionally. No solemnity, no formal preparations; she was only a humble Christian doing a religious act; she did discreetly and secretly saintly things.

In the early morning she attended to the care of her room, in the Tuileries almost as she did in the Temple.

She never spoke of the painful and bleeding things of her youth, unless to a very few persons in her intimacy. The 21st of January and the 16th of October, the death days of her father and mother, she shut herself up alone, sometimes sending, to help her in passing the cruel hours, for some person with whom she was in harmony of mourning and piety,— the late Mme. de Pastoret, for example.

She was charitable to a degree that no one knows, and which it is hard to fathom; those who were best informed as to her alms and other deeds were constantly discovering others, which came up, it were, as from underground, and of which they knew nothing. In that she was of the true and direct lineage of Saint Louis.

Her life was very regular and very simple, whether in the Tuileries or elsewhere in exile. The conversation around her was always very natural. At moments, when misfortune made truce for a while, it was noticed that she had in her mind or in her nature a certain gaiety, of which, alas! she could make too little usage. Still, on her best days and in privacy she would let herself go, if not to saying, at least to hearing, things that were gay. When she felt herself in safe and friendly regions a certain pleasantry did not frighten her, and when on festivals she was expected to order plays for her theatre she did not choose the most serious.

Even amid the habit of pain there rose to the surface a sort of joy, such as comes to tried and austere souls, whom religion has guided and consoled throughout all time.

Politics were not for her; she did not like public affairs. No influence affected her. Her policy, which if it came from herself would have been judicious, was ruled completely by the desires of the king. She thought that when the king decidedly wished anything it was not permissible to resist it, however good a royalist one might be. MM. de Villèle and Corbières in resisting the king displeased her quite as much as the liberals themselves could have done.

She was educated, in the style of the instruction of Louis XVI.; she read books of history, travels, morality, and religion. If her reading lacked that which is vivifying in a worldly and literary sense, in the political and profane sense, if the breath and the intelligence of the new epoch never crossed the lines of her horizon, can we wonder at it? can we pity her for it? did she not gain far more than she lost through her fixed faith and the stability of her confidence in Heaven?

The letters that are quoted as hers, and probably all those that she wrote, are simple, sensible, a little stiff and dry, and presenting nothing remarkable.

Few good sayings of hers have been repeated, although her heart occasionally suggested one. Apropos of the war in Spain, when she heard of the deliverance of King Ferdinand by a French army, she exclaimed: "So it is proved that an unfortunate king *can* be saved!"

During her last exile at Frohsdorf she was visited (December, 1848) by a French traveller, M. Charles Didier, who ventured to say to her: "Madame, it is impossible that you should not see in the fall of Louis-Philippe the finger of God." "It is in all things," she replied with simplicity, but also with a tact which came from religion, and from the heart as well.

It was the same moral delicacy which, in her union with the Duc d'Angoulême made her constantly ignore what there was of inequality between them. She took pains to put him forward on the front line, — a delicacy the more real because it was never known whether she was conscious of it.

I have told the class of sentiments to which we must limit ourselves in seeking her and admiring her. Do not ask of that soul, so early wounded and despoiled, either coquetry of mind or the lighter graces. She would have thought it profanation and indeed a sacrilege to have made her sorrows and those of her parents, her virtue and the respectful interest she inspired, a means of policy, success, or attraction for what she believed to be the "good cause." She would have blamed herself for so doing before God; and when the memory of all that she had lost came back to her she could only veil herself and withdraw into her soul with sobs and tears.

Enough said to indicate that august nature, that none have been tempted to misconceive: solidity, good sense, kindness, a certain background, as I have said, of gaiety, and a perfect simplicity, — those are the chief traits which composed that nature. Religion with charity placed upon it a seal sublime. Her religion was the most uniform, the most practical, and absolutely foreign to all effect on others and all worldly considerations. No one ever bore more simply, naturally, or with more Christianity a greater woe.

The Duchesse d'Angoulême died at Frohsdorf October 19, 1851, aged seventy-three years and four months, and in the twenty-first year of her last exile. Her preceding exile lasted eighteen years (not counting the Hundred Days). They were preceded by imprisonment in the Temple for three years, and a forced confinement in the Tuileries in the midst of riot and danger for three more. That was the frame of this destiny of sorrow and sacrifice, on which Antiquity would have shed its poesy and its idealism, while we see only its inner beauty, half-veiled, as becomes Christianity.

APPENDIX I.

Montreuil.

IN 1792 the Commune of Versailles took possession of Madame Élisabeth's much loved Montreuil, which was thenceforth called the "Maison d'Élisabeth Capet." Seals were placed upon it until inventories were made and the property in it sold by the agents of the National Domain. After that it was let to various persons, and used for various purposes until finally it fell into a state of dilapidation and was sold, on the 6th of May, 1802, as a National domain by the Commune of Versailles to Citizen Jean-Michel-Maximilien Villers, living in Paris, rue de l'Université, No. 269, for the sum of 75,900 francs.

Some of Madame Élisabeth's servants remained on the place for a time to take care of it for their new masters. But her faithful Jacques Bosson and his wife, who had charge of the cows and dairy, being obnoxious to the revolutionaries on account of their nationality (Swiss), were thrown into prison, where, being foreigners and friendless, they languished for some years. Among the archives of Versailles is a pathetic letter to the municipality dated March 7, 1793, from one of Madame Élisabeth's servants asking for food for her dogs; he says they are three *large* dogs, and he no longer has the means to feed them. The cows were sold, the hens died for want of care, the garden was torn up and devastated, the fruit stolen.

Some of the inventories of the property (made by order of the Department of National Domain in October, 1792) are very interesting, especially those of the garden and grounds, and of the library. There were 487 plants in the greenhouses, of 145 different species. Of these 35 were orange-trees, and 15 pomegranates. Many of the plants, the Latin names of which are given, are choice varieties of their kind even at the present day.

In the nursery grounds were 14 kinds of young trees and shrubs; 1413 in all; of which 300 were Scotch pines, 250 ash-leaved maples, 150 *Arbres de Sainte-Lucie* [?] spireas, dogwoods, syringas, lilacs, cherries, etc.

The library contained 2075 volumes; a remarkable collection for that period, with a wide outlook in history, memoirs, biography, and essays on the political condition of France. Of history, there were 406 volumes, among them Hume's England, Robertson's Scotland, Gibbon's Roman Empire, histories of all the countries of Europe, of Constantinople, Japan, the Ottoman Empire, Arabia, Siam, etc. Of memoirs and biography, 203 volumes. These were chiefly French, beginning with Villehardouin and coming down to Mme. de Staal-Delaunay and the Letters of Mme. de Pompadour. There were many classics, chiefly translated; the Bible in 31 volumes; all the great poems (among them "Le Paradis Perdu") and the chief French dramatists; also 42 volumes of Fairy tales; the Arabian Nights, Robinson Crusoe, and a small, a very small sprinkling of novels. But most interesting of all are the books she bought in the last year of her living life, before the tomb of the Temple closed upon her. Among them were: —

Reflections on the Revolution in France by Mr. Burke, 1791.

Speeches and Letters of Mr. Burke, 1790, 1791.

The Constitution of England.

Rights and Duties of a Citizen.

Political Situation of France, and its present Relations with all the Powers of Europe, 1789.

The Evil and its Remedy; Memorial on the Militia of the Army, 1789.

The True Patriot.

The King's Household: what it was, what it is, and what it should be, 1789.

Principles opposed to the System of M. Necker, by M. de Favras, 1790.

Present situation of France, 1791.

The *Naviget antyciras*, or System without Principles, 1791.

The reign of Louis XVI. placed before the Eyes of Europe, 1791.

Impulse of the Heart and Mind, or Justice rendered to the Queen, 1791.

Plan for a Free and Happy Constitution, 1790.

Among a mass of papers preserved in the archives of Versailles, sad and sorrowful reading as they are, there is one amusing little record of Madame Élisabeth's extravagance in a detail of dress. It is a bill of her shoemaker, named Bourbon, rue Neuve des Augustins, Paris, for shoes supplied to her nearly every other day from April 6, 1792, to June 30, a short three months; never more than two pairs at a time were sent, and the dates are given. There were 27 sendings and 32 pairs of silk shoes [*taffetat*] : 16 pairs of black, 5 pairs of gray, 3 of blue, 2 of russet, 2 of puce, and one each of carmelite and green — all of silk. It is true that Madame Élisabeth mentions having walked for three or four hours in the garden, and speaks of "the shocking mud," *crotte indigne*, so perhaps it is no wonder that silk shoes lasted only two days.

APPENDIX II.

First Examination of Madame Élisabeth by Fouquier-Tinville, May 9, 1794. From the Official Record.

THIS day, twentieth floréal, year two of the Republic, before Antoine-Quentin Fouquier . . . we have asked the name, age, profession, place of birth, and residence of Élisabeth Marie Capet, sister of Louis Capet, age thirty, born at Versailles.

Q. Did you conspire with the late tyrant against the safety and liberty of the French people?

A. I am ignorant to whom you give that title; but I have never desired anything but the happiness of the French people.

Q. Have you maintained correspondence with the internal and external enemies of the Republic, especially with the brothers of Capet and yourself? and have you furnished them help in money?

A. I have known none but those who loved France. I have

never furnished help to my brothers; and since the month of August, 1792, I have received no news of them, nor have I sent them any.

Q. Did you not send them diamonds?

A. No.

Q. I call your attention to the fact that your answer is not correct as to the diamonds, inasmuch as it is notorious that you sent your diamonds to be sold in Holland and other foreign countries, and that you sent their proceeds, by your agents, to your brothers, to help them in maintaining their rebellion against the French people.

A. I deny the charge, because it is false.

Q. I call you to notice that in the trial which took place in November, 1792, relatively to the theft of diamonds made from the *ci-devant* crown property, it was established and proved that a portion of the diamonds with which you formerly adorned yourself came from there, and it was also proved that the price for which they were sold was sent to your brothers by your orders; that is why I summon you to explain yourself categorically on those facts.

A. I am ignorant of the thefts of which you speak. I was at that period in the Temple, and I persist in my previous denial.

Q. Did you not have knowledge that the journey determined upon by your brother, Louis Capet, and Antoinette, to Saint-Cloud on April 18, 1791, was imagined only to seize the occasion to leave France?

A. I had no knowledge of that journey further than that my brother wished for change of air, not feeling well.

Q. Was it not at your solicitation and that of Antoinette, your sister-in-law, that Capet fled from Paris on the night of the 20th of June, 1791?

A. I learned during the day of June 20 that we should start that night, and I conformed in that matter to the orders of my brother.

Q. The motive of that journey was it not to leave France and unite yourselves with the *émigrés*, and the enemies of the French people?

A. Never did my brother, or I, have any intention of quitting our country.

Q. I observe to you that that answer does not seem correct, for Bouillé had given orders for several bodies of troops to be at a point agreed upon to protect your escape, and enable you, your brother, and others to leave French territory.

A. My brother was on his way to Montmédy, and I never knew him to have any other intentions.

Q. Have you knowledge of the secret conferences held in the apartments of Antoinette, *ci-devant* queen, with those who called themselves the Austrian committee?

A. I have perfect knowledge that none such were ever held.

Q. I call you to observe that it is, nevertheless, notorious that they were held between midnight and three in the morning, and those who attended them passed through what was then called the Gallery of Pictures.

A. I have no knowledge of it.

Q. What did you do on the night of the 9th and 10th of August, 1792?

A. I remained in my brother's room; we did not go to bed that night.

Q. I call your attention to the fact that, having each your separate apartments, it seems strange that you should collect in that of your brother; no doubt that meeting had a motive, which I call upon you to explain.

A. I had no other motive than to be always near my brother when there was disturbance in Paris.

Q. That night did you not go, with Antoinette, into a hall where the Swiss Guard were making cartridges, and especially were you not there between nine and ten o'clock that night?

A. I was not there, and I have no knowledge of that hall.

Q. I request you to observe that your answer is not correct; it has been proved at several trials, that Antoinette and you went several times in the night to the Swiss Guards, that you made them drink, and urged them to continue the making of cartridges, several of which Antoinette bit off herself.

A. That never happened; I have no knowledge of it.

Q. I represent to you that the facts are too notorious for you not to remember them, and not to know the motive which assembled troops of all kinds at the Tuileries that night. That is why I again summon you to declare if you still persist in your denials, and in forgetting the motives for this assembling of troops.

A. I persist in my denials, and I add that I know no motives for that assemblage. I know only, as I have already said, that the constituted bodies charged with the safety of Paris, came to warn my brother that there was an uprising in the faubourgs, and on that the National Guard assembled for his safety, as the Constitution prescribed.

Q. At the time of the escape of the 20th of June, 1791, was it not you who brought out the children?

A. No; I came out alone.

Reading being made to her of the present interrogatories, she persisted in her replies, and signed with us and the clerk.

ÉLISABETH MARIE,   A.-Q. FOUQUIER,
DELIÉGE,   DUCRAY, Clerk.

APPENDIX III.

Extract from the Deliberations of the Commissioners of the Commune on the Service of the Temple.

December 22, 1792, Year I. of the Republic.

At six in the evening the Council assembled to deliberate on the two subjects here following: —

1st. Louis Capet appears to be inconvenienced by the length of his beard; he has spoken of it several times. They proposed to shave him. He manifested repugnance, and showed a desire to shave himself.

The Council thought yesterday that it might give him the hope that his request would be acceded to to-day; but this morning it was discovered that Louis Capet's razors are no longer in the Temple. On that, occasion was taken to discuss the matter again; it has been amply argued and the result is a unanimous resolution to submit the matter to the Council-general of the Commune, which, in case it judges proper to permit Louis Capet to shave himself, will direct that there be given to him one, or two, razors, of which he will make use before the eyes of four commissioners, to whom the said razors shall be immediately returned, and who will register the fact that the return has been made to them.

2d. The wife, sister, and daughter of Louis Capet have asked that scissors be lent to them to cut their nails.

The Council having deliberated thereon has likewise voted unanimously that this request shall also be submitted to the Council-general of the Commune, which is hereby asked, in case it gives its consent, to fix the method to be employed in the matter.

It is decreed that the present deliberation shall be sent to the Council-general of the Commune this day, and early enough for the answer to reach the Council of the Commune in the Temple before night.

And the following do sign the registers.

MAUBERT, DEFRASSE, JON, ROBERT MALIVOIR, and DESTOURNELLES.

APPENDIX IV.

Signs agreed upon to make known to the Princesses the Progress of the various Armies, etc.; and sundry Communications from Madame Élisabeth to M. Turgy.

[THE queen and Madame Élisabeth arranged a system of signs with Turgy, the faithful waiter who brought up their meals. These with several written communications from Madame Élisabeth, conveyed to him in a variety of ways, Turgy took to Vienna in 1796, and gave into the hands of Madame Marie-Thérèse de France. The following (in the French) was copied from those originals].

The English put to sea: right thumb on right eye; if they land near Nantes, put it on right ear; if near Calais, left ear.

If the Austrians fight on Belgian frontier, forefinger of right hand on right eye. If they enter France, on right ear. If on the Mayence side, same with middle finger.

Savoyards, fourth finger, same signs. Spaniards, fifth [little] finger, same signs.

Be careful to hold the fingers to the place more or less time according to importance of the losses.

When they are within 15 leagues of Paris keep the same order for the fingers, but lay them on the mouth.[1]

---

[1] Remembering all that Count Fersen tells of the delays and the callous indifference of the Powers, each pretending to wait for the others, it is piteous to think of these women watching daily for signs of a deliverer who never came, but left them coldly to their one deliverer, Death. — TR.

If the Powers speak about us, lay fingers on the hair, using the right hand.

If the Assembly pays attention to them, the same, using the left.

If it adjourns [*s'en allait*], the whole hand over the head.

If the *rassemblements* [collections of *émigrés*] advance here, and gain advantages, the finger of right hand on the nose for one advantage, and the whole hand when they are within fifteen leagues of Paris.

Use the left hand only for the advantages of the French.

In answer to all questions use the right hand only, not the left. [Here three lines are undecipherable]. Is there a truce, raise your collar. Are they asking for us on the frontier, hand in coat pocket. Are they negotiating, in waistcoat. Paris, are they provisioning it, hand on chin. Has General la Marseille gone, on forehead. Are the Spaniards trying to join the Nantes people, rub the eyebrow.

Is it thought we shall still be here in August? After supper go to Fidel (Toulan); ask him if he has news of Produse. If he has good news, napkin under right arm; if none at all, under left. Tell him that we fear his denunciation may bring him into trouble. Ask him whenever he has news of Produse to tell you, and then sign it to us.

Can you not, if anything new happens, write it to us with lemon-juice on the paper they use to stopper the water-bottle, or put over the cream? or perhaps you could put it in a ball, which you could throw down in the room when you are there alone. Get possession of the paper on the bottles whenever I blow my nose as I leave my room. The days when you use that means, lean against the wall as I pass you.

If it is thought we shall still be here in August hold the napkin in your hand. We hope you will not be harassed again.

Do not fear to use the left hand for bad news of the armies; we prefer to know all. If the Swiss declare war the sign is a finger on the chin. If the Nantes people reach Orléans two fingers on the chin.

What are they crying under our windows? ... (*several*

words illegible) received his pardon yesterday. . . . Has he an idea that we are informed? and will he not redouble in attentions to prevent it? Whatever wrong the poor man has done it can only inspire pity, all the more because his repentance followed immediately upon his fault. God has punished him very severely. We pity him.

Is it true that fear has seized the Parisians, especially young men? My sister may soon ask for almond-milk. . . . Has the Commune been changed? Is Tison's wife as crazy as they say she is? Do they mean to send any one to us in her place? Is she well taken care of?

Consider carefully the disadvantages of T's (Toulan's) demand, and do not let your zeal lead you to do anything to your injury; if you yield, let it be only after you are urged, and promised the greatest secrecy. Are you not expressly forbidden to speak to him? Consider all that. Try to find out if they are not trying to throw the disturbances on my companion [the queen] and take her *property* (Louis XVII.) more than two leagues away from her. It was Fidel (Toulan) who gave us the newspaper I mentioned. The manner in which you serve us is our consolation. Ask Mme. de S. (Sérent) for answer on Miranda.

We saw a newspaper yesterday which spoke of Saumur and Angers as if the *R* were still mistress; what does that mean? Is Marat really dead? has it made an excitement?

Tell Fidel how touched we are by his last note; we do not need his assurances to rely wholly and always upon him; his signals are good. We only want *Aux armes, citoyens!* in case they intend to reunite us. But we hope that such precautions will not be necessary. Is your fate decided? answer this question. If it is necessary that we should get your note quickly, lean towards us and lower your napkin. Tison sometimes hinders our taking it at once. But we will watch for it; do not be uneasy. This is only to be when you have something urgent to say to us.

Who is the municipal whom they suspect of being in correspondence with us? Is it by writing, or merely by giving news? Who said it? Have they no suspicion of you? Take care.

You must give this, Tuesday, to the person to whom you went Saturday; it is the woman. Give her something to bring out the ink. Send no answer until Tuesday, so as not to multiply packages.

Give Fidel this note from us, and say to him that because my sister has told you that she sees the little boy go up the staircase, through the window of the cabinet, this is not to keep him from sending us news of him. Why do they beat the drums every morning at six o'clock? Answer this. If you can without compromising Mme. de Sérent [one of Madame Élisabeth's ladies], or yourself, tell her, that I beg her not to remain in Paris for me. The proposal at the Cordeliers against the nobles worries me for her. If anything happens at the Federation do not fail to let us know. What foundation is there for all the victories they have been crying for the last three days? If you have need of almond milk, hold your napkin low when I . . .

What has become of the English fleet? and of my brothers? Have we a fleet at sea? What do you mean when you say that all goes well? Is it hope of a quick end, of a change in the public mind? or are things really going well? Are these executions of persons whom we know? We hear them cried in the street. How is Mme. de Sérent, and my abbé [Edgeworth de Firmont]? *Constant* [M. Huë]? does he know by chance any news of Mme. de Bombelles, who is living near St-Gall in Switzerland? What has become of all the persons at Saint-Cyr? Tell me if you have been able to read all this; and cover the water-bottle with good paper that we can use.

As for Mme. de Sérent, as soon as the law about the *émigrés* is wholly finished let her know, and continue to give me news of her.

This is for Fidel. What you tell me about that person [the queen] gives me great pleasure. Is it the gendarme, or the woman, who sleeps in her room? Could she hear through the latter anything more than news of those she loves? If you cannot be useful to her there, put yourself in some place whence you will not be forced to move ; but let me know where, in case we have need of you. I do not consider what concerns me, but if you cannot be useful to that person come and join me in case you are needed.

I cannot yet believe that you are going away. Try to let me know what is decided ; whether you remain and Tison's wife returns. Could you throw a paper into the basket, or put it in a loaf of bread? Tell me if it is through Mme. de Sérent that you hear news of a being who, like me, knows how to appreciate faithful men [the Abbé Edgeworth de Firmont]. It is with deep regret that I see you taken from me; the last and only one that remains to me.

I am much distressed; save yourself for the days when we may be happier, and able to give you some reward. Carry with you the consolation of having been useful to kind and unhappy masters. Advise Fidel not to risk too much for our signals. If chance lets you see Mme. Mallemain [one of Mme. Élisabeth's waiting-women] give her news of me and tell her I think of her.

Adieu, honest man [Turgy] and faithful subject.

My little girl [Madame Royale] insists that you made her a sign yesterday morning ; relieve me of anxiety if you still can. I have found nothing. If you put it under the bucket it must have flowed away with the water and will certainly never be found. If there is any news for us, let me know it if you still can.

Have you read my second bit of paper, in which I spoke of Mme. Mallemain? Tell Constant [Huë] that I am convinced of his sentiments ; I thank him for the news he gives me, and I am much grieved at what has happened to him.

Adieu, honest man and faithful subject ! I hope that the God to whom you are faithful will support you, and console you in what you have to suffer.

APPENDIX V.

Louis XVI.'s Seal and Ring.

[CLÉRY did not continue in the service of the dauphin, as the king requested. He was compelled to give up the above-named articles to the Council of the Commune, and they remained in the council-room of the Tower until they were mysteriously stolen. This was done (as will be seen by the Narrative of Marie-Thérèse de France) at the instigation of the queen, who was passionately desirous of rescuing these memorials of her husband for her son. Eventually, after the queen's death, Turgy took the seal to *Monsieur*, and the ring to the Comte d'Artois, as will be seen by the following Note to Cléry's Journal.]

Having started from Vienna on my way to England, I passed through Blankemburg with the intention of doing homage to the king [Louis XVIII.] and presenting to him my manuscript. When His Majesty reached this part of my Journal, he searched in his secretary and showing me with emotion a seal, he said to me: "Cléry, do you recognize it?" "Ah! Sire, it is the very one." "If you doubt it," said the king, "read this note." I read it trembling, and I asked the king's permission to print the precious document. The following is a copy from the original: —

"Having one faithful being on whom we can rely, I profit by him to send to my brother and friend, this deposit which can be intrusted to no hands but his. The bearer will tell you by what miracle we have been able to obtain these precious pledges. I reserve to myself to tell you some day the name of him who has been so useful to us. The impossibility, up to this time, of giving you any news of us, and the excess of our sorrows, makes us feel even more keenly our cruel separation. May it not be much longer! I embrace you meantime as I love you, and you know that that is with all my heart.

"M. A. [Marie Antoinette]."

"I am charged for my brother and myself to embrace you with all our hearts.

"M. T. [Marie-Thérèse]. Louis."

"I enjoy in advance the pleasure you will feel in receiving this pledge of friendship and confidence. To be reunited with you, and to see you happy is all that I desire; you know if I love you; I kiss you with all my heart.

"E. M. [Élisabeth Marie]."

The ring was sent with a packet of the king's [Louis XVI.] hair to Monseigneur le Comte d'Artois. Here is the note that accompanied it:—

"Having at last found means to confide to our brother one of the two sole pledges that remain to us of the being whom we all mourn and cherish, I thought you would be very glad to have something that came from him; keep it as a sign of the tenderest friendship with which I embrace you with all my heart.

"M. A."

"What happiness for me, my dear friend, my brother, to be able after so long a space of time to speak to you of my feelings. What I have suffered for you! A time will come, I hope, when I can embrace you, and tell you that never will you find a friend truer and more tender than I; you do not doubt it, I hope.

"E. M."

INDEX.

ANGOULÊME (Duc d'), 209; marriage to Marie-Thérèse, Madame Royale de France, 290, 291.

AOSTA (Duke of), suitor to Mme. Élisabeth, 9.

ARTOIS (Charles, Comte d'), characteristics, 14, 15; relations with Mme. Élisabeth, 21, 22; she disapproves of his intimacy with Calonne, 58; relations with his family during the Revolution, 69-71, 73; letters from Mme. Élisabeth, 76, 77, 324.

AUGUST 10, 1792. Cléry's account of it, 112-118; Madame Royale's account of it, 236-243.

BAILLY (Jean Sylvain), astronomer, author of "History of Astronomy," mayor of Paris, 215.

BARNAVE (Antoine-Pierre-Joseph-Marie), goes to Varennes to bring back the king, 226, 227.

BEAUCHESNE (M. A. de), his "Vie de Madame Élisabeth," 1.

BOMBELLES (Marquise de), one of Mme. Élizabeth's friends and correspondents, 10; Mme. É.'s letters to her and others, 33-89; Mme. É. inquires for her in her last days, 321.

BOUILLÉ (Marquis de), and his son, their failure at Varennes, 221, 222.

BRAZIL (Infant of Portugal, Prince of), suitor to Mme. Élisabeth, 8.

BRETEUIL (Baron de), his powers from Louis XVI., 74.

CALONNE (Charles-Alexandre de), 34, 35, 58.

CAUSANS (Marquise de), superintendent of Mme. Élisabeth's household, 10.

CAUSANS (Mlle. Marie de), Mme. Élisabeth's letter to her, 38-40.

CAUSANS (Marquis de), correspondence with Mme. Élizabeth lost, 10.

CHAUMETTE (Pierre-Gaspard), 274; brutal questioning of Madame Élisabeth and her niece, 275, 276.

CHAUVEAU-LAGARDE (M.), his defence of Mme. Élisabeth, 92, 101, 102; and of the Queen, 277.

CHOISEUL (Duc de), at Varennes, 221, 222.

CLÉRY, Louis XVI.'s *valet de chambre*, his "Journal of the Temple," 2, 111-206; his account of August 10, 1792, 112-118; admitted to the Tower of the Temple to serve the king and dauphin, 119-121; massacres of Sept. 2 and 3; Madame de Lamballe's head brought to the Temple, 122-124; description of the small tower of the Temple, 125; life of the royal family, 126-129; character and insolence of their jailers, 130-137; instances of pity, 134, 135; description of the great Tower of the Temple, 148, 149; narrative of events in the Tower till the king's condemnation, 150-165; same till his death, 175-206; mentioned in the Narrative of Marie-Thérèse de France, 252, 254, 259, 260; his interview with Louis XVIII. at Blankemburg, 323.

CLOTILDE DE FRANCE (Madame), Queen of Sardinia, sisterly relations with Mme. Élisabeth, 3, 4; their sorrowful parting, 7.

DUMOURIEZ (Charles François), 261.

ÉLISABETH DE FRANCE (Philippine-Marie-Hélène, Madame), birth, early character, self-will, and pride, 2, 3; gradual change under wise management, 4-6; Marie-Antoinette's judgment of her as a child, 7; her household formed, proposals of marriage, 8, 9; attachment to her young friends, 10-12; plans her life, her personal appearance, 16; enthusiasm for the war of independence in America, 17, 18; the king's gift to her of Montreuil, and her life there, 19-22; devotion to her brothers, especially the king, 5, 21, 22; her fears for and of him in the future, 22; her spirit of faith, 23; her last day at Montreuil, Oct. 5, 1789, her firm and wise advice to Louis XVI., 24; her farewell to Montreuil, 25; life and anxieties in the Tuileries till June 20, 1791, 25, 26; the same till June 20, 1792, 27, 28; Resignation; her last letter, 31; August 10, 1792, her last appearance to the world until her execution, May 10, 1794, 32; her letters to friends from 1786 to August 8, 1792, 33-89; fac-simile of her writing, 87; of her seals, 89; the record of her life in the Tower of the Temple told by her niece and by Cléry, 90; the municipality of Paris demands her arraignment, 90, 91; she is taken from the Temple and examined by Fouquier-Tinville, 92, and Appendix, 313-316; indicted and arraigned with twenty-four others before the Revolutionary Tribunal, 93-95; her examination, 95-101; sentenced to death; Fouquier-Tinville's remark upon her, 103; inspires and strengthens those who are to die with her, 104, 105; her death, 106; Cléry's account of her life in the Tower of the Temple, 118, 122-124, 126-129, 135, 137, 141, 150, 151, 154, 156, 159, 160, 164, 166, 169-171, 177, 178; the parting from Louis XVI., 199, 200; account given of her in the Narrative of her niece, Marie Thérèse de France, on October 5, 1789, 210, 213; on the flight to Varennes, 216, 218; on June 20, 1792, her bravery and speech, 232, 234, 239; in the Tower of the Temple, 253, 261, 264, 267, 269, 272; her examination in the Temple, 274-276; life in the Tower from the queen's death to her own martyrdom, 278-283; her examination at the Conciergerie by Fouquier-Tinville, 313-316; her system of signs and notes of communication in the Temple with Turgy and Toulan, 318-322; last words to *Monsieur* and the Comte d'Artois, 324.

FALLOUX (Comte de), description of the Duchesse d'Angoulême just before her death in 1851, 291.

FAVRAS (M. de), execution of, 25, 45; book by him, 312.

FAYETTE (Marquis de la), his conduct on the 5th and 6th of October, 1789, 24; made governor of the Tuileries and keeper of king's person after return from Varennes, 27; convinced of his mistaken course, becomes willing to save the king, 29, 49; commands the rioters October 5, 1789, and compels the king to go to Paris, 211, 213-215, 218; sends in pursuit of the king to Varennes, 222, 228, 229, 246.

FERRAND (Antoine), Minister of State, and peer of France, his Éloge Historique de Madame Élisabeth de France, 1.

FERSEN (Axel, Count), the flight to Varennes, 218, 219.

FIRMONT (the Abbé Edgeworth de), becomes Mme. Élisabeth's confessor, 59; extract from his Memoirs, 59, 60; summoned by the king after his condemnation, 194, 195; is with the king the last evening of his life, 198;

INDEX. 327

says mass on the last morning, 201, 202, 257; last words to Louis XVI. on the scaffold, 258; Marie Thérèse, Duchesse d'Angoulême, nurses him in his last illness, 321, 322.

ouquier-Tinville (Antoine-Quentin), examination and arraignment of Madame Élisabeth, 92-96, 313-316; his remark upon her, 103.

oguelat (M.), 64, 221.

omier, jailer at the Temple, appointed after 9th Thermidor, his kindness to the dauphin, 287.

ustavus III., King of Sweden, his murder and death, 79.

ue (François), the Narrative of the Duchesse d'Angoulême given to him, 209, 248.

seph II. of Austria, Emperor of Germany, a suitor to Madame Élisabeth, 9.

ne 20, 1791, Varennes: account of it in the Narrative of Marie Thérèse de France, 216-230.

ne 20, 1792, assault on the Tuileries, account of it in same Narrative, 230-236.

mballe (Marie-Thérèse-Louise de Savoie-Carignan, Princesse de), tries to brighten the queen's life in the Tuileries after October 6, 1789, 25; leaves the Tuileries with the royal family, August 10, 1792, 32; goes with them to the Tower of the Temple, 115, 118; horrible indignities to her head and body after her murder, September 3d, 122-124, 130; mention of her by Marie Thérèse de France, 233; in the Temple, 244, 245, 248, 249.

sne, jailer in the Temple who succeeds Laurent, takes the greatest care of the dauphin, 288.

urent, appointed after 9th Thermidor jailer to the dauphin and Marie-Thérèse, his kindness, 285-289.

Louis XVI., becomes king at the age of 19, 7; his character, 12, 13, 15; his reforms, 7, 8, 16, 17; gives Montreuil to Mme. Élisabeth, 18, 19; his need of her, 22; October 5, 1789, his weakness and indecision, 24; urged by Mme. Élisabeth to firmness and action, 25, 27; his weak letter to his confessor, June 20, 1792, 28; vainly urged by the Constitutionals to form a National party and put himself at the head of the army, 29-31; abandons the Tuileries against the will of his wife and sister, August 10, 1792, 31, 32; his character transformed in the Tower of the Temple, 32; signs the Constitution, 67, 68, 71; his life in the Tower described by his valet, Cléry, 119-165; the books he read, 150; is summoned for trial before the National Convention, 166-172; obtains counsel, 173; is separated from his family, 175; his Will, 180-184; appears the second time before the Convention, 185; his sentence to death, 188-194; his conduct under it, 194 *et seq.*; sends for the Abbé Edgeworth de Firmont, 195; the parting with his family, 198-200; prepares for death, 201-204; leaves the Temple for the scaffold, 205; his daughter's account of him on October 5, 1789, on the flight to Varennes, on June 20, 1792, on August 10, 1792, 210-243; from the imprisonment in the Tower of the Temple till his death, 243, 259; the parting with his family, 257; *Fils de Saint-Louis, montez au ciel*, 258.

Louis Charles (Dauphin), Cléry's account of him in the Tower of the Temple, 119; the king educates him, 127; his prayers, 129; his games, 150, 167; his goodness of heart and thoughtfulness, 160-162; separated from his father, 168, 169; the final parting from his father, 199, 200, 257; rough treatment the beginning of his illness, 263, 264; torn from his mother and family, 266, 267; his mother watches daily for hours to see him through a chink in the wall, 267, 288; given over to the brutal care of Simon, 268; is degraded by him, 270, 271; his most dreadful life, 280, 281, 284; after 9th Thermidor his keepers, Laurent, Gomier, and Lasne, were very kind to him, 286, 287; his health destroyed, he dies of dirt, neglect, and cruelty, June 9, 1795, at 3 P.M., 288, 289.

LUBERSAC (Abbé de), letters from Mme. Élisabeth to, 42, 65, 84, 87; massacred September 2, 1792.

MACKAU (the Baronne de), Mme. Élisabeth's second governess, her wise treatment of the child, 4, 6.

MALESHERBES (Chrestien de Lamoignon de), failure of his reform ministry, 8, 30; his letter to Pres. of National Convention offering to be the king's counsel, 173, 174; consultations with the king, 175-177, 187, 184; informs the king of his sentence to death, 188, 189; denied access after that to the king, 190, 192, 256, 257.

MALOUET (M. de), his Memoirs of the Constituent Assembly relate the efforts made to induce Louis XVI. to leave Paris and form a National Party, 29-31.

MANUEL, prosecutor of the Commune and member of National Assembly, his insults to the king, 151-153, 244, 252.

MARIE-ANTOINETTE (Queen), became queen at 18 years of age, 7; aids the king in giving Montreuil to Mme. Élisabeth, 19, 20; life in the Tuileries after October 6, 1789, 25; shares Mme. Élisabeth's fear of the king's weakness, but looks for help from Austria, 27; her noble speech, August 10, 1792, 31; her last appearance to the eyes of men until her condemnation and death, October 16, 1793, 32; Mme Élisabeth's remarks about her in letters, 36, 37; taken to the Tower of the Temple, 118; attempt to make her see the head of Mme. de Lamballe, 122-124; her life and occupations in the Temple described by Cléry, 125-130 et seq.; her terrible parting from the king, 198-200; her daughter's account of her, 211-213, 216, 217, 221, 232, 234-236, 238, 245, 249, 252, 253, 255, 257, 258, and until her death, 259-278, 286; apostrophe to her written by Marie-Thérèse on the wall of her room in the Tower, 289, 290.

MARIE-THÉRÈSE DE FRANCE, Duchesse d'Angoulême, her Narrative, 2; taken with her family to the Tower of the Temple, 118; Cléry's account of her life there, 125 et seq., 150, 151; faints on parting with her father, 199; her Narrative, 209-295; of the first uprising, October 5, 1789, 210-216; of the flight and stoppage at Varennes, June 20, 1791, 216-230; of the assault on the Tuileries, June 20, 1792, 230-236; of August 10, 1792, 236-243; of the imprisonment in the Tower of the Temple till the death of the king, 243-259; of the life in the Tower from the death of the king to that of the queen, 259-278; of the same until the death of Mme. Élisabeth and the dauphin, 278-289; her release from the Temple, marriage, exile, and portrait, 290; Napoleon's remark upon her, 291, 306; the close of her life at Frohsdorf, 291; the words upon her tomb, 291; Sainte-Beuve's essay on her life and character, 294-310.

MARSAN (Comtesse de), Mme. Élisabeth's first governess, 3.

MIRABEAU (Honoré-Gabriel-Riquetti Comte de), 54; his death, 60, 61.

MONTIERS (Marquise de), letter from Mme. Élisabeth to, 50-52.

MONTMORIN (M. de.), his efforts with others to induce the king to leave Paris, August 7, 1792, and form a National party, 29-31.

MONTREUIL, 19-22, 25, 36, 44; its fate

INDEX.

after Madame Élisabeth's imprisonment, its greenhouses, library, etc., 311, 312.

MORRIS (Gouverneur), his efforts to influence Louis XVI. to action, 30.

NECKER (M.), 22, 24.

OCTOBER 5th and 6th, 1789, beginning of the French Revolution, and the end of the Monarchy, 210–216.

ORLÉANS (Philippe Egalité, Duc d'), 49; conduct on the 5th October, 1789, 212, 213; votes the king's death, 194; his death, 278.

PÉTION (Jérôme), goes with Barnave and others to compel the king's return from Varennes, 226, 227; conduct as Mayor of Paris, 234, 236, 242, 249.

PROVENCE (*Monsieur*, Comte de), afterwards Louis XVIII., 12; characteristics, 14; his friends, 15; at Montreuil, 21; corrects the Narrative of Marie-Thérèse, Duchesse d'Angoulême, 209; she shares his exile after her release from the Tower, 290, last letters of the family in the Tower to him, 323.

RAIGECOURT (Marquise de), one of Madame Élisabeth's friends and correspondents, 10; charming story of Mme. É.'s love for her, 11; Mme. É.'s letters to her and others, 33–89.

ROCHEFOUCAULD (Duc de La), his account of the king and royal family leaving the Tuileries, August 10, 1792, 32.

SAINTE-BEUVE (C.-A.), his essay on the Duchesse d'Angoulême, 294–310.

SANTERRE, brewer, and Commander of the National Guard, 128, 196; fetches the king for the scaffold, 205, 233, 244.

SÉGUR (Vicomte de), 36.

SÈZE (M. de), one of the king's counsel for his defence, 177; defends him, 185.

SIMON, shoemaker, jailer at the Tower, his insolence, 132; brutal treatment of the little dauphin, 268; depraves him, 270, 271.

SWISS GUARD (The), their splendid devotion and butchery, August 10, 1792, 31.

TARGET (M.), refuses the king's request to defend him, 173.

TISON, employed in the Tower of the Temple, 151, 245; Mme. Tison becomes insane from remorse, 265, 266.

TOULAN, a municipal at the Temple faithful to the royal family, his death in consequence, 157, 158; notes to him from Mme. Élisabeth, 321; rescues the king's seal and ring for the queen, 323.

TOURZEL (Marquise de), accompanies royal family to the Temple, 32, 115, 118; the dauphin prays for her, 129; Madame Royale's account of her, 217–221, 238, 239, 244.

TRONCHET (M.), accepts the king's request to defend him, 173, 175, 176, 184.

TURGOT (Robert-Jacques), failure of his reform ministry, 7.

TURGY, seeks employment in the Temple to serve the imprisoned royal family, 143, 144, 177, 178, 212, 272; signs agreed upon and notes passing between himself and Mme. Élisabeth, 318–322; carries the seal and ring of Louis XVI., with notes from the royal family to *Monsieur* and the Comte d'Artois, 323, 324.

CPSIA information can be obtained
at www.ICGtesting.com
Printed in the USA
LVHW020311300120
645188LV00011B/332